CENTRAL LIBRARY
SWINDON
Tel: 463238

D1632679

# Brief Histories

*General Editor: Jeremy Black*

*Titles published in the Brief Histories Series:*

| | |
|---|---|
| Modern Greece | Thomas W. Gallant |
| Czechoslovakia | Maria Dowling |

*Titles published or in preparation for the Brief Histories Series include:*

| | |
|---|---|
| The Caribbean | Gad Heuman |
| Christianity after the Reformation | Nigel Aston |
| Eastern Europe 1945–2000 | Mark Pittaway |
| Empire of the Sultans | Gabor Agostan |
| Genocide in the Twentieth Century | Mark Levene |
| The Holocaust | Frank McDonough |
| Latin America in the Twentieth Century | Jean Grugel |
| Magic and Superstition | P G Maxwell-Stuart |
| Modern Southern Africa | Bill Nasson |
| Nationalism in the Modern World | A W Purdue |
| The Origins of the First World War | Thomas Otte |
| The Reformation | John Edwards |
| The Romanov Empire 1613–1917 | Alan Wood |
| Twentieth Century Russia | Peter Waldron |

# Czechoslovakia

## Maria Dowling

A member of the Hodder Headline Group
LONDON
Co-published in the United States of America by
Oxford University Press Inc., New York

6 354 960 000

First published in Great Britain in 2002 by
Arnold, a member of the Hodder Headline Group,
338 Euston Road, London NW1 3BH

**http://www.arnoldpublishers.com**

Co-published in the United States of America by
Oxford University Press Inc.,
198 Madison Avenue, New York, NY10016

© 2002 Maria Dowling

All rights reserved. No part of this publication may be reproduced or
transmitted in any form or by any means, electronically or mechanically,
including photocopying, recording or any information storage or retrieval
system, without either prior permission in writing from the publisher or a
licence permitting restricted copying. In the United Kingdom such licences
are issued by the Copyright Licensing Agency: 90 Tottenham Court Road,
London W1P 0LP.

The advice and information in this book are believed to be true and
accurate at the date of going to press, but neither the author nor the publisher
can accept any legal responsibility or liability for any errors or omissions.

*British Library Cataloguing in Publication Data*
A catalogue record for this book is available from the British Library

*Library of Congress Cataloging-in-Publication Data*
A catalog record for this book is available from the Library of Congress

ISBN 0 340 76369 8 (pb)

1 2 3 4 5 6 7 8 9 10

Production Editor: James Rabson
Production Controller: Bryan Eccleshall
Cover Design: Terry Griffiths

Typeset in 10/13pt Utopia by Charon Tec Pvt. Ltd, Chennai, India
Printed and bound by MPG Books Ltd, Bodmin, Cornwall

What do you think about this book? Or any other Arnold title?
Please send your comments to feedback.arnold@hodder.co.uk

# Contents

List of maps                                                                          vi

Preface                                                                               vii

Introduction: Czechs and Slovaks in Austria–Hungary                                   ix

1   1918: The World War and the Making of a State                                      1

2   The First Czechoslovak Republic, 1918–1938                                        19

3   1938: Foreign Policy and the Munich Agreement                                     39

4   World War II: Resistance, Propaganda and National Survival                        58

5   1948: Communist Coup and Stalinist Rule                                           80

6   1968: Prague Spring and the Soviet Invasion                                      103

7   Normalisation and Dissent: 1968–1988                                             121

8   1989: The Velvet Revolution                                                      141

Epilogue: 1992 : The Velvet Divorce                                                  160

Suggestions for Further Reading                                                      168

Index                                                                                175

# List of maps

1. Czechoslovakia 1918–1938                              18
2. Czechoslovakia after Munich 1938–1939                 57
3. Czechoslovakia 1945–1992                              79

# Preface

The history of Czechoslovakia, characterised as it is by the themes of nationalism, democracy and authoritarian rule, offers insights into the nature of government, power and culture in twentieth-century Europe. In many ways it was unique. It was not a historic state, but was born out of two regions of the collapsed Austro-Hungarian Empire in 1918. It attempted to create a single nation out of two distinct though kindred peoples. Between the world wars, in contrast to its neighbours in Central and Eastern Europe, it resisted the allure of both Communism and fascism; as a functioning parliamentary democracy, it aimed to act as a political, ideological and cultural bridge between East and West.

Yet the paradox and tragedy of Czechoslovakia was that, though its orientation was western in terms of democratic tradition, economic advancement and societal development, it was of no strategic importance to the West. Consequently its independence was sacrificed to Nazi Germany at Munich in 1938, while during and after World War II the Western allies recognised that Czechoslovakia lay within the Soviet sphere of influence. In 1948 the newly re-established democracy succumbed to a Communist coup.

The Stalinist regime that followed was similar in many ways to those that were established in the rest of the Soviet bloc. Czechoslovakia, however, again showed its uniqueness in the nature of its Communist revolution, the phenomenon of Prague Spring in 1968, and the lively movements of dissent which plagued the authorities until the velvet revolution of 1989. Thus the history of Czechoslovakia affords a study of similarity and contrast to the rest of Europe.

This survey of Czechoslovak history is intended for English readers. Consequently the bibliography contains only primary and secondary sources available in that language. In both the Czech Republic and Slovakia there has been a spate of publication of both collections of documents and secondary works, and there is a lively historiographical debate on a number of events and issues. Unfortunately, comparatively little of this material has been translated from Czech or Slovak.

A related matter is the question of diacritic marks (accents). These have been omitted, as it is felt that English readers would find the complex diacritic marks of Czech, Slovak, Hungarian and German more confusing than helpful.

I would like to thank my colleagues in the History Programme at Strawberry Hill for their generous professional and moral support, particularly in view of their own commitments to scholarship and publication projects. I am especially grateful to Ruth Mellor for preparing the maps. In addition Edmund Green is to be thanked for lively and useful discussion of many issues, and Joan Henderson for her enthusiastic interest. Lastly, this book is dedicated to Maureen, Susan and Julia, who shared my adventures in Czechoslovakia.

Maria Dowling
October 2001

# Introduction

## Czechs and Slovaks in Austria–Hungary

Czechoslovakia was created in 1918 out of the ruins of the Austro-Hungarian Empire. It was thus not a historic state, but an attempt to create a single nation out of two distinct yet kindred peoples. Almost from its birth it was depicted as an artificial state, particularly by Germans both from within Czechoslovakia and from Germany itself. Most notoriously, Hitler was wont to describe Czechoslovakia as 'the bastard child of [the treaty of] Versailles'. In the 1930s the appeasers of the Western democracies were prepared to accept this view, and even during World War II the viability of a reconstituted Czechoslovak state was questioned. The 'velvet divorce' of 1992 between Czechs and Slovaks might seem to lend credence to this view. Yet for more than 70 years, in the face of real and threatened aggression by their neighbours, the Czechs and Slovaks did attempt to forge a nation state.

Furthermore, particularly in the era of the First Republic (1918–1938), the Czechoslovaks were able, with justice, to depict their country as a bridge between East and West. Though Czechs and Slovaks belonged to the Slavonic world, their state was the only example in the Central European region of a functioning parliamentary democracy on the Western European model. (Indeed, by 1938 it was one of the few liberal democracies on the European mainland.) Yet ties of blood, culture and sentiment also linked them to the Slavs of Southern Europe, and to the Soviet Union itself.

What makes a nation? Nationalism as an ideology was a product of the Enlightenment and of the French revolution. By the nineteenth century there had developed two broad variants of nationalism. The first was the argument from historic right, which based its claims on the past existence of a power entity (usually a kingdom) which might be revived. The second variant was romantic nationalism which, following the theories of Herder, Fichte and other German thinkers, perceived the nation as an organic entity, identified and unified by ties of blood, language and soil. The paradox of Czechoslovakia was that it based its claims on both types of nationalism, yet truly it could not be identified with either. In making the case for the existence of a Czechoslovak nation both a national mythology and a national myth were utilised. (Here 'mythology' refers to legends about the nation's unwritten past, while 'myth' means the fashioning of historical fact to reflect the nation's destiny.) Both had particular application to the Czechs, but were later extended to include the Slovaks. Consider the Czech composer Bedrich Smetana's great symphonic poem *Ma Vlast* (My Country). This is romantic in the extreme, drawing on the natural beauty of Bohemia (forests, fields, the river Vltava); the legends of the dark ages (Sarka and her band of maiden warriors); and the historic Hussite defenders of Tabor and the knights of Blanik. With these last history is mingled with legend. Like Arthur for the British and Barbarossa for the Germans the knights sleep under a mountain, ready to wake at the nation's hour of need. Sadly, the knights of Blanik slumbered through all the crises of the twentieth century.

Now that the Czech and Slovak peoples have gone their separate ways it is time to analyse and evaluate the history of the sovereign state which they shared for the best part of a century. In order to do so it is necessary to call on both concrete history and nationalist theory, and to evoke the very different historical experience of Slovaks and Czechs.

As far as the Slovaks are concerned this is relatively straightforward. The shadowy and largely undocumented empire of Great Moravia, inhabited by Czechs as well as Slovaks, came to an end about the year 1000 when it was overrun by marauding tribes from the east, notably the Magyars. Great Moravia itself has been depicted as an invention of nineteenth-century Czechoslovakists who were anxious to find a precedent for the union of the two peoples into one state. The nature and extent of Great Moravia has yet to be determined by scholars of the early medieval era. What is indisputable, however, is that the land of the Slovaks was subsumed into the lands of the Hungarian crown of St Stephen, its inhabitants alternately treated as an insignificant minority or subjected to relentless Magyarisation.

This was not mere mindless repression, but represented real and understandable fears on the part of the Hungarians. In September 1840, for example, Count Karoly Zay was appointed inspector general of the Lutheran Church in Hungary, including Slovakia. His aim was to make Hungarian the official language of the Church and its educational institutions, and to forge a union with the Calvinists. His great fear was of Russian imperialism disguised as pan-Slavism, with which he identified the Slovak patriots. For Zay, the choice was between Magyar and Slav, freedom or the cossack's whip. Zay's colleague Ferenc Pulszky was rather less exalted, when he described the Slovaks as composed of the basest material of civilisation.

In the eighteenth century came the first stirrings of a Slovak national awakening, thanks to the work of the Jesuit Antonin Bernolak (1762–1813). Bernolak made a case for a Slovak national identity, though not for an independent state or even for autonomy. Rather, he saw the Slovaks as a distinct nationality under Habsburg and Hungarian rule, which would afford protection to the small nation and its language. Bernolak was the first to attempt a formulation of Slovak as a literary language. His codification of 1787 was based on the western dialect, with some elements of central Slovak. Among his works were a Slavic grammar (1790), and a dictionary in Slovak, Czech, Latin, German and Hungarian (published posthumously, 1825–1827).

Bernolak's followers over three generations formed the Slovak national intelligentsia; they turned Slovak into a literary language, using it for educational, religious and fictional writing. Indeed, there followed something of a Slovak literary renaissance, for example with the poetry of Jan Holly (1785–1849), like Bernolak a Catholic priest. His first works were translations from Greek and Roman classics, in particular the *Aeneid* of Virgil. Later and more notably he composed a series of heroic and patriotic epics: *Svatopluk* (1833), which told the story of the princely ruler of Great Moravia; *Cirilo-Metodiana* (1835), which concerned the early Christian missionaries to the Slavs; and *Slav* (1839). Holly's achievement was to demonstrate the poetic potential of the Slovak language.

A contrasting patriot and poet to Holly was Jan Kollar (1793–1852). Kollar was pastor to the Lutheran Slovaks in Pest from 1819 to 1849 and professor of Slavic archaeology at Vienna university from 1849 to 1852. His most famous poetic work was *Slavy Dcera*, which can be translated as 'daughter of glory' or as daughter of the goddess Slava. This was a highly patriotic poetic cycle whose final version was published in 1832. Kollar also produced collections of folk songs, partly in collaboration with the scholar Pavol Safarik. Heavily influenced by Herder's romantic nationalism, he believed that Slovaks and Czechs were descended from the same Slavic tribe. Thus he rejected Bernolak's Slovak language, writing in Czech with an admixture of central Slovak. Though this 'Czechoslovakism' was criticised by later Slovak autonomists, Kollar was influential in the formation of Slovak national consciousness in nineteenth-century Hungary.

Another early 'Czechoslovak' was Pavol Jozef Safarik (1795–1861), the friend of the Slovak Kollar and the Czech Palacky. Safarik was a Slovak by birth, spent much of his life teaching in Hungary, and ended as professor of Slavic philology and director of the university library in Prague. He wrote at a time when Slovaks and most other Slavonic peoples were deemed to be people without history or culture. His scholarly works on Slavic language and literature (1826), antiquities (1837) and ethnography (1842) were important in correcting this view. Safarik also wrote poetry and translated German classical literature, as well as writing extensively on the history, language and literature of the South Slavs. Though by no means a pan-Slav in the political sense, Safarik was a pioneer of Slavonic studies, and his works contributed greatly to the growth of national consciousness among Czechs and Slovaks as well as the Slavs of Southern Europe.

There was a second major attempt after Bernolak's to make Slovak a literary language. This was the work of Ludvit Stur (1815–1856), the most important and influential of the Slovak national awakeners. In 1843 he re-codified the language, basing it on the central Slovak dialect and using an orthography adapted from the Czech; this became the basis of modern Slovak. Importantly, he rejected the Czecho-Slavism advocated by Kollar, believing, like Bernolak's followers, that the Slovaks were a separate racial entity from the Czechs. This would leave an enduring legacy among some literate and informed Slovak patriots. Highly active in the most important events of the 1848 revolution, Stur called finally for an autonomous Slovakia divorced from Hungary and under the protection of Vienna. After the failure of the revolution he lived under virtual house-arrest, writing poetry and political works which showed his disillusion with the Habsburgs and adherence to a form of pan-Slavism.

While the Slovaks had found that their land had become mere 'upper Hungary', with a majority population of Slovaks and a Hungarian minority, the Czechs had enjoyed a historic legitimacy of undisputed value. The medieval crown of Bohemia had grown from a minor fiefdom of the Holy Roman Empire, as exemplified by the rule of Prince or Saint Vaclav (Wenceslas) in the tenth century, into a hereditary kingdom and an electorate of the said empire. The kingdom comprised the provinces of Bohemia, Moravia and Silesia. It reached its apogee in the fourteenth century with the reign of Charles IV Luxembourg, king and emperor. All the arts and most of the crafts flourished at the court of Charles, while Bohemia was a major factor in international politics. The rule of his son and successor Vaclav IV was both weak and violent, and was followed by the Hussite wars. The kingdom was finally pacified in 1458, under the reign of the Czech king Jiri of Podebrady. The dynastic changes and marriage contracts which followed Jiri's reign are too tedious to relate here. Suffice it to say that in 1525 Ferdinand of Habsburg, brother of the emperor Charles V, claimed and eventually won the kingdom. From then on until 1618 it formed virtually a part of the Habsburg family inheritance.

Just as World War I had Serbia and the assassination at Sarajevo as its start-ing point, so the Thirty Years War (1618–1648) began in Bohemia with the revolt of the Protestant Estates against Ferdinand II. Bohemia's part in the war ended two years later in defeat at the battle of White Mountain. The brutal, nasty but short repression of the rebellion became incorporated into the Czech national myth as 'three hundred years of darkness', during which Czech virtually disappeared as a written language and the people were oppressed by a foreign nobility and an alien faith. That there was more than an element of exaggeration in this picture goes, of course, without saying. Nowadays the Czechs are more appreciative of the artistic heritage bequeathed to them by the age of Baroque, particularly in terms of architecture. Nonetheless the kingdom became in fact what it had long been in practice, a mere possession of the Habsburgs. The native nobility all but disappeared, noble titles and estates being awarded to foreigners, notably Germans and Austrians.

The defeat at White Mountain also accelerated the trend to immigration by Germans of all types, professions and classes. Germans had been trading with and settling in Bohemia since the eleventh century; by the mid-nineteenth, they formed a large minority of two-fifths of the population of the Czech lands. In theory Czech and German had parity as official languages, for example, in courts of law. In practice, it was the German that predomin-ated. Ambitious Czechs would have to be bilingual; similar Germans rarely troubled to learn the language of a 'subaltern people'. As a result, Czech virtu-ally ceased to be a written language.

Into the 'national darkness' of the Czechs following White Mountain came light, in the shape of the national awakening of the late eighteenth and early nineteenth centuries. Among the outstanding Czech awakeners were Dobrovsky, Jungmann, Palacky, Havlicek-Borovsky and Rieger. Josef Dobrovsky (1753–1829) was a Jesuit and a linguist. Among other works he composed an Old Slavic grammar in Latin, a German–Czech dictionary, and a history of Czech language and literature in German. He has been hailed by more than one commentator as the founding father of Slavonic studies. Josef Jungmann (1773–1847) was the author of a five-volume dictionary of Czech and German, a history of Czech literature written in the Czech language, and the translator into his mother tongue of works by Milton, Pope, Goethe and Chateaubriand.

Foremost among the political thinkers of the national awakening stands the historian Frantisek Palacky (1798–1876). Employed at the national museum in Prague, Palacky wrote his great *History of the Czechs* first in German, then in a more expanded Czech edition. Together with his son-in-law, Frantisek Rieger (1803–1918), and the political journalist Karel Havlicek-Borovsky (1821–1856),

Palacky would be pre-eminent among the political theorists of the 1848 revolution in the Czech lands.

The national awakening of both Czechs and Slovaks achieved its culmination in this year of 1848, when most regions of mainland Europe experienced revolution based on political, social, economic and national grievances. The Habsburg monarchy was an obvious target for the liberal, constitutional and national demands of the revolutionaries; and the empire was threatened with dissolution. Representatives of the German states assembled at Frankfurt and demanded unification of all German lands, including Austria. The king of Piedmont-Sardinia vowed to drive the Austrians out of the Italian peninsula. The Hungarians rose in revolt, first demanding autonomy and then outright independence. Even the Viennese had brought about the downfall of Metternich, the reactionary chancellor, and were agitating for a constitution.

The position of small Slavonic nations like the Czechs and Slovaks was not an easy one. To espouse pan-Slavism would have been to throw in their lot with the repressive tsarist autocracy, something which was patently undesirable. Havlicek-Borovsky, for example, had been cured of his youthful Russophilism by a visit to Russia, where he observed the squalor and brutality of life under the tsar. On the other hand, the Germans were exerting direct pressure for union with Austria, and the Frankfurt assembly despatched a letter to Prague inviting the Czechs to join the future united Germany.

This invitation was answered by a well-known letter from Palacky, and in it he expressed what came to be known as Austro-Slavism. There was no place for the Slavs in a united Germany, he observed. Yet such small nations were too weak to stand alone. The solution was for them to take shelter in a reformed Austrian empire, which would protect them against pan-Germanism, pan-Slavism and Magyarisation. Most famously, he declared that if Austria had not existed it would have been necessary to invent her.

These sentiments were not shared by the Slovak Stur, who felt that the Slavs had rotted under Austria, which was in any case decrepit and under a curse. More directly, the Slovaks, like the Croats and other Slavonic peoples, were threatened by the ambitions of Lajos Kossuth and the other Hungarian nationalist leaders. While demanding equality with the Austrians, the Magyars refused the same rights to their subject peoples, on the grounds that the lands of the crown of St Stephen were indivisible. This attitude rebounded on them when they were defeated in part by the Croatian armies of Ban Jellacic, allied to the Habsburgs who were also assisted by tsarist forces. The Slovaks, whose leaders had been in negotiations with the Croats, took the side of Austria, and in the autumn of 1848 they raised the standard of revolt against the Hungarians. The imposition of martial law prevented the rebellion from becoming widespread. It was bloodily repressed, with many Slovak patriots dying on the 'Kossuth gallows'.

It would take several more months before the Hungarians were finally subdued; meanwhile, Prague had been bombarded into submission by the armies of General Windischgraetz in June. Despite a heroic defence by 1200 citizens and 500 national militia, they were overwhelmingly outnumbered by the General's forces of 10,000 men.

The resurgent Habsburgs, under a new emperor, Franz Josef, were quite ready to take revenge on the leaders of their rebel subjects. Stur and Palacky were virtually confined to their homes. The latter renounced his Austro-Slavism, famously declaring some years later: 'Before Austria was, we were, and when Austria no longer is, we shall be.'

A greater vengeance was exacted on Havlicek. In December 1851 he was exiled to the Tyrol, where he remained until April 1855. He returned to Bohemia a sick and impoverished man, and died in July 1856. His funeral was the occasion of patriotic demonstrations; a wreath of thorns was placed on the coffin. His penniless young daughter Zdenka was adopted as the 'daughter of the nation', and a lottery was organised to raise funds for her dowry. Sadly, she died unmarried in 1872, at the early age of twenty-four.

The triumph of the forces of conservatism meant rigorous repression of both liberal constitutionalism and nationalism. This was exercised nowhere more harshly than in Slovakia. The Hungarians feared a resurgence of rampant pan-Slavism which would put the crown of St Stephen in particular and Europe in general at the mercy of imperial Russia. Accordingly a policy of ruthless Magyarisation was imposed on the Slovaks, and their treatment was exacerbated by the *Ausgleich* (Compromise) of 1867 which made Austria and Hungary equal partners in the new Dual Monarchy and gave each of them authority over their subject nationalities. It was to escape this persecution, as well as the grinding poverty that was the lot of most of the population, that some 80,000 Slovaks emigrated from the homeland in the 40 years before World War I.

From 1867 until the end of the Austro-Hungarian monarchy there were no state secondary schools for Slovaks in Slovakia. The entire state system was Magyarised, and measures were taken to reduce the numbers of the few denominational schools which offered instruction in the Slovak language. There was a university in Pressburg (later Bratislava), named after the Empress Queen Elisabeth, so beloved of the Magyars. Naturally it was only for Hungarians and Magyarised Slovaks. In 1874 the three Slovak gymnasia were dissolved. The same fate befell the cultural institution of the *Matica Slovenska*, whose property and endowments were merely confiscated by the Hungarian authorities. In answer to a parliamentary question as to whether these funds and assets should not be returned to the Slovak nation, the prime minister, Koloman Tisza, notoriously declared, 'There is no Slovak nation.'

Indeed, Slovaks were very poorly represented in the Budapest parliament. It has been estimated that, as a proportion of the population of Hungary, the Slovaks should have been entitled to about 40 seats. In the 1906 elections, however, only seven were permitted to be returned. Three of these – the Catholic priest Ferdinand Juriga, the lawyer Milan Ivanka, and the agrarian Milan Hodza – received prison sentences of varying lengths. A fourth, another priest named Jehlicka, became a Magyar agent and was bribed to leave parliament for a university chair. In the 1910 elections only three Slovaks were returned to parliament, and one of these was soon forced to resign. In 1916 Edvard Benes claimed that there was only one parliamentary delegate in Budapest to represent three million Slovaks.

Slovak political aspirations found expression in the Slovak National Party, re-founded in 1905. This was not so much a tight political organisation as a loose conglomeration of Slovak nationalist views. In it three trends could be discerned. The first was liberal-progressive, whose members are sometimes known as Hlasists after their journal *Hlas* ('Voice'). The outstanding members of this group were Vavro Srobar, Pavol Blaho (both physicians), Ivan Derer (a lawyer), and Antonin Stefanek and Igor Hrusovsky (both journalists). They were ardent believers in Czechoslovak unity and identity, and were greatly influenced by T.G. Masaryk, one of the founding fathers of the future Czechoslovak state.

The other two trends in Slovak national political thinking were populism and agrarianism, represented respectively by Father Andrej Hlinka and Milan Hodza. Hlinka's name has been blackened by its posthumous appropriation by fascist Slovak separatists. In fact, Hlinka was not hostile to the idea of Czechoslovak unity, though he expected autonomy for the Slovaks in any political union with the Czechs. Hodza was an able politician who saw shrewdly that if the Slovak national cause were to succeed, appeal must be made to the peasants who made up the majority of the population.

The Czechs fared rather better than their Slovak brothers, though they claimed many national grievances. Czechs as well as Bohemian Germans had political representation in the Austrian parliament (*Reichsrat*) in Vienna. For much of the nineteenth century they were divided into two political parties, the Old Czechs and the Young Czechs, who were rather more alike than their names would suggest. From 1863 to 1879 the Czech deputies led by the Old Czech Frantisek Rieger boycotted parliament. This was largely over the unfairness of the franchise, which favoured the Germans of Bohemia, but it had no effect whatsoever.

Ethnic tension between the two groups escalated into violent confrontation over the Badeni laws of 1897. Count Kasimir Badeni had been appointed chief minister of Austria with a brief to tackle the problems of Bohemia. The laws in question were two language ordinances which required officials in the Czech lands to be bilingual. While this presented little difficulty to the Czechs, German-speakers in Bohemia and elsewhere in the empire feared that they would be forced to learn the local language, so that Austrian linguistic, ethnic and cultural supremacy would vanish. The Badeni laws led to filibustering in parliament by German-speaking liberals and nationalists, and to rioting in Vienna and other cities. Badeni was forced out of office by popular pressure and his laws were rescinded in 1899. Henceforward it would be the Czechs who engaged in parliamentary filibustering.

All the same the Czechs, unlike the Slovaks, were able to benefit from the introduction of universal manhood suffrage in the Austrian part of the monarchy in 1906. This gave them adequate representation in the Vienna *Reichsrat*, and hence parliamentary and political experience. In immediate terms, however, they were constantly frustrated in their parliamentary battles with the Austrian and other German-speaking deputies.

In addition to renewed (if not altogether fruitful) political activity, there was a genuine indigenous cultural revival in the Czech lands. The arts were represented by writers such as Alois Jirasek, Jan Neruda, Karolina Svetla and Bozena Nemcova; painters like Josef Manes and Mikulas Ales; and composers such as Bedrich Smetana, Antonin Dvorak, and the Moravian Leos Janacek.

Another manifestation of Czech national and cultural life was the *Sokol* ('Falcon') movement. This was a gymnastic organisation founded in 1862 by Miroslav Tyrs (1832–1884) and Jindrich Fugner (1822–1864). While it had parallels with the German *Turnenverein* it was not merely a pale imitation. According to its statutes the aim of Sokol was the revival of the homeland through the education of body and spirit, through physical energy and art and science. At crucial points in the history of the Czechoslovak state – notably, 1938 and 1948 – the annual mass display of Sokol gymnasts was to be an occasion of nationalist and democratic demonstrations.

The story of the national theatre (*Narodni Divadlo*) in Prague exemplifies the cultural aspect of the Czech national struggle. Since funds were not forthcoming from the Habsburg authorities, the building of the theatre was financed by voluntary contributions collected from towns and villages throughout the Czech lands. (This explains the motto on the proscenium arch, which states that the theatre is a gift to the nation from itself.) Likewise the foundation stones were gathered from sites of historic importance. These stones were laid in 1868 by Palacky and by Smetana, whose patriotic opera

*Libuse*, recounting the tale of the legendary princess who founded Prague, was played on the opening night in June 1881. Two months later the building was virtually destroyed by fire; undeterred, the Czechs collected money and started to rebuild.

Indeed, many of the public buildings and monuments of Prague attest to the vigour of Czech culture on the eve of independence. While the national theatre was built in neo-renaissance style, the municipal house (*Obecni dum*) is an outstanding example of the Czech version of *art nouveau*. Completed in 1911, it was designed as a cultural centre for the Czechs (as opposed to the Germans) of Prague. Cubism was also well represented in Prague before World War I, a notable architectural example being the house at the black Madonna in the old town. This was originally designed as a department store by Josef Gocar, one of the foremost Czech cubists, and was completed in 1911–12.

This resurgence of language, literature and art at both elite and popular levels was welcomed by neither the Austrian authorities nor the Bohemian German population. Besides grosser punishments for greater offences petty punitive measures were introduced, of which one example will suffice; a schoolboy who spoke Czech in class would be presented with a small wooden donkey, which stood on his desk as a symbol of stupidity, stubbornness and shame.

The wars and troubles of the fifteenth and seventeenth centuries furnished the Czechs with two national heroes. The first was the scholar and preacher Jan Hus, burned at the stake for heresy in 1415.

Hus became a national hero for a number of reasons. Chiefly, he was seen (somewhat anachronistically) as a martyr for the cause of the individual's freedom of conscience. In addition, he had championed the cause of the Czech 'nation' at Charles university in Prague, which had been underrepresented in the voting system where predominance was given to the Germans. Hus and his colleagues managed to obtain the decree of Kutna Hora from King Vaclav IV in 1409; this assigned three votes to the Czech nation and only one to all the foreign nations. This stance of Hus was often invoked in nineteenth-century university politics in Prague. His death at Constance, through the treachery of the 'German' Emperor Sigismund (Zikmund), in reality the son of Charles IV and brother of Vaclav IV, added fuel to the Czech national myth.

The second Czech national hero was Jan Amos Komensky or Comenius (1592–1670), a Protestant scholar and pedagogue known as the 'teacher of nations'. A pastor belonging to the Unity of Czech Brethren, Komensky was forced into exile in 1628 after the defeat of the Protestant estates at White Mountain. He came to symbolise Czech scholarship, independence of mind and tenacity. His confident prophecy was inscribed on the plinth of the

Hus monument in Prague: 'I too believe before God that when the storms of wrath have passed, to thee shall return the rule over thine own things, O Czech people!'

Both these men were invoked at times of national crisis by the Czechs or Czechoslovaks. When he left the Austrian empire during World War I to begin his task of founding the Czechoslovak state, T.G. Masaryk took with him the Hussite bible of Kralovice and the testament of Comenius, from whence comes the quotation above.

During World War II Komensky served the exiled Czechoslovak government well as propaganda for the national cause. A volume of essays and addresses was published in 1941 to commemorate Komensky's visit to England. Among the contributors were Edvard Benes, the exiled president of Czechoslovakia, and Oskar Kokoschka. Thus the lie was given to the Nazi German propaganda that stated that the Czechs were a people without history or culture. Also during World War II, in a particularly insulting gesture, the occupying Germans draped the Hus monument in swastika flags. In 1968 the people of Prague draped it in black, as a protest against the Soviet occupiers. In that year, too, Komensky put in an appearance, as the source of a patriotic pop song which topped the charts and annoyed the occupiers as much as it comforted the occupied population.

In political terms the Czechs of the nineteenth century were a thorn in the side of Austria. The *Ausgleich* or Compromise of 1867 had transformed the Austrian Empire into the Dual Monarchy of Austria–Hungary, much to the benefit of the Magyars. No such concessions were made to the Kingdom of Bohemia, despite the fact that the Czech lands were the most modernised and industrialised region of the whole Monarchy. From the Austrian point of view there was no need to treat the Czechs as the Hungarians had been. This was a fatal oversight, and would serve the Austrians and Hungarians ill during World War I. In 1918 the history of Czechoslovakia began in reality, but not without the exercise of much heroism, intrigue, suffering, statesmanship and audacity, as the following chapter will show.

# 1918

# The World War and the Making of a State

Czechoslovakia was born out of the pressure of a world war and the collapse of the Habsburg Empire. As one of its founding fathers, T.G. Masaryk later remarked, perhaps the most extraordinary thing about its birth is that it took place, not on home soil, but abroad.

Before embarking on the astounding story of the making of the state, it would be as well to say something of the triumvirate who founded Czechoslovakia: Tomas Garrigue Masaryk, Edvard Benes and Milan Rastislav Stefanik. Masaryk was the most senior and the most decisively influential. His career needs some discussion here, as his thought and experiences contributed greatly to the making and shaping of the Czechoslovak state.

Masaryk was born in 1850 in Moravia to a Slovak father and a Czech mother; this circumstance alone might have inclined him to Czechoslovakism, but in fact his thought on the subject was the fruit of many years of meditation. His family background was humble, and as a young boy he was apprenticed in turn to a locksmith and a blacksmith. All the same his considerable intellectual gifts were recognised, and after a period as a pupil-teacher at high school and four years at the grammar school in Brno he went to study in Vienna. However, he was rejected for training for a career in politics and diplomacy because of his lowly background. Instead he became a professor, and in 1883 went to teach in the Czech branch of Charles University in Prague. He was a deputy for the Young Czech Party in the Austrian parliament from 1891 to 1893, and in 1907, after the introduction of universal manhood suffrage in the Austrian part of the monarchy, sat again as a representative of his own Czech Realist Party.

Masaryk was an extraordinary and controversial figure. As a delegate in the Vienna parliament he led two successive small parties, the Realist and the Progressive, which quarrelled with both the Old Czechs and the Young. A deeply religious man, he was branded an atheist for his opposition to clericalism in politics; as a democratic liberal he believed firmly in the separation of church and state, and saw religion as a private, not a public matter. He was howled down by patriots of all types when he proved that some recently discovered 'medieval' manuscripts which demonstrated a rich cultural life in old Bohemia were, like the donation of Constantine, merely pious forgeries. Masaryk's view was that such pretensions did more harm than good, and that a nation should base its claim to independence on the truth about the past. Nationalists and clerics alike denounced him for his defence of Leopold Hilsner, a Jewish tramp falsely accused of ritual murder in the last great blood ritual trial of the modern era. Most unusually for the time, he espoused the cause of women's rights, taking his wife Charlotte's maiden name as his own middle name and advocating the political, social and cultural emancipation of women. Above all, Masaryk was a democrat, seeing democracy as the only political system which was consonant with the dignity of humankind.

Like most Czech or Czechoslovak nationalists Masaryk originally advocated Palacky's Austro-Slavism, seeing the Empire as a protection for the small nations of Central and Eastern Europe from the twin menaces of Russia and Germany. This was far from being blind loyalty, however, but rather the choice of the least of three evils. Masaryk was well aware of the shortcomings of Austrian and Hungarian justice, for example, when applied to the Slavonic peoples of the Monarchy. In 1909 he had intervened in the Zagreb 'treason trial' to show that the evidence against the accused was forged. This was largely the work of the historian Heinrich Friedjung, who was prosecuted by the former Zagreb defendants that same year. So embarrassing was Masaryk's demonstration of the falsity of Friedjung's evidence that the trial had to be ended on a compromise. Masaryk's involvement in these matters would stand the Czechoslovak cause in good stead with the South Slav brothers during the Great War. As it was, the attitude of the Austrian authorities at the start of that conflict would demonstrate to Masaryk that Austro-Slavism was no longer an option.

In his work of foundation of the state Masaryk was assisted by two younger men, both of them his disciples at Charles University. Edvard Benes was born to a Czech peasant family in 1884. He acquired two doctorates in law, one Czech and the other French, and while studying in Paris worked as a journalist for the Czech press. During the war he was able to put his journalistic skills as well as his knowledge of law and politics at the service of the Czechoslovak action abroad.

Masaryk's other assistant was Milan Rastislav Stefanik, a Slovak, and the son of an impoverished Lutheran pastor, born in 1880. After schooling in Slovakia and Hungary he studied at Charles University, where he received the diploma of doctor of philosophy. In 1904 he went abroad, his nationalistic leanings having come to the attention of the Hungarian authorities. He studied astronomy and worked as an astronomer and meteorologist in several countries, including Switzerland, Italy and, chiefly, France. He obtained employment at the French observatory, and took part in astronomical expeditions in the Sahara and, notably, Tahiti. When war broke out in 1914 he volunteered for the French air force so as to be able to fight against the Habsburgs. He also persuaded the French authorities that soldiers of the subject peoples of the Empire, though classed officially as Austrians or Hungarians, should be regarded as Allied soldiers. Eventually he took French citizenship, and rose to the rank of general. Broadly speaking, Stefanik assisted Masaryk in a military capacity while Benes served him in a political and propagandic one.

The international crisis of summer 1914 gave hope to members of all the subject nations of Austria–Hungary that the pressure of war would bring them, if not complete independence, then at least an improved position in the Empire through its reorganisation or even federalisation. Indeed, in 1909 Masaryk himself had voiced the Czech demand for a federal empire, declaring that, with a powerful German Reich as a neighbour and with a German minority population in Bohemia and Moravia, the Czechs could not enjoy a political existence independent of Austria. Any hope which Masaryk and other Czech patriots might have harboured on the subject was destroyed by a conversation he had with a former prime minister of Austria, Ernst von Koerber, in December 1914. Masaryk asked von Koerber whether an Austrian victory would bring about reform of the Empire. The unequivocal answer was that it would not. Indeed, victory would give the upper hand to the military, who would further centralise and Germanise the Austrian part of the Empire. Naturally, no reform was to be expected from the Magyars, for historical and cultural reasons.

This conversation with von Koerber confirmed Masaryk in his determination to leave the Empire and begin the struggle for freedom. From the outset he realised that, for the Czechs and Slovaks, this would be a war on two fronts; resistance at home and diplomatic persuasion and military action abroad. The home front was soon organised (indeed, Masaryk had taken steps in this direction before he went abroad for the last time late in 1914), and in February 1915 there took place the first meetings of the chief resistance organisation, known as the 'Maffia'. Its leaders were the Russophile Karel Kramar, Alois Rasin, Pavel Samal, Josef Scheiner, head of the Sokol gymnastic and patriotic organisation, and (before his escape from Austria–Hungary) Edvard Benes. Secret channels of communication were swiftly established between the Maffia and Masaryk and the other activists abroad. A complex network of secret messengers was created, and letters and newspapers sent home from abroad in a variety of skilfully constructed items of furniture.

An important agent in conveying messages and in spying on the enemy was the American Czech Emanuel Voska. In September 1914 he returned home from Prague via London, where he conveyed messages and information from Masaryk to the British secret service. This resourceful man set up a network of 80 Czech immigrants in several cities who collected information from Austrian and German embassies, consulates, businesses and shipping lines. Spies for the Central Powers in the United States were unmasked, and subversive activities there uncovered. All of this was passed to the Allies, including the information that the Germans were shipping weapons to Mexico in oil tankers and coffins; information that contributed to the United States' entry into the war, and ensured sympathy for the Czechoslovak cause.

The position of the Czech and Slovak patriots was a strange one. Technically they could be considered as traitors to Austria–Hungary, and as having no homeland. While Czechoslovak agitators, like Polish or South-Slav ones, might have some nuisance value for the Allies, there was ever the fear that the Habsburgs would make a separate peace with the Allies which would ignore the rights of the subject peoples. Connected with this was the problem of legitimacy; who or what could Masaryk and his colleagues be said to represent? Some sort of recognition by the Allied governments would be necessary if the objective of independence were to be attained.

In December 1914 Masaryk, then aged 64, left the Austrian Empire for the last time; when he returned four years later, it was to the infant but independent Czechoslovak state. First he visited the neutral powers of Italy and Switzerland, to gather news and gauge international opinion. He was actually on the point of returning to Prague in February 1915 when he received a secret and urgent message telling him that he would face arrest and possibly execution as a traitor at the border. This news was confirmed by Benes, who managed to meet him at Geneva. Wisely, Masaryk decided not to return home.

On 6 July 1915 he gave a public lecture in Geneva on the medieval Czech preacher Jan Hus, burned at the stake 500 years before; this was to raise the standard of revolt on behalf of the Czechs and Slovaks. The importance of Hus as a national symbol for the Czechs was not lost on the Habsburg authorities. The great monument to the martyr on Old Town Square in Prague had been commissioned in 1900 for this very quincentenary, but the Austrians refused permission for an official unveiling ceremony. In protest, Czech patriots covered the statue in flowers. On the other side of the Atlantic American Czechs also commemorated Hus' anniversary. Across the United States small meetings and large-scale rallies celebrated the martyr and propagated the cause of Czech freedom.

After these demonstrations and his own lecture Masaryk was warned unequivocally that it would not be safe for him to return to the Empire. In September Benes joined him in Switzerland, having made a dramatic escape from Austria–Hungary. The two then went to Paris, where they made contact and joined forces with Stefanik.

Naturally enough the Austro-Hungarian authorities were both vigilant and repressive when dealing with Czech and Slovak resistance on the home front. In September 1914 Vaclav Klofac, leader of the Czech National Socialist Party, was arrested and imprisoned. In May 1915 it was the turn of the Maffia leaders Kramar, Scheiner and Vincenc Cervinka; they were followed into prison by Rasin. All were convicted of treason and imprisoned under threat of execution. Nor were female patriots spared; both Masaryk's daughter Alice and Benes' wife Hanna were imprisoned in September 1915.

The process whereby the leadership abroad achieved recognition by the Allies as official representatives of the Czechs and Slovaks was long and quite complex. On 14 November 1915 the Czech Foreign Committee was formed in Paris and immediately declared independence for the Czech lands. This manifesto was addressed to Russia as the great Slav nation; to England as the home of constitutional government; to Italy as the birthplace of Cavour, Mazzini and Ferrero; and to the France of the great revolution. It declared that the Habsburgs had abdicated by reason of their subservience to the Prussian Hohenzollerns; and it was signed by Masaryk, Jaroslav Durich and representatives of Czech and Slovak organisations in Europe and North America.

The Czech Foreign Committee became the National Council of the Czech Lands in February 1916, with Masaryk as President, Stefanik and Durich as Vice-Presidents, and Benes as General Secretary. Later that year, however, a rival puppet Czech committee led by Durich was set up in Petrograd under the auspices of the tsarist authorities. In March 1917 this body was repudiated by the revolutionary Russian provisional government. In January of that year the proclaimed Allied war aims included, for the first time, the liberation of the 'Czechoslovaks'. Full recognition of the Paris body as the agency authorised to represent the Czechoslovak cause abroad was only accorded by France on 13 July 1918 and by Britain on 9 August. The United States recognised it as a de facto belligerent government as late as 3 September 1918.

Recognition was achieved by patient and untiring work in the three areas of propaganda, diplomacy and military activity. In particular the changing international situation, with the Russian revolutions on the one hand and the entry of the United States into the war on the other, had to be assessed and used to advantage. There was also the problem of Italy (who entered the war in 1915) and the South Slavs. The former was anxious to gain territory in the Balkans at Austria–Hungary's expense; the latter wished for a united South Slav state which would include that territory. The complication for the Czechoslovaks was that Italy at first was resistant to all claims for independence on the part of subaltern nations, as this would seem to support the pretensions of the South Slavs. In addition, the leaders of the Czechoslovak action abroad had to coordinate their activities with those of the Maffia at home and of émigré organisations of Czechs and Slovaks, particularly in North America.

Propaganda had to cope with the fundamental difficulty that neither the leaders nor the populations of the Allied countries had much knowledge of Czechs and Slovaks or of their homeland. At the higher levels the exiled leaders were able to use contacts made through academics and journalists such as Ernest Denis in France and the Englishmen R.W. Seton-Watson and Wickham Steed. It was through Professor Denis' good offices that Masaryk was able to give his lecture on Hus in Geneva, and through the persuasion of Professor Seton-Watson that he agreed to accept the first chair of Slavonic studies at London University in October 1915. Immense publicity for the Czechoslovak cause was generated by his inaugural lecture on the rights of small nations. Masaryk gave a similar lecture on the Slavs at the Sorbonne in February 1916. On the more popular level, the Czechoslovaks in London rented a shop in Piccadilly Circus which acted as an information centre. In its window were displayed maps of Central Europe, news about the Czechoslovaks, and refutations of Austrian propaganda against them.

The main points of the Czechoslovak counter-propaganda were summarised in a pamphlet by Edvard Benes, published in Paris in 1916 and entitled (in French) 'Destroy Austria–Hungary!' This short work was designed to persuade the Allies, especially the French, that a drastic reorganisation of Central Europe was vital if a future war caused by Germanic aggression were not to occur. Its arguments stemmed from the time of the national awakening of Czechs and Slovaks, but were augmented by the experience of the past 50 or so years.

Benes began by rehearsing the whole history of oppression by the Habsburgs and the two dominant and favoured nationalities in the Empire, the German-Austrians and the Hungarians. Curiously, he alluded to 'The Czecho-Slovaks, or quite simply the Czechs'. This was doubtless to stress the ethnic and linguistic closeness of the two peoples, and by adding the three million Slovaks to the seven million Czechs of Bohemia and Moravia to create a still small yet viable nation fit for a nation-state.

In the old Kingdom of Bohemia the Czechs had been at odds with their Catholic, Germanic overlords since the time of Jan Hus, whom Benes ingeniously (if not altogether accurately) identified with the struggle for freedom of the individual conscience which culminated in the French revolution of 1789. The religious struggle of the Hussite wars had also become a national struggle, and the same was true of the revolt of the Bohemian estates in 1618 which precipitated the 30-years-war. From the time of Ferdinand II in the sixteenth century to that of Maria Theresia and Joseph II in the eighteenth the Czechs had been the victims of Habsburg centralisation. Following the Czech defeat at the battle of White Mountain in 1620 a period of '300 years of darkness' had set in, with the Czechs suffering national, cultural and religious oppression. This 'darkness' had been briefly illuminated by the national awakeners and by the revolutions of 1848, which Benes described as the Czech national 'renaissance'. Yet ironically, at that date the Czechs had to take refuge in Palacky's concept of 'Austro-Slavism'; the Empire was the only shelter for such small nations from the depredations and ambitions of Russia in the East and Germany (which seemed to be on the point of unification) to the West. However, after more than half a century of Habsburg broken promises and renewed oppression Palacky's formula no longer held true. Moreover, since German unification under Bismarck the Austrians had been in political and spiritual thrall to their Prussian brothers, and the two ambitious powers were determined to Germanise the whole of Central Europe. If they succeeded, small nations like the Czech would suffer national extinction, while Western Europe would never be free of the threat of further aggression and general war. Indeed, of all the great powers Austria–Hungary bore the most guilt for starting the present terrible war.

The Austrians had been assisted in their work of tyranny by the Hungarians, who had destroyed the Czecho-Slovak state of Great Moravia at the turn of the tenth century, since which time the Slovaks had been enslaved by them. The Czechs, too, had suffered from Magayar domination since the Habsburgs acquired the crowns of Bohemia and Hungary in the sixteenth century, though less directly and to a lesser extent than the Slovaks. These last had also had their moment of revolutionary glory in 1848, only to be ruthlessly repressed and subjected to a rigorous and cruel policy of Magyarisation. In particular language rights were ignored. There were almost no Slovak national elementary schools and no secondary or higher education in the Slovak language. The three million Slovaks were represented by one delegate to the Hungarian parliament in Budapest. The courageous stance of Kossuth and other Hungarian heroes against the Habsburgs in 1848 had only served to deceive liberal opinion in Western Europe, for while the Magyars were brave in defence of their own national, historic and linguistic rights they denied these same rights to the Slavic and Latin peoples of their part of the Empire. It was time, Benes declared, that the truth about this was known.

In terms of diplomacy and political argument, the Czechoslovaks abroad faced three fundamental questions. These were the projected role of Russia in the liberation of Czechs and Slovaks; the Allied attitude to Austria–Hungary and its future; and the basis for arguing the national right of Czechs and Slovaks to a common homeland.

The Russian question arose because of the prevalence of Russophilia, particularly among Czechs. If Austro-Slavism had to be rejected because of the intractability of the imperial authorities as regards reform, then small nations like the Czech could look to the Slavic 'big brother' for protection. Karel Kramar, leader of the Czech National Democrats and one of the most prominent members of the Maffia, had long envisaged the resurrection of the Kingdom of Bohemia under the rule of a prince of the house of Romanov. For Kramar, the Austro-Hungarian monarchy had lost the right to his allegiance by its aggression against Serbia; Russia was absolutely justified in its defence of the South Slav kingdom. Masaryk, however, was determined not to play the Russian card alone. He was influenced in this not only by his distaste for and distrust of the corrupt tsarist autocracy, but by his knowledge of the parlous state of the Russian army. Therefore while not speaking openly against the Russians, he was careful to keep open negotiations with the Western Allies and to work hard to win American opinion over to the Czechoslovak cause.

The problem with Austria–Hungary was that the Allies did not regard that state with the same degree of animosity as they felt for Germany. (In particular, the widespread sympathy for such romantic nationalist Hungarians as Kossuth has already been noted.) From the very outset of the war there were plans to separate Germany from Austria in strategic terms, by moving Russian troops into the Czech provinces; and there were also hopes of facilitating a political division by means of a separate peace. These hopes were revived in early 1917 by the secret peace negotiations initiated by the new emperor, Karl. In March of that year Karl received a secret message from Count Otakar Czernin, one of the joint foreign ministers, that it was essential for Austria–Hungary to conclude peace by late summer, or face total ruin. (This message was intercepted and soon reached the Allies by clandestine channels.) Accordingly Karl approached the Entente powers secretly through his brother-in-law, Prince Sixtus of Bourbon-Parma. On 30 May he reconvened the *Reichsrat*, which had not met in three years, as a forum for the subject peoples of the monarchy.

Masaryk was deeply concerned that Austria–Hungary would win a separate peace, and thus avoid dismemberment as an entity, at the cost of some token reorganisation of the Empire. Accordingly in February 1916 he visited Aristide Briand, the French prime minister, and persuaded him that for the sake of general security Central Europe would have to be reorganised after the war; this would mean the disintegration of the Austro-Hungarian Empire into its constituent parts. Masaryk's statement was reported in several Paris and

London newspapers, and did much to win support for the rights of small nations. In his pamphlet of 1916 already cited, Benes appealed to the Entente powers for such a dismemberment of Austria–Hungary. He suggested autonomy for Poland, the union of the South Slavs under Serbia, the return of Transylvania from Hungary to Rumania, and of course, the creation of a Czecho-Slovak state. (So dangerous was this revolutionary plan that the French censor refused to allow publication of a map of Benes' new Europe, and thus two pages in the pamphlet are left blank.) Such a reorganisation of Central and South-Eastern Europe would constitute an impregnable barrier to any future aggression by the two Germanic powers.

Masaryk later claimed that he had intended to work for union of the Czech lands with Slovakia from the moment he left Prague in 1914. There were problems, however, both theoretical and practical. Most Czech nationalist politicians based their arguments for independence on the concept of historic right; that is, the revival of the historic kingdom of Bohemia. Masaryk certainly took this line, but also went back to the writings of the national awakening to argue a case from natural right. The two peoples, Slovaks and Czechs, were closely allied by blood and language. Moreover, as they were both small nations it was only practical in economic and security terms that they should be united in a single state. (Masaryk was perhaps less frank about another practical matter; in a Czech state which excluded the Slovaks the Czechs would be roughly equal in population to the Bohemian Germans; the Slovaks were needed to ensure a clear Slavonic majority in the new country.)

The chief difficulty lay in the fact that Slovakia formed part of Hungary, and that there was much sympathy for the Magyars in Allied circles. Moreover the Hungarians employed a similar historic-right argument in relation to the lands of the crown of St Stephen as the Czechs used for those of the crown of St Vaclav. However difficult the argumentation, Masaryk, Benes, Stefanik and their supporters eventually won the day, and the liberation of the 'Czechoslovaks' was announced as part of the Allied war aims on 10 January 1917. Two factors helped to bring this about; the Czechoslovak military contribution to the war effort, and the mobilisation of the opinion and influence of the Czech and Slovak colonies abroad.

The story of the formation and contribution to the war effort of the Czechoslovak legions is a long, complex and often heroic one. In the autumn of 1914 a Czech military unit was formed in Russia. The initiative for this 'legion' came from the Czech colony in Moscow, though these Russians of Czech origin were soon joined by volunteer prisoners of war. Indeed, on the eastern front men were deserting in droves to the Russians, the most spectacular incident being the surrender of the entire 28th Regiment, known as the 'children of Prague', at Dukla in the Carpathians on 3 April 1915. These men had marched through Prague on their way to the front singing *Hej Slovani*, the pan-Slav anthem, but with an additional verse that ran, 'We march against the Russians, but no one knows why'. At Dukla they went over to the Russians with flags flying and the regimental band playing, and soon found themselves transferred to Kiev.

Other troops met with reprisals from their own officers. The 11th Pisek regiment refused to march against the Serbs; it was decimated twice by the Austrian commanders, and the survivors were massacred by the Magyar artillery. The 36th Czech regiment, from Mlada Benesov, was massacred in barracks after the men mutinied; the 88th regiment was destroyed in crossfire between German troops and Hungarians in the Carpathians. Men of the 102nd Benesov regiment communicated and fraternised with the Serbs in the opposing trenches and contributed to the Austro-Hungarian defeat in the Balkans. The 35th Plzen (Pilsen) regiment, as Benes recounted, was transported by train to the Galician front; within half an hour of their arrival many of the troops were in the Russian trenches receiving a warm welcome; the rest were massacred by the Germans and Austrians. Meanwhile, Czech and Slovak volunteers joined the French armed forces in the west, though obviously not in such spectacular style or numbers. All the same, almost 3000 American Czechs and Slovaks joined the Czechoslovak legion in France, with others going to Italy and Russia. After the entry of the United States into the war in April 1917 about 40,000 Americans of Czech and Slovak origin served in the American forces.

The Czech troops in Russia faced difficulties posed by the tsarist authorities, who understandably wanted a reliable Russian army rather than some foreign units who were chiefly interested in fighting their own corner. Accordingly they demanded that the Czech troops take Russian nationality, and that they be under the command of Russian officers. Stefanik managed to gain official permission for the formation of a Czech division, but this was soon rescinded. Despite the best efforts of Stefanik and the French military mission in Petrograd to persuade them to organise the Czech troops otherwise, matters stood thus until after the February revolution of 1917. It was only on 24 April that the provisional government agreed to the organisation of the Czechoslovak army, though many details were left undecided until the coming of Masaryk, who arrived in Petrograd in May, on a false passport supplied by the British authorities.

Masaryk and Stefanik had agreed that there should be a real army, not the merely propagandist organisation that the Russians wanted, and that it should be despatched to France as soon as possible. Masaryk had friends in high places in revolutionary Russia, and Milyukov, Lvov and Kerensky were all sympathetic to his cause. However, what really established the Czechoslovaks' fighting reputation and indeed, the right to existence of a Czechoslovak military force, was their distinguished participation in the battle of Zborov in July 1917. This was the last engagement of the second Brusilov offensive, was observed by Alexander Kerensky and by delegates of Allied military missions, and resulted in unmistakable victory. After the battle the Czechoslovaks, who had fought for the first time as a brigade, transformed themselves into the 'First Czechoslovak Infantry Division of Hussites'.

As was only to be expected, the Bolshevik revolution of November merely complicated matters. However, Masaryk was determined that the Czechoslovak legion should hold aloof from Russian internal affairs and depart for the western front. Accordingly in February 1918 the Czechoslovaks made a treaty with the Bolsheviks. This recognised the legion as a regular and independent army and guaranteed its armed neutrality and its right to leave Siberia for France. In order to strengthen its international position Masaryk declared that the legion was part of the French army. The agreement once concluded, Masaryk preceded the legion to Vladivostok, whence he travelled by way of Tokyo to the United States.

The successful establishment of the Czechoslovak legion in Russia stimulated military organisation elsewhere. Stefanik organised the recruitment of volunteers from the United States in 1917, while Benes negotiated with the French authorities; the upshot of this was a French decree of 16 December which established a Czechoslovak army in France. The political concomitant was a convention signed by Benes and Clemenceau, the French premier, in early 1918, which assured the Czechoslovaks of a place at the forthcoming peace conference.

In 1918 the Czechoslovak legionaries in Russia began their famous 'anabasis', which Lloyd George was later to describe as one of the greatest epics of history. This was indeed an epic journey from Western Russia and the Ukraine to Vladivostok, where they took ship for Western Europe via the Suez canal. The situation in Russia had been complicated by two factors. The first was the treaty of Brest–Litovsk, a separate peace between the Bolsheviks on the one hand and Germany and Austria–Hungary on the other. This affected the legionaries in that the Russians were now not able to countenance anti-Austrian activity on their territory. The second factor was the start of the Russian civil war, with both sides eager to take advantage of the Czechoslovaks' military potential. Accordingly the legionaries had to fight their way across the Trans-Siberian railway, engaging alternately with the Reds and the Whites. Armed neutrality, indeed.

Although the Czechoslovak army in Russia arrived too late to engage in combat on the western front, it managed to return in remarkably short order. The first transport left Vladivostok on 9 December 1919 and the whole operation was completed on 30 November 1920, with the general staff arriving in Prague on 17 June. According to Masaryk's own figures there were 92,000 Czechoslovak troops in Russia, with a further 12,000 in France and 24,000 in Italy, making a total of 128,000 men. Indeed, the French President Raymond Poincare declared at the opening of the Paris peace conference that the legionaries had conquered their right to independence.

The Czechoslovaks' military contribution to the war effort was obviously crucial in justifying the creation of the new state. Of equal importance was the utilisation of Czech and Slovak colonies outside Austria–Hungary, particularly in North America. Many were economic migrants, though in their own minds they connected the lack of economic opportunity at home with the lack of political freedom under the rule of Vienna and Budapest. Masaryk was able to draw on their continued interest in the homeland. Even before he left the Empire in 1914 Masaryk had organised fundraising on a large scale in the United States, and was thus possessed of an independent means of financing the Czechoslovak action abroad.

Also in 1914 the Czechs in emigration showed anti-Austrian and pro-independence sentiment. In July the Czechs of Paris hauled down the Austrian flag from the embassy there and decided to volunteer for the French army. (They were granted permission to join the French foreign legion on 20 August.) There were anti-Austrian demonstrations by Czechs in Chicago on 27 July and in London on 3 August. The initiative taken by the Czech colony in Moscow to form an army in Russia has already been noted.

The largest section of the Czech and Slovak emigration was concentrated in North America. As early as 27 August 1914 a Czecho-American Committee for Independence and Support of the Czech Nation was formed in New York, and on 2 September the Czech National Alliance was founded in Chicago. On 13 January 1915 a congress of this organisation met in Cleveland, Ohio. The American Slovaks had been even quicker off the mark. The Slovak League was founded in 1907 by emigrant miners in Pittsburgh. Originally this body aimed at Slovak autonomy within Hungary, but in October 1914 its chairman wrote a newspaper article which declared that a 'United States' of Bohemia, Moravia and Slovakia would be best for the Slovaks.

The American Czechs and Slovaks were to be influential in deciding the shape of the new state, something that became controversial over the course of time. On 19 June 1918 Masaryk was received for the first time by President Woodrow Wilson; on 30 June he signed the 'Czechoslovak convention' between

American Czechs and Slovaks in Pittsburgh. This agreed on the union of the two peoples, and on an autonomous administration, representative assembly and judicial system for Slovakia within the new state. In later years Slovak separatists of the Hlinka Party would claim that 'Czechoslovakia' had been foisted on them by foreigners who were not representative of the people at home.

In point of fact the Pittsburgh convention had been preceded in time by the Liptovsky Svaty Mikulas declaration in favour of union with the Czechs by Slovak patriots at home. This declaration was read out by Vavro Srobar at a Social Democratic Party rally on 1 May 1918 (international workers' day). It demanded self-determination for all subject peoples of Austria–Hungary, including 'the Hungarian branch of the Czechoslovak family'. On 24 May the Slovak National Party met at Turciansky Svaty Martin. On this occasion Hlinka himself announced that the thousand-year marriage of Slovaks with Hungarians had failed, and urged his followers to declare themselves for a Czechoslovak orientation. It remains only to add here that on 30 October 1918 the Slovak National Council meeting at the same place agreed that Slovakia should join the new state.

A similar situation obtained with regard to the Ruthenes of North America. Sub-Carpathian Ruthenia (also known as Sub-Carpathian Russia or Carpatho-Ukraine) was a backward region of Hungary inhabited by Slavs who were closely allied by race to the Ukrainians. The American Ruthenes were determined to free their homeland from Hungarian rule, and debated at length what the future of the region would be. Finally, at a congress held in Scranton, Pennsylvania on 19 December 1918, they voted to join the new state of Czechoslovakia on a federative basis.

Czechs, Slovaks and Ruthenes were not, of course, alone among the subject nations of the Habsburg Monarchy to aim at independence. A meeting in Prague on 13 April 1918 was attended by Croat and Slovene delegates; here a 'national oath' was read out by the distinguished Czech novelist Alois Jirasek and approved by the gathering. In addition four congresses of the oppressed peoples of Austria–Hungary were held, in Rome on 8 April 1918, in Prague on 16 May, in Ljubljana in Slovenia on 18 August and in New York on 15 September. The most important issue was the South Slav question, since Serbs, Croats and Slovenes sought independence in a unified state; this would not only necessitate the break-up of the Habsburg monarchy, but would also affect Italian territorial ambitions. In addition the Poles aimed at the revival of their state, which had been divided among their greater neighbours since the eighteenth century, while Romania hoped to gain Transylvania from Hungary. All these nations viewed President Wilson's concept of self-determination with hope and satisfaction.

Well before the international meetings, on 6 January 1918 the Czechs met in Prague for the 'Epiphany convention'. The choice of the feast of the three kings might or might not have been a coincidence; but the word 'epiphany' means a showing or revelation, and certainly the manifesto produced by the convention revealed the Czechs' nationalist aspirations. The manifesto demanded a sovereign state for Czechs and Slovaks, 'within the historic boundaries of the Bohemian lands and of Slovakia'. It condemned the Hungarians' oppression of the Slovaks, and for the first time demanded that Czechs and Slovaks be represented at the forthcoming peace conference. Later in the month, in a gesture of solidarity with the Austrian workers, the Czech socialists declared a general strike. All this did nothing to ease the lot of the Austrian authorities.

In the summer and autumn of 1918 the events which led to the birth of Czechoslovakia gathered momentum. On 28 June the French became the first to recognise the Czechoslovak National Council in Paris as the supreme organ of the nation and the basis of a future Czechoslovak government. American recognition of the Czechoslovak National Council came on 2 July. On 9 August the British recognised the Czechoslovaks as co-belligerents and the National Council as the supreme organ of the interests of the nation and trustee of its future government. On the home front, the Czech Catholic clergy circulated a statement endorsing Jirasek's 'national oath' and describing the future Czechoslovak state as 'an act of God's historic justice'.

Meanwhile on 13 July a Czechoslovak National Committee had been established in Prague, in defiance of the Habsburg authorities. There was now a danger of divided authority which might give the Austrians a chance to challenge the legitimacy of the national movement. Accordingly, on 26 September, after prolonged discussions with the home Czechoslovaks and with the Allies, the National Council in Paris was proclaimed as the provisional Czechoslovak government. Masaryk was named as president of the government and of the council of ministers and minister of finance, Benes as foreign minister and minister of the interior, and Stefanik as minister of national defence.

This development was necessary in view of the Habsburgs' plans to try to save the Empire by making it into a federation with some degree of autonomy for the subject nationalities. Indeed, hearing that the Emperor Karl was preparing a statement on the federalisation of Austria (though not Hungary, which would have left the Slovaks under Magyar domination), Masaryk hastened to make the Czechoslovak declaration of independence on 18 October in Washington.

This extraordinary document condemned the proposed Habsburg federation as a sham and denied the theory of the divine right of kings as blasphemous. It affirmed belief in democracy and in the principles of President Wilson, and outlined the character of the new Czechoslovakia:

> The Czechoslovak State will be a republic. In a continuous effort for progress it will guarantee full freedom of conscience, religion, science, literature and art, speech, press, assembly and of petition. The church will be separated from the state. Our democracy will be based on an equal right to vote; women will be politically, socially and culturally made equal with men. The rights of minorities will be secured by proportionate representation, national minorities will enjoy the same rights ... privileges of the nobility will be abolished.[1]

Given the extremely democratic tenor of this declaration, it is not surprising that Czechoslovak independence was immediately recognised by the United States.

In his book *The Making of a State* Masaryk duly acknowledged the role played by international events in securing Czechoslovak independence, while at the same time emphasising the efforts of the Czechoslovaks themselves:

> Our independence is a fruit of the fall of Austria–Hungary and of the world conflagration. In vanquishing Germany and Austria, the Allies won our freedom and made it possible. At the peace conference the victors established a new order in Western and Central Europe. We took part in these conferences from beginning to end and signed the treaties, since the Allies, recognizing and accepting our programme of liberation, had admitted us during the war into the areopagus of belligerent nations in whose hands the decision lay. And our former enemies presently recognized our independence in their turn by signing and by giving constitutional ratification to the Peace Treaties. Yet it was only by our resistance to Austria–Hungary and by our revolt against her that we earned our independence. As President Poincare tersely said, we won it by fighting in France, Italy and Russia.[2]

In addition, a revolution of sorts took place in Prague in October. The National Committee continued to exercise authority and to keep order in the

Czech lands, anxious to avoid demonstrations which the Austrians could treat as 'provocations'. By the end of September the National Committee had obtained the cooperation of both the 'socialist council' and of the Czech Catholic People's Party. On 19 October the National Committee proclaimed that the Czech question was no longer internal, but international.

The 'Prague revolution' was far from bloody or violent, though German street signs were torn down, and the victory column of the Virgin on Old Town Square, symbol of Habsburg victory at the battle of White Mountain, was toppled. While these largely symbolic demonstrations took place, representatives of the national committee conducted negotiations with the Austrian governor for a peaceful transfer of power. These were successful, and on 28 October the declaration of independence was signed at the municipal house and also proclaimed at the Vaclav (Wenceslas) monument in Prague. At last the Czechs found themselves masters in their own house. Once again, however, events at home had been pre-empted by developments abroad.

Once independence had been declared and recognised, two questions of great significance confronted the founders of Czechoslovakia; the existence of two governments or sources of authority in Prague and in Paris; and the constitutional form the new state would take. These two matters were settled by negotiations in Geneva in late October between Benes as representative of the provisional government and members of the Prague national committee led by its chairman, Kramar. Agreement was reached between them on 31 October; the two governments were to be merged, and (as had been stated in Masaryk's declaration of independence in Washington on 18 October), the new state was to be a republic.

In a separate and quite independent development, the Slovaks meeting at Turciansky Svaty Martin declared their intention of adhering to the new state. On 5 November Kramar proclaimed a free, independent and democratic republic in Prague, and by 14 November the revolution was complete. On that date the new Czechoslovak national assembly formally deposed the Habsburgs and elected Masaryk as first president of the republic by acclamation. It also elected a provisional government, with Kramar as premier, Benes as foreign minister and Alois Rasin as minister of finance; thus the new government included the foremost members of the previous governing bodies in Prague and Paris.

Masaryk finally returned home to enormous demonstrations of popular acclamation on 20 December 1918. He had left an Austrian province in 1914; four years later he returned to a free, independent Czechoslovakia that he himself had been largely instrumental in creating.

## Notes

[1]   Printed in Vera Laska, ed., *The Czechs in America 1633–1977, A Chronology and Fact Book* (New York, 1978), pp. 117–18.

[2]   T.G. Masaryk, *The Making of a State, Memories and Observations 1914–1918* (London, 1927), p. 333.

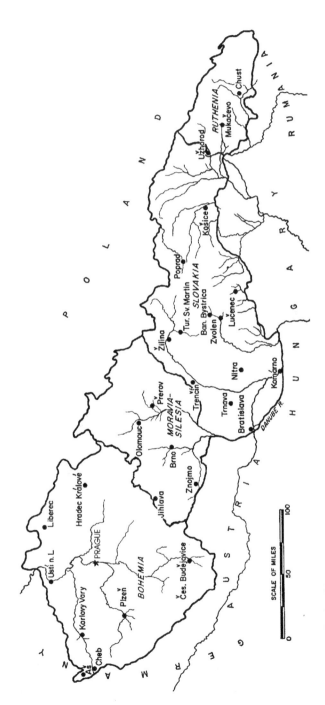

*Map 1 Czechoslovakia, 1918–1938.*

# 2 The First Czechoslovak Republic, 1918–1938

In retrospect the First Czechoslovak Republic has been viewed almost as an ideal state, an island of democracy in a sea of fascist and authoritarian regimes. During the Communist era in particular, Czechoslovaks were wont to look back nostalgically at this 'golden era' ruled over by Masaryk, who was simultaneously the 'President Liberator' and the 'little father'. This image is in vivid contrast, of course, to the view of the appeasing Western democracies in the late 1930s, who saw a corrupt subaltern people exploiting and oppressing a noble and suffering German minority. More recently, revisionist historians such as Zbenek Zeman have questioned both the virtue of the Republic and the integrity of Masaryk and his associates.

This chapter will offer a considered appraisal of both the achievements and shortcomings of Czechoslovakia as a democracy between the world wars. It will consider the constitution and party political system; the economy and social reform; relations between Czechs and Slovaks, and between Czechoslovaks and the national minorities, notably the Germans and Hungarians; and intellectual, artistic and cultural life.

First of all, however, it is essential to consider the circumstances of the birth of Czechoslovakia. As the previous chapter has shown, diplomatic and military activity abroad combined with a bloodless revolution at home had resulted in the making of the state. However, Central Europe at the end of World War I was far from settled or peaceful. The conflicting claims of the successor states to the Habsburg Empire and the determination of the formerly dominant nations to retain their advantages were set in the context of troop movements, an influenza pandemic and general uncertainty and displacement. The chaotic circumstances of the collapse of Austria–Hungary should not be understated. Consequently the first task of the newly liberated Czechoslovaks was to secure the territory of the new state.

A major problem encountered was the ambition and policy of the German population of both Austria proper and the Czech lands. These last, subsequently and inaccurately called 'Sudeten Germans', were determined to preserve at least their autonomy, if not their accustomed superiority. Consequently their leaders refused to cooperate in the establishment of the new Czechoslovak state, believing that it would be a short-lived political and territorial arrangement. Instead they nailed their colours to the mast of Austria's ailing ship. On 21 October 1918 in a pre-emptive strike the Bohemian German deputies joined their Austrian brothers in voting to turn the *Reichsrat* into the German–Austrian assembly. This body then proclaimed the German-populated areas of the historic Czech provinces to be an integral part of Austria. This was followed by the creation of four separate 'German' provinces in the Czech lands which were quite isolated from each other and could not possibly form a viable political entity. The prospects of the Bohemian Germans as a unit in Central Europe were changed, however, when the Austrian–German National Assembly voted for *Anschluss* or union with Germany on 12 November.

Such an aggrandisement of the German Reich was against the interests of both the Czechoslovaks and the western Allies, particularly the French. For the former, the creation of an Austro-German entity would mean fragmentation of their own state (an Austrian law of 22 November incorporated the Bohemian German provinces into German Austria) and ultimately national extinction. For the latter it was unthinkable that the German aggressors who (in French eyes particularly) had started the world war should benefit territorially in the post-war settlement. Accordingly, while Czechoslovak armed forces occupied the Bohemian German provinces the French informed the Austrians that Czechoslovakia as one of the Allied nations should be in possession of the historic Czech lands at least until the peace conference. The British and Americans supported this interim arrangement, and there the matter rested.

A problem of equal moment was the attitude of the other formerly dominant nationality of Austria–Hungary, the Magyars. It had long been an axiom of Hungarian nationalism that the lands of the crown of St Stephen were sacred and indivisible, regardless of the ethnic composition of their populations. It was not therefore likely that the Hungarians would abandon Slovakia, which they continued to call upper Hungary, without a struggle.

On 1 November 1918 Hungary seceded from the Dual Monarchy. Immediately there were riots and revolts in Slovakia, but the Slovak National Council at Turciansky Svaty Martin hesitated to assert its authority. Consequently Vavro Srobar was sent from Prague with a small military force and a very small provisional Slovak government to try to take control. Matters were complicated by the Belgrade armistice between Hungary and the Allies which was vague in the extreme as to the fate of both Slovakia and Transylvania. On 11 November, the date of the armistice, the Hungarians invaded Slovakia in order to secure it. The Slovak National Council was broken up and its leaders arrested, and Srobar's small Czechoslovak contingent of troops was pushed back to the border with Moravia. Military weakness led Benes, still in Paris, to negotiate with the French on Slovakia's behalf. Meanwhile Milan Hodza, the Czechoslovak representative in Budapest, complicated matters even further by separate negotiations with the Hungarians which agreed on a demarcation of territory different to that which Benes had agreed with the French. This arrangement was disowned by the authorities in Prague. On 19 December the situation was finally resolved when the French ordered the Magyars to evacuate Slovakia as far as Benes' line of demarcation. By mid-January an increased Czechoslovak army composed of returning legionaries had occupied the whole of Slovakia.

An apparently peripheral matter, but one that would continue to cause bad blood between Czechoslovaks and Poles throughout the existence of the First Republic, was the Silesian duchy of Tesin (Cieszyn in Polish, Teschen in German), with its coal mines and prosperous town. In ethnic composition it was overwhelmingly Polish, with Czech and German minorities. The new Polish Republic claimed the area on ethnic and historic-right grounds, the Czechoslovaks by reason of historic right and economic considerations. An early agreement between the two sides failed to satisfy either, and in January 1919 Czechoslovak forces settled the matter by military occupation of the region. To their surprise the Czechoslovaks did not receive the unequivocal support of the French on this issue, and were ordered to evacuate Tesin and divide it again with the Poles by a provisional agreement which would last until the peace conference decided the matter.

The peace conference opened in Paris on 18 January 1919. The claims of Czechoslovakia had been considered and dealt with by early April, though the treaty of St Germain was not signed with Austria until 10 September, and the treaty of Trianon with Hungary was not signed until 4 June of the following year. The delay in settling the affairs of Hungary was due to Bela Kun's Bolshevik uprising, which culminated in the establishment of a Hungarian Soviet Republic which was intent, among other matters, on reclaiming Slovakia. A Czech comrade of Kun's, Antonin Janousek, proclaimed a Slovak Soviet Republic at Presov in May 1919. This allied itself with Hungary against Czechoslovakia, but fortunately for Czechoslovak unity it collapsed shortly after Kun was forced by an Allied ultimatum to withdraw his troops from Slovakia.

The Czechoslovak delegation to the peace conference was led by Benes and Kramar, respectively foreign minister and premier of Czechoslovakia. Benes' experience in wartime diplomacy made him the chief negotiator, and he put forward the Czechoslovak claims to the Czech lands and Slovakia as well as other parcels of territory. The crown lands of the ancient Czech kingdom (Bohemia, Moravia and Silesia) were claimed on the basis of historic right. Slovakia was claimed for historic, ethnic, economic and strategic reasons. In addition he claimed two other Slavonic areas, Sub-Carpathian Ruthenia and Lusatia. Masaryk had already agreed with the American Ruthenes at Scranton that Sub-Carpathian Ruthenia should leave Hungary and join the future Czechoslovak state on a basis of autonomy. Benes argued further at Paris that possession of Ruthenia would give his country the advantage of a frontier with Romania. Benes' rather weak claim to Lusatia was that it had been a province of the old kingdom of Bohemia until the seventeenth century and that its Slav inhabitants, the Sorbs, would rather be citizens of Czechoslovakia than of Germany. He also asked for a 'corridor' across Hungary (similar to the 'Polish corridor' across German territory) which would give Czechoslovakia a border with Yugoslavia. There remained, of course, the outstanding dispute with Poland over Tesin.

Most of Benes' claims for Czechoslovakia were approved by the peacemakers at Paris, with the exceptions of the corridor to Yugoslavia and Lusatia. With regard to Ruthenia, its own leaders decided to bring the region into the Czechoslovak state on 8 May 1919. It was recommended that the question of Tesin be settled by direct negotiations between Czechoslovakia and Poland. In addition to having its territory delineated, Czechoslovakia was bound by the peace treaties to respect the rights of its national minorities and to pay a substantial sum by way of liberation payments which applied to all the successor states of Austria–Hungary.

In ethnic terms the new Czechoslovak Republic contained about seven million Czechs, two million Slovaks, over three million 'Bohemian' Germans (mainly in the Czech lands and the larger Slovakian towns), three quarters of a million Hungarians (chiefly in Slovakia), 500,000 Ruthenes and some 80,000 Poles. As will be shown, all this along with the government's centralising tendencies would result in competition, tension and resentment.

Much later, in the early 1930s, Masaryk told the Czech writer Karel Capek: 'The new Europe is like a laboratory built over the great graveyard of the world war, a laboratory which needs the work of all. And democracy – modern democracy – is in its infancy.'[1] The First Czechoslovak Republic has often been hailed as the very model of a working parliamentary democracy in a Europe which by and large preferred more authoritarian forms of government. In order to determine the truth of this picture it is necessary to examine the constitution and its workings; party politics; and the administration of the state with particular reference to Slovakia and to treatment of the national minorities.

A provisional, unicameral national assembly was established in November 1918, together with the provisional government. On 14 November the assembly deposed the Habsburgs, proclaimed the Republic, and elected the absent Masaryk as president by acclamation. On the previous day a provisional constitution had been approved by the national committee which vested ultimate political authority in the national assembly. This body was to elect the president, who was to have severely limited powers and was not even to have the right to dissolve the assembly. It was also to choose the prime minister and government, who were answerable to the assembly. In effect this body was a constituent assembly, charged with the drafting of a permanent constitution.

Initially, the Czech parties were represented in the assembly according to their electoral strength in the last elections to the Austrian *Reichsrat*, held in 1911, and were divided into seven 'clubs'. Of the 268 deputies 55 were members of the Agrarian club; 53 were Social Democrats; 46 belonged to the State-Rights (later National) Democrats. The Czech (later National) Socialists had 29 deputies and were joined in their club by the six Progressive Party delegates; the Czechoslovak People's Party (which was Catholic and clerical) had 24. There was also a Slovak Club of 40 (later 53) deputies. These Slovak members were selected personally by Vavro Srobar, who was a trusted follower of Masaryk. The different means of choosing Czech and Slovak deputies can be accounted for by the marked lack of parliamentary experience among the Slovaks, who had been accorded very little representation under the Hungarian crown.

Perhaps the greatest shortcoming of the provisional constitution was that the national minorities of both Slovakia and the Czech lands were excluded from representation in the provisional national assembly. To balance this it must be borne in mind that the loyalties of the minorities were not above suspicion; and that chaos reigned in Slovakia until the withdrawal of Bela Kun's forces in June 1919 and the subsequent collapse of the anti-Czechoslovak 'Slovak Soviet Republic'. In addition, the German minority refused to accept the legality and authority of the provisional national assembly, and instead wanted to vote in the elections to the Austrian Republican parliament. The Czechoslovak authorities naturally refused to allow them to participate in these elections in a foreign state, so on polling day, 4 March 1919, they demonstrated in large numbers. Although the Germans were apparently unarmed they were fired on in several localities by the nervous Czechoslovak police, who overreacted to apparent danger. Altogether 52 demonstrators were killed and 84 wounded. This tragedy did not bode well for future German–Czechoslovak relations.

As might be expected for one of his forceful and didactic temperament, Masaryk was dissatisfied with his role of a figurehead. He was not content to 'stay above the clouds' (in Kramar's hopeful phrase), but argued successfully for an augmentation of the presidential powers. Although there was some opposition to this in the national assembly, an amendment to the provisional constitution was passed on 23 May 1919.

The new, permanent constitution was approved by the provisonal national assembly on 29 February 1920. The new national assembly was to be bicameral, with a senate (150 members) elected for eight years and a chamber of deputies (300 members) for six. The government was to be responsible to the chamber, and the whole national assembly was to elect the president, for a term of seven years. The president himself was to have quite wide executive powers. There was to be both universal suffrage and proportional representation. The electorate was to vote for a party, not a personality, and a senator or deputy would have to give up his seat at his party's request; this ensured both stability and inner-party discipline. Parliamentary elections were held in April, and Masaryk was elected president on 27 May. He took up residence in Prague castle, formerly the seat of Czech kings, and adopted as the Republic's motto the words of Jan Hus, *Pravda Vitezi* ('Truth Prevails').

The Czechs have often been characterised as a sober, bourgeois nation. Ferdinand Peroutka remarked on his people's staidness and sensible lack of heroics, while even today Czechs use the term *cesky maly clovek*, meaning the little Czech 'bloke' who gets on with his business and quietly achieves his results, whatever the authorities might dictate. It has been said that they stand in contrast to the 'gentry' nations like Poland and Hungary. 'My aristocracy and your bourgeoisie', was the frequent comment of the Polish General Sikorski to the Czechoslovak President Benes during World War II, as they strove to negotiate better relations between their two peoples.

The Czechs and for that matter the Slovaks are not without heroic figures from both the historic and legendary past; but there is a concrete reason for the bourgeois character of Czechoslovak democracy during the First Republic. After the battle of White Mountain the native Czech gentry and aristocracy had been virtually wiped out by dint of execution, expropriation and exile. Their titles and lands had been given to foreigners, who were German-speaking and identified themselves (when convenient) with Vienna and the Habsburgs. These aristocrats played little part in the affairs of the Czechoslovak Republic; the land reform of the 1920s curtailed their incomes and estates, and they had no separate political representation in the national assembly. While the Slovaks were described as peasantry rather than bourgeoisie they, too, lacked a native gentry and aristocracy. Their lords and landlords were either Hungarian or of Magyarised Slovak families.

The system of proportional representation meant that a large number of parties were represented in the national assembly, though only five of them were of any real importance. Indeed, the collaboration of these five parties was required to ensure a working majority in the assembly. Consequently all 17 governments up to 1938 were coalitions. Parliamentary politics at least in the First Republic tended to be moderate, and the only government minister to be assassinated was the unfortunate Alois Rasin, murdered by a Communist student in 1923.

The five decisive parties were the Agrarians, the National Democrats, the National Socialists, the Social Democrats and the Populists (People's Parties). Despite the confusing similarity of some of their names each party had a distinctive ideology and a well-defined constituency.

The Agrarian Party was the largest, and found support among Slovaks, Ruthenes and some minorities as well as among Czechs. Its official title was the Republican Party of Agriculturists and Small Peasants, and it was able to use the land reform of the 1920s to gratify this traditional constituency. However through its involvement in banking and in local government bureaucracy it also managed to become the party of middle-class interests in general. Its leader in the earlier years of the Republic was Antonin Svehla, who was prime minister from October 1922 to March 1926 and again from October 1926 to February 1929. Among its more prominent members were the Slovaks Vavro Srobar and Milan Hodza; this last was prime minister from November 1935 until the Munich crisis.

The National Democratic Party, descended from the Young Czechs of the nineteenth century, was the most conservative grouping. Indeed, it moved so far to the right that it fought the 1935 elections on a common platform with the small and ineffectual Czech National Fascist League. The leader of the National Democrats was Karel Kramar, Russophile and originally monarchist in his sympathies; he was the first prime minister of the Republic, holding office from November 1918 to July 1919. The party was nationalist in the extreme and also anti-clerical, and most of its electoral support was in Bohemia. Chiefly it represented the upper bourgeoisie, and was highly influential through its control of much of the press and its infiltration of the upper echelons of the government bureaucracy. As it came increasingly to represent the interests of the rich commercial and industrial classes a breakaway movement was formed, the Small Traders and Artisans Party.

Most confusingly, the National Socialist Party bore no resemblance to its German near-namesake. Rather, it had been founded in 1897 as a specifically Czech, nationalistic socialist party and as a rival to the Marxist and internationalist Social Democratic Party, founded in 1878. Though Edvard Benes was formally a member (he was ordered by President Masaryk to join a party, though he felt no strong party affiliation), the leaders of the National Socialists were its founder Vaclav Klofac, the same politician who was arrested and imprisoned by the Austrians during World War I, and Jiri Stribny, who was later a fascist. The Social Democratic Party, being Marxist, was at the opposite end of the political spectrum. While members some of the National Socialist Party did incline to fascism until their expulsion in 1926, the Social Democrats aided by the Moscow-inspired demands of the Comintern, engineered the secession of their Communist wing in 1920. As time went on the two parties moved closer together, though there was no question at this point of their amalgamation.

The final major parties to be considered were the People's Parties or Catholic-clerical parties. The character of the Czech and Slovak parties differed markedly from each other, and after 1921 they went their separate ways, with the Czech party participating in government and the Slovak being usually among the opposition. The Czech People's Party was led by Monsignor Jan Sramek, and was in ideology somewhat right of centre. The Slovak People's Party was led by Monsignor Andrej Hlinka, a fervent Slovak patriot who had been imprisoned under the Habsburgs for his active opposition to the policy of Magyarisation. He was co-founder and chairman of his party in 1913, and in 1918 was also co-founder and executive member of the Slovak National Council. As such, he signed the Turciansky Svaty Martin declaration expressing the will of the Slovaks for a common state with the Czechs. However in August 1919 he tried to raise the question of Slovak autonomy at the Paris peace conference, and was imprisoned briefly for this on his return to Czechoslovakia. Until his death in 1938 he remained chairman of his party which was renamed the Hlinka Slovak People's Party in 1925. The party itself contained moderate conservatives, but also had a right wing which tended towards fascism or at least authoritarianism. As will be seen, Hlinka was the chief spokesman in the struggle for an autonomous Slovakia.

The five parties of government (excluding the Hlinka party) dominated political life and cooperated closely with President Masaryk. Indeed, the relationship between the *Pet* (Five) and the *Hrad* (Castle) has been criticised for exerting a stranglehold on politics and preventing the organic development of parliamentary democracy. Masaryk himself has been depicted as an authoritarian rather than a democratic figure who exercised too much power as president because of his dominant personality. Given the plethora of parties spawned by the system of proportional representation and the need for coalition government; given, too, Masaryk's immense personal standing; it seems reasonable that a degree of collaboration between the parties and the head of state should have occurred.

Political stability was also assisted by the fact that Masaryk continued as president until his resignation on grounds of ill health, at the age of 85, in December 1935. (He had been re-elected to office for the third time in May 1927.) He was succeeded as president by his chosen heir, Edvard Benes, the national assembly bowing to the wishes of the outgoing President Liberator. Rather like his German counterpart Stresemann, Benes had held office briefly as prime minister but was Foreign Minister up to 1935. Thus there was continuity in foreign policy. Benes was mostly active at the League of Nations in Geneva and did not have much of a profile at home in Czechoslovakia. Furthermore his character and public persona lacked the grandeur of Masaryk's, being somewhat cold, dry and lawyer-like. Consequently a plethora of publications was launched to present his personality, achievements and policies to the Czechoslovak public. Among others, an appreciation was published to mark his 50th birthday the previous year. Despite the contrast between himself and Masaryk, Benes earned respect, and was accorded the sobriquet of 'President Constructor'.

While the five mainstream parties kept parliamentary politics respectable, there were two groupings on the extreme fringes of the political scene which were able to exert at best a certain nuisance value, at worst a destructive influence. The Communists were particularly insidious. Formed as a breakaway faction of the Social Democrats in 1921, they took their orders from the Communist International, particularly after Klement Gottwald took over the leadership from Bohumir Smeral as Stalin's own nominee in 1927. By and large they were ineffectual both in parliamentary politics and as revolutionaries, though the assassination of minister Rasin by a young Communist has been mentioned. Significantly, the Czechoslovak authorities saw no need to proscribe the party and drive it underground; indeed, it was the only legal and parliamentary Communist party in the region.

At the other end of the political spectrum the Czech fascists formed two small and ineffectual groups who were never strong enough to participate in government. The larger of the two was the National Fascist League, founded in 1926. This group was led by General Radola Gajda, the Siberian legionary who had been one of the heroes of the battle of Zborov in 1917. Among its more eminent members was the poet Viktor Dyk. The League took its inspiration from Mussolini's Italian model, and had a youth organisation and a small trade union section. Anti-Nazi, anti-German and anti-Semitic, it was motivated by a romantic and unrealistic pan-Slavism. Its aim was to destroy the Soviet regime and then, together with a Russia purged of Communism and Marshal Pilsudski's authoritarian Poland, to form a Slavic federation. The League also advocated state control of the economy (in a hazy way akin to

Italian Fascist corporatism), and land reform. Gajda became a parliamentary deputy in 1929, but a plan to seize an army barracks in 1933 proved abortive. The elections of 1935 saw the League poll only 2 per cent of the vote. The other, smaller fascist group was the Czech National Camp (*Vlajka*), which was overtly pro-Nazi and possibly numbered some 30,000 by the late 1930s.

Potentially far more dangerous than either the Communists or the fascists were the parties of the national minorities. Most ominous were the German Nationalist Party and the German National Socialist Party. This last was a direct copy of Hitler's party in Germany, even down to the identical banners and uniforms it adopted. The party followed the German example in being racist, anti-Semitic, pan-German and anti-democratic. As such, it hated the Czechoslovak Republic. In 1920 Bohemian German Nazis attended a pan-German conference at Salzburg which was addressed by Hitler. They were dejected by the failure of the Munich Putsch in 1923 and elated when Hitler was released from prison late in 1924. In 1929 they founded their own version of the German Nazi SA for young men, the *Volkssport*. In 1932 seven members of this group were put on trial for plotting armed rebellion, the destruction of the Republic and a pan-German union. The charges were really too broad to stick, and the accused received derisory prison sentences. The Czechoslovak authorities were probably wise in not making martyrs; only after Hitler and the Nazis came to power in Germany did the Nazis of Czechoslovakia pose a serious threat to the Republic.

Although initially most Bohemian Germans were hostile to the Czechoslovak state, a number of parties recognised the need for cooperation with the authorities and then saw the advantages of participating in government. These parties and politicians were termed 'activist', as they had recognised the political reality of the Republic and had reconciled themselves to working within it. Activism included liberals, Catholics and Social Democrats, while the specifically German Communist Party soon merged with the Czechoslovak national party. From 1926 activist politicians participated in government, members of the Christian (Catholic) Socialist, Agrarian and Social Democratic Parties holding cabinet posts.

No such activism could be expected from the Hungarian parties in Slovakia. This was chiefly because of the irredentist stance of Horthy's Hungary, which refused to relinquish its historic claims to Slovakia, Ruthenia, or for that matter any of the former lands of the crown of St Stephen. Indeed, there is evidence that Budapest was active in fanning discontent and even encouraging treason towards Czechoslovakia. In contrast, in 1926 the able foreign minister of Weimar Germany, Gustav Stresemann, made it clear that he would not quarrel with Czechoslovakia over its ethnic Germans; for him, issues outstanding between Germany and Poland were far more important.

In terms of administration the Czechoslovak Republic was governed as a unitary and highly centralised state. There were solid practical reasons for this, but nonetheless it not unnaturally engendered resentment among Slovaks, Ruthenes and the national minorities. Their grievances will be reviewed below, after national economic and social policy has been discussed. These are particularly important areas, given that Communist propaganda during and after World War II constantly castigated the First Republic for promoting social and economic inequality and even injustice.

After World War I Czechoslovakia along with the other successor states of Austria–Hungary faced financial difficulties due to the vast over-inflation of the old Austrian crown. By 1922 the new Czech crown had been stabilised, but stringently deflationary measures had to be taken by the minister of finance, Alois Rasin, in order to raise its international value. These measures were unpopular as unemployment rose, and Rasin paid for them with his life. However, they saved the Czechoslovak economy from the worst effects of the hyperinflation which ravaged neighbouring Austria and Germany in 1923.

In the long term the economic prospects for Czechoslovakia looked good. The Czech lands at least had not suffered much war damage and were endowed with mineral resources, developed industries and an industrial infrastructure, while there was fertile farmland in Slovakia as well as in the historic Czech provinces. Czechoslovakia inherited between 70 and 90 per cent of the old Empire's sugar refining, brewing, glass, textile, ceramic, leather, chemical and paper industries, as well as the lion's share of coal mining and the building and construction industries. In 1921 nearly 34 per cent of the population was employed in industry and handicrafts, compared with nearly 40 per cent employed in agriculture. A higher proportion of the population was employed on the land in Slovakia and Ruthenia, and a lower one in industry in these relatively undeveloped areas. The chief problem for industry and commerce was to find new outlets, now that the secure internal market of the old Empire had gone. The main difficulty for agriculture was that many smallholdings were too small to be profitable (indeed, many agricultural labourers were landless), and some form of land reform was urgently needed.

The land expropriation law was passed on 9 April 1919, and was designed to redistribute the great landed estates among the rural population. Large estates were to be put at the disposal of the state, their owners being permitted to retain no more than 500 hectares. The question of compensation to these owners was deferred, although none was to be granted to members of the Habsburg family, citizens of an enemy state, or those who had committed grave offences against the Czechoslovak nation during World War I. Tenants with long leases could buy no more than 80 hectares of the lands they farmed. Priority in the land redistribution was to be given to legionaries, war wounded and returning Czech and Slovak emigrants.

A further law of June 1919 established the land office, to be supervised by a board of control selected by the national assembly. Finally, the compensation law was passed in April 1920. Compensation was to be paid to former owners, but at a low rate. They were to receive the value of their land as it was estimated in 1913–1915, calculated in pre-war Austrian crowns but paid in postwar Czech crowns. The price was to be lowered by 10 per cent for every 100 hectares over 1000. Former employees of the great estates were to be compensated by land, a suitable job, a money payment or a pension. Naturally the complex of claims meant that compensation was a slow and cumbersome process, and it was still in train as late as 1937.

On the whole the land reform has been seen as a moderate measure. Thanks to the efforts of the Agrarian Party the land issue was settled in the sense of private property in the shape of smallholdings, though many forests, fishponds and pasture lands were awarded to rural communities and co-operatives. In practice the 500-hectare limit on land retained by the owners was not rigorously enforced; families such as the Schwarzenbergs as well as the Catholic Church managed to retain a good deal of property. However, nearly all the great estate owners were Germans and Hungarians, as were many of their employees. As was to be expected, the national minorities claimed that the land reform was simply an instrument of ethnic injustice, and that they faced unjust discrimination in the matter.

The record of the Czechoslovak Republic on social and industrial legislation was quite creditable. As early as December 1918 the provisional national assembly legislated for the 8-hour working day. In July 1920 came the child labour law, which totally prohibited the employment of children under 14 and forbade the employment at heavy labour of boys under 16 and girls under 18. In addition, young people under 16 and women were not to be employed in dangerous industries such as mining.

Sickness and accident insurance legislation was passed in 1924. Employers were obliged to register all their employees in a health insurance fund, and equal contributions were to be made to this fund by both parties. Sickness benefit was paid out for a period up to 52 weeks, and workers on sick leave could not be dismissed. Accident insurance covered the whole industrial or commercial concern rather than the individual, who might receive up to 26 weeks of benefit if injured in an industrial accident. A law providing for old age pensions for white-collar workers was passed in 1926. In this case, too, employers and employees made equal contributions to the fund. Workers would be pensioned off after the age of 65 in some schemes or after 35 years' service in others, and would receive on average half their monthly salary on retirement.

The lot of women improved immensely under the First Republic. The constitution denied recognition of any privilege based on sex, birth or occupation, women received the vote along with men and some were even elected to the national assembly. There was absolute equality of education for the sexes right up to university level. All posts in state and local administration were open to women. After 1930 they could be appointed as judges, and law required that one-third of candidates in a pool of jurors should be women. In contrast to other European states including Britain, women teachers were not required to retire on marriage, as had obtained under Austria–Hungary. At the insistence of the Czechoslovak feminist organisation women were not privileged in the matter of working hours. On the other hand, they could receive 12 weeks' paid maternity leave, a benefit that was extended even to women in cottage industries such as laundering, dressmaking and lace and bead work.

Social welfare provision was looked on as one of the great achievements of the First Czechoslovak Republic. Indeed, in 1943 the government in exile in London would publish a pamphlet entitled *Social Security in Czechoslovakia*. This was partly propaganda but was also a contribution to the British debate on the Beveridge plan. It was illustrated with photographs of (among other subjects) a modern swimming pool in a Slovakian spa, convalescent and children's homes, a sanatorium, and the enormous card index at the Social Security Institute for Workmen in Prague.

All this legislation notwithstanding, there were inequalities among the population and the mode of governing the country engendered resentment, not only among ethnic Germans and Hungarians, but also among Slovaks and (to a less marked extent) Ruthenes. Much has been made of the 'Note on the regime of Nationalities in the Czecho-Slovak Republic', drawn up by Benes and presented to the Paris peace conference on 20 May 1919. In this document reference was made to acceptance by the new state of the principles applied in the constitution of the Swiss Republic as a basis for national rights. This allusion was subsequently interpreted as a promise by Benes that Czechoslovakia would be a confederation on the Swiss model, though it seems doubtful that either he or Masaryk would ever have contemplated such a constitutional arrangement. For one thing, they were rightly mistrustful of the loyalty of the German and Magyar minorities, who in any case were not concentrated in sufficiently large numbers in homogeneous areas to make autonomy feasible. For another, both Slovakia and Ruthenia were considered by the Czechs to be too backward and lacking in either political experience or economic strength to govern themselves; a state of affairs they blamed on the former Hungarian rulers.

Thus the First Republic was proclaimed as a unitary, centralized state governed directly from Prague. It was the home of the 'Czechoslovak' nation, 'Czechoslovak' was its official language. Consequently all other groups were merely 'minorities'. It is not hard to imagine the indignation this would arouse in the former dominant nationalities, the Magyars and Germans. It should be added, however, that these minorities had full political, economic and religious rights together with the majority Czechoslovaks.

The Slovaks and Ruthenes, Slavonic brothers of the Czechs, had agreed to join the new state in the expectation of autonomy, and they were highly resentful of the Czechs' well intentioned but heavy handed efforts to modernise them and their territory. Centuries of enforced Magyarisation had left both regions economically backward, culturally impoverished and politically inexperienced. Nonetheless national traditions and sentiment had developed among the Slovaks and, to a lesser extent, the Ruthenes. Resentment and frustration could only result from Prague's decision to run the regions as colonies. In addition, in Slovakia differences developed between centralists and autonomists which tended to poison regional politics.

Subsequent history might have been different if not for the tragic death of the Slovak founding father of Czechoslovakia. Milan Rastislav Stefanik was killed on 4 May 1919 when the plane carrying him to his liberated homeland crashed near Bratislava. Though little known inside Slovakia, his military exploits had given him the status of a hero. Possibly his authority might have served to compose internal quarrels.

As has been seen, the provisional Czechoslovak government sent Vavro Srobar to take charge of Slovakia late in 1918. Srobar was Masaryk's devoted disciple and a leading member of the Hlasist ('Voice') group among Slovak nationalists. In January 1919 he dissolved the Slovak National Council and various regional committees and established Bratislava as the capital of Slovakia. 'City of the glory of the brothers' was the new name for the old capital of Hungary (Poszony in Hungarian, Pressburg in German). It was chosen as the capital despite the predominance of Magyars and Germans among the population because of its good communications, particularly the railway.

Srobar was an energetic and forceful politician who could be high-handed, if not authoritarian. He faced a formidable task. The bureaucracy and regional government had been entirely in the hands of Magyars or Magyarised Slovaks ('Magyarones'), who Srobar considered too untrustworthy for continued employment. In addition, he favoured the Slovak Protestant minority over the Catholic majority, as he felt that they would be more loyal to a centralised Czechoslovak state. Partly (though not entirely) as a reaction to this favouritism the Catholic politicians became increasingly autonomist.

In the aftermath of the world war and the Hungarian invasion Slovakia faced severe economic problems. For one thing, food had to be requisitioned for the Czech lands from Slovakia, a matter which did little to further Slavonic brotherhood. For another, the severance of the connection with Hungary severely disrupted what industry there was in Slovakia. Srobar was increasingly blamed for these difficulties. His fall was finally brought about by a violent incident during the first Czechoslovak elections, in March 1920. A number of people were killed and wounded when police fired into a crowd of striking farmhands at the village of Rumanova. Srobar's party, the Agrarians, performed poorly in the elections, and he was jettisoned.

After Srobar two men dominated the Slovak political scene. Milan Hodza was one of the founders of the Slovak Agrarian Party, and its leader even after it merged with the Czech party in 1922. Originally he came out strongly as a Czechoslovak centralist, but as an astute and skilled politician he learned to temper his pronouncements in order to satisfy autonomists and centralists alike. He held several posts in the Prague government, and indeed was the last prime minister of pre-war, independent Czechoslovakia.

A politician of quite a different kidney was Andrej Hlinka. A Catholic priest and a passionate patriot, Hlinka had been bitterly disappointed that the provisions of the Pittsburgh agreement regarding Slovak autonomy were not implemented. His career in the 1920s and 1930s was often stormy as he was frequently at odds with the government in Prague. Nonetheless, in his political testament of August 1938, written when he was dying and the Republic was under attack from Slovak separatists as well as German Henleinists, he stated unequivocally that Czechoslovakia was the natural homeland for the Slovak nation.

In practical as well as 'national' terms, the Slovaks were undoubtedly better off in Czechoslovakia than they had been in Hungary. In 1910 out of a total of 6185, only 154 local government officials had been Slovaks, while there were only 150 Slovak lawyers out of a total of 1879. None of the 59 secondary schools had Slovak as the language of instruction, and the only university, the Elisabeth University in Bratislava, was for Hungarians only. The *Matica Slovenska*, the cultural institution which had done much to foster the Slovak national awakening, had been closed down by the Budapest government in 1875. This was re-established, and a new university, named after Jan Amos Komensky (Comenius), the Czech 'teacher of nations', was founded in

Bratislava in 1919. By 1928 there were 65 secondary schools of which 48 taught in Slovak. Illiteracy rates fell from 34.9 per cent in 1910 to 8.16 per cent in 1930. There was a similar success story in fields such as health care.

At first the colonising Czech teachers, lawyers and doctors were welcomed, but once suitably educated and qualified Slovaks were available to fill their posts, they found their chances of employment obstructed by the colonisers. This, too, would breed resentment.

The most backward and impoverished region of Czechoslovakia was Sub-Carpathian Ruthenia, formerly a province of Hungary. As the previous chapter has shown, the impetus for its inclusion in the Czechoslovak state came from the American Ruthene community in agreement with Masaryk. Certainly, there was little manifest political or national consciousness in the region itself before its inclusion in the First Republic.

As with Slovakia, modernisation of Ruthenia was heavily dependent on an army of Czech teachers, doctors, lawyers, bureaucrats and other qualified professionals. The results in the field of education were astonishing. Before World War I there were only 47 schools in the whole of Hungary which taught in the Ruthenian language. By 1931 in Sub-Carpathian Ruthenia there were 45 nursery schools, 425 lower elementary schools, 16 higher elementary schools, and three teacher-training colleges. Indeed, at Uzhorod, the regional capital, there was even a school for Roma (Gypsy) children.

Attempts were made at economic improvement, such as new methods of cultivation of arable land and vineyards. Nonetheless, Ruthenia remained desperately poor, its revenue being equal to half its expenditure. The reason for this was the poverty of resources of the region, which was rich only in timber (being heavily forested) and possessed of only one mineral, salt.

As in Slovakia, the new political freedom was used to express discontent with the Czechoslovak democratic system. In the parliamentary elections of 1935 the Communist party took over a quarter of the vote, and the autonomist bloc nearly 15 per cent. Once more the American Ruthenes intervened in home affairs. The Ruthenian Council of National Defence in the United States protested at Czechoslovak policy in a memorandum to the League of Nations. Their grievances were that the autonomy promised in the Scranton agreement had not materialised (a fair point which Benes conceded, justifying this on the grounds of the backwardness of the region); that the Ruthenes of Slovakia had not been united with the motherland; and that there were too many Czech officials in the region. All this notwithstanding, Ruthenia was indeed too poor, weak and backward to stand alone. In 1939 it was reabsorbed by Hungary, and after World War II was incorporated into the Ukrainian Soviet Republic by Stalin.

By far the most discontented elements of the population, however, were the Hungarian and German minorities. These formerly dominant nationalities found difficulty in adjusting to rule by a subaltern people. The 'Sudeten Germans' in particular voiced many grievances. 'Sudetenland' was the name given to one of the four German provinces briefly established late in 1918, in the area including the Sudeten mountains. From the mid-1930s the name came to be applied to the whole German population, thus deliberately giving the false impression that they were a homogeneous population. In fact Czechs and Germans were often intermingled. For Masaryk the question was whether there was more injustice in making a fragment of the German race live in a non-Germanic state than in making the entire Czechoslovak nation live in a Germanic one. In addition, and as *Anschluss* with Austria was expressly forbidden by the peace treaties, many German industrialists realised the economic sense in becoming part of Czechoslovakia. Moreover, such people preferred rule from bourgeois Prague rather than 'red' Vienna or Berlin.

The new state's obligations to its minorities were outlined at the Paris peace conference and finally embodied in the minority treaty which Czechoslovakia, like all the successor states, was obliged to sign with the victorious Allies. The Czechoslovaks, however, went further than anyone else in taking on extra obligations, for example providing higher education as well as elementary schools for the minorities. Their rights were also enshrined in the constitution of 1920. Differences of language or religion were not to affect an individual's equal standing before the law nor bar him or her from government service or from any trade or profession, while any type of denationalisation was declared to be a criminal offence. In the event the Germans protested that the constitution had been foisted on them, as they were not represented in the national assembly, though they forbore to explain that this was so because they boycotted the assembly until April 1920. More justified was their protest at Masaryk's first presidential message to the nation, which described the original German inhabitants of Bohemia as emigrants and colonists.

In general, most authorities agree that the Czechoslovak state did not pursue a policy of discrimination against the ethnic German minority. Indeed, Czechoslovakia was more scrupulous than most states in observing the provisions of the minority treaty and other international agreements. However, it was probably unwise to turn the Germans and Hungarians into mere minorities, as this was bound to be provocative. It must also be said that on the local bureaucratic level Sudeten Germans did suffer discrimination at the hands of petty Czech officials. Whether this was sufficient grievance for them to demand incorporation into Nazi Germany, however, is open to doubt.

In artistic and cultural terms the First Czechoslovak Republic enjoyed a vigorous life. The Barrandov studios in Prague produced films that matched well the calibre of their Berlin counterparts. In literature there were world class writers such as Kafka, Karel and Josef Capek and Jaroslav Hasek. The visual arts were represented by such artists as Alfons Mucha, while the music of Janacek and Martinu was adventurously experimental. Yet all too often the culture of Czechoslovakia is overlooked, overshadowed by that of the neighbouring Weimar Republic, or simply and wrongly claimed as part of Germanic culture. In terms of literature and film the language barrier must have played a part (few foreigners even engaged in business or diplomacy with Czechoslovakia felt the need to learn the Czech or Slovak language). However, some Czechoslovak artists have achieved recognition outside Central Europe.

Franz Kafka, of course, is a special case, since he wrote in German and his works have been translated into foreign languages, including English. He became known posthumously through the editorial and biographical work of his friend, Max Brod. His father Hermann was a Czech-speaking Jew (he took as his trademark the jackdaw, *kavka* in Czech), who 'bettered himself' by marrying a woman of the German-speaking yet socially advanced minority in Prague. (In 1910 they numbered about 34,000 out of a population of 450,000.) Franz Kafka grew up bilingual but was sent to a German school. Despite chronic ill health (he died of tuberculosis in 1924 aged 40) and employment as an insurance clerk he wrote prolifically, though most of his work remains unfinished. He is best known for his novels and tales of alienation such as *The Castle, The Trial, Metamorphosis* and *In the Penal Settlement*. These works are heavily introspective, and are marked by an abhorrence and yet respect (if not awe) for the workings of bureaucracy. Indeed, he once commented that the shackles of tormented mankind were forged out of red tape.

Kafka's most famous love affair was with Milena Jesenska, and his letters to her have become a literary classic. Yet it is not widely known that Jesenska was a highly influential and respected democratic journalist in her own right during the First Republic. An outspoken advocate of democracy, she died in Ravensbruck concentration camp in 1944.

A very different writer to Kafka was Jaroslav Hasek; the two men knew each other through the Czech Young Men's Club in Prague. Hasek's life was quite as picaresque as that of his famous fictional creation, the good soldier Svejk (Schweik). He had a series of short-lived jobs as chemist's assistant and bank employee but mainly he devoted himself to travelling and writing fiction, producing 16 volumes of short stories. An irrepressible practical joker, as a writer for the journal *Animal World* he amused himself by inventing whole new species before readers' complaints earned him dismissal. In 1912 he stood in the Austrian elections as a candidate for the purely imaginary Party for Moderate Reform Within the Bounds of the Law; Kafka attended one of his 'rallies'. Like Svejk he served in Galicia during World War I. Captured by the Russians, he was allowed to join the Czechoslovak legion, but later deserted to the Bolsheviks. In 1920 he returned to Prague with a Russian wife whom he had married bigamously. But years of hard drinking had broken his health, and his satirical masterpiece *The Fortunes of the Good Soldier Svejk in the World War* remained unfinished at his death in 1923. Svejk, brilliantly drawn by the artist Josef Lada, became a Czech national hero, the little man whose seeming idiocy brings chaos to the authorities. Under Nazi occupation and Communist rule he would become a symbol of devious and ironic resistance.

Karel Capek achieved fame as a writer of plays, novels and stories which often had a fantastic element. These were sometimes written in collaboration with his brother Josef, an artist and sculptor. The plays included *RUR*, which gave the word 'robot' to the English language; and *The Makropoulos Case*, which concerned a 300-year-old woman who had drunk the elixir of eternal youth. Among the novels was the satirical *War With Newts*. Karel Capek died on 25 December 1938; Erika Mann declared that he could neither stay in mutilated Czechoslovakia after Munich, nor could he outlive his unhappy homeland. Josef Capek was arrested by the Nazis in September 1939 and held successively in the concentration camps of Dachau, Buchenwald, Sachsenhausen and Bergen-Belsen, where he died.

Some Czech artists became famous for their work abroad, such as Alfons Mucha in painting and Bohumil Martinu in music. Mucha made his name in Paris in the 1890s but returned to Prague to concentrate wholly on his epic *Slavonic Epoch*, a series of 20 enormous historical pictures painted between 1910 and 1928 and commissioned by President Masaryk's American friend Charles R. Crane. Martinu largely resided in Paris but composed *Czech Rhapsody* in 1918 and *First Symphony* for the tenth anniversary of the First Republic in 1928. Also in music Leos Janacek challenged operatic tradition to produce modern music drama of a deep psychological intensity. Among his works are *Jenufa*, *Katya Kabanova* and an adaptation of Karel Capek's play *The Makropoulos Case*.

As befitted a bourgeois democracy Czechoslovak industrialists were often patrons of the arts. The Barton family of textile magnates were notable in this respect; their castle at Nove Mesto nad Metuji (Eastern Bohemia) was built in the Renaissance style on the lower storey, baroque on the top, with the whole interior furnished and decorated with in the modernistic style of the First Republic. Surprisingly, none of these architectural and ornamental elements jars with another. In the late 1920s Tomas Bata rebuilt the town of Zlin in

Moravia for the workpeople of his shoe factory. The architect he employed for the town and the shop fronts was Frantisek Gahura, a pupil of Jan Kotera. The slogan at Zlin was 'work together, live individually', and indeed, detached private houses were designed as well as public buildings. Another architect and pupil of Kotera who was active during the First Republic was the cubist Josef Gocar. Together with Pavel Janak he developed the Czechoslovak 'national style', a good example of which is the bank of the Czechoslovak legionaries in Prague. Among other projects he was responsible for the 'new town' in Hradec Kralove, which is strikingly innovative.

The First Republic was also notable for its philosophers, from Karel Capek through Ferdinand Peroutka to Masaryk himself. Indeed, Masaryk as president consciously created the image of Plato's philosopher–king, a noble figure ruling with justice and wisdom. If in reality his personality was more human than the image suggests, he bequeathed his small country a great legacy. Masaryk wrote that democracy is the best political system since it is the only one that is suited to the dignity of man. It is fortunate that his death in 1937 saved him from experiencing the destruction of the democratic Republic he had built at the hands of totalitarian barbarians.

**Notes**

[1]   Karel Capek, *President Masaryk Tells His Story* (London, 1934), p. 299.

# Foreign Policy and the Munich Agreement

The experiment in parliamentary democracy that was the First Czechoslovak Republic endured for a mere 20 years. While it is true that the state faced a number of significant internal problems, there can be no doubt that the causes of its demise lay in external, international affairs. In order to understand this it is necessary to review European diplomacy between the world wars and the foreign policy of Czechoslovakia itself.

In 1924 Edvard Benes presented a review of Czechoslovak foreign policy to the chamber of deputies of the national assembly. In this speech he stressed the moral foundations of that policy:

> Our principles issued and issue from our faith in democracy, from resistance to every absolutism and aristocracy in all its medieval survivals; we believe in respecting the human personality in everyone and everywhere, and in our policy we are guided by this principle. We condemn oppression in every shape and form, whether it be the material oppression incorporated in the governments of the old pre-war regime, or the material or spiritual oppression practised in our own days in the exaggerations of nationalism, or of sheer revolutionism and terrorism.[1]

In practical terms Czechoslovak foreign policy during the First Republic was conditioned by a number of factors: the origins of the state; its geographical position; the ambitions and attitudes of its neighbours; and great power relations. Czechoslovakia was a small successor state in the very heart of Europe. It had reason to fear the revanchist and irredentist ambitions of the shrunken Austrian Republic and the truncated Kingdom of Hungary. There were constant problems with Poland, especially over the Tesin region. Bolshevik Russia was an unknown but quite possibly dangerous quantity. Relations between the Entente powers, France and Great Britain, and defeated Germany, would also have a bearing on the affairs of Central Europe.

Europe after World War I was in trauma, divided and embittered after four years of conflict. Two powerful empires – the Russian and the Austro-Hungarian – had been destroyed by the strain of the war, while a third, the Ottoman, decrepit for decades, had finally collapsed, too. In addition, the German Reich had become a republic, and had lost all its overseas possessions as well as a considerable amount of territory in Europe.

In place of the old empires there were established a number of successor states. Most (though not all) of the South Slavs were united in the new Kingdom of Serbs, Croats and Slovenes, soon to be renamed Yugoslavia. Poland reappeared on the map of Europe for the first time since the late eighteenth century, its territory taken from the old partitioning powers, Austria, Russia and Prussia. Czechoslovakia, as has been shown, was created out of both Austrian and Hungarian territory. All these 'successor states' were meant to fulfil President Woodrow Wilson's principle of self-determination. Such was the ethnic mix in these new countries, however, that substantial national minorities remained; in the Czech lands, for example, there were Bohemian Germans, and in Slovakia a Magyar minority. In the Republic as a whole there were also Poles, Ruthenes, Jews and Roma (Gypsies). All the subject nationalities were meant to be protected by the minorities' treaty which formed part of the peace settlement and of the covenant of the League of Nations.

Naturally enough, the losers in World War I were embittered by the harsh peace terms imposed on them, by their loss of prestige and of territory. Revision of the peace treaties posed a potential danger to the successor states. Ironically in view of future events, it was not revision of the treaty of Versailles with Germany which initially seemed to threaten Czechoslovakia, but the revisionist and revanchist aims of Austria and Hungary.

Yet it was not merely a question of victors and vanquished. The United States most famously washed its hands of Europe and withdrew into isolationism. Great Britain and France, too, were war-weary and the former in particular had had enough of European affairs. The Italians, who had 'rushed to the aid of the victors' belatedly in 1915, were disappointed in their share of the spoils, and even before the advent of Mussolini were demanding more territory, particularly on the Adriatic and at the expense of Yugoslavia.

To complicate matters further, there was Bolshevik Russia to consider. Lenin's government had made a separate peace with the Central Powers in January 1918 and, despite the preoccupations of the Russian civil war, continued to clamour for world revolution. The reality of the Bolshevik menace seemed to be revealed by the formation of the short-lived Hungarian and Slovakian Soviet Republics in 1919 and by the Spartacist uprising in Berlin in January of that year. Accordingly, Soviet Russia was treated as a pariah by the international community. The former Allies intervened militarily (if ineffectually) in the Russian civil war. Moreover Russia, like Weimar Germany, was not allowed to join the League of Nations and was effectively excluded from diplomacy.

In addition to their political problems, most European countries suffered to a greater or lesser degree from the physical and psychological aftermath of the war. There was material damage and loss of life, civilian as well as military in many areas. There was famine in parts of Europe, economic dislocation and pandemics of diseases such as influenza and typhoid. Inflation and unemployment were major problems for most European countries in the early 1920s, and economic factors were bound to be a complicating factor in international relations.

The direction of Czechoslovak foreign affairs between the wars was almost consistently in the hands of one man, Edvard Benes. Except for a brief period as prime minister, from 26 September to 7 October 1922, Benes was Foreign Minister until he succeeded Masaryk as president on 18 December 1935. Even after that date, when Kamil Krofta succeeded him as foreign minister, he continued to have a controlling interest in foreign policy. He was extremely proactive, making no fewer than 50 visits abroad between 1920 and 1928. He was especially prominent in the League of Nations at Geneva, serving six times as chairman of the council and once as president of the assembly, besides chairing numerous committees and acting as rapporteur. In particular, he chaired the committee that drafted the protocol of Geneva in 1924. Based on the principles of arbitration, security or sanctions, and disarmament, this agreement was designed to prevent international disputes from escalating into conflict. Czechoslovakia was the first state to ratify the protocol, but ominously, the reluctance of the British government and Dominions to become involved too closely in European affairs led to its rejection and replacement by the treaty of Locarno in 1925.

The League was at the heart of Czechoslovak foreign policy until the early 1930s when Germany, until this time not really regarded as a threat, came under Nazi control and the whole complexion of international affairs changed. Germany had been admitted to the League in 1926 but was withdrawn from it by Hitler in 1933. Thereafter, and at his dictation, diplomacy was conducted outside the framework of the League. Even so, collective security was ever Benes' goal, and he pursued it through the League, the maintenance of the peace treaties and the creation of the Little Entente.

In addition, and probably uniquely among democratic statesmen, Benes believed that collective security could only be assured if Soviet Russia were to return to the comity of nations. In this respect, he believed, Czechoslovakia could continue Bohemia's historic role as a bridge between East and West, a Slavonic nation firmly committed to liberal and democratic traditions.

In its earlier years the greatest potential threat to Czechoslovakia came from Austria and (to a greater extent) Hungary, the two defeated remnants of the Habsburg monarchy. The danger from Austria was greatly lessened when it became clear that the victorious Allies were determined to prevent its *Anschluss* or union with Germany. The German lands of Austria proper were established at Allied insistence as a republic, Karl of Habsburg being compelled to renounce the Austrian throne, though not that of Hungary. The Czechoslovaks under the guidance of Benes worked consistently for cooperation with the new sister-democracy.

In January 1920 Dr Karl Renner became the first of several Austrian chancellors to negotiate with the Czechoslovaks when he visited Prague at Benes' invitation. Their talks were positive, and in December 1921 a treaty of Austro-Czechoslovak friendship was signed. This agreement provided for peaceful relations, economic cooperation, recognition of the status quo in Central Europe, and settlement of any future disputes by a court of arbitration. Subsequently Czechoslovakia made a much-needed loan to Austria and intervened on its behalf at Geneva over the question of its financial stabilisation. Indeed, Benes served at Geneva on the special council committee of the League of Nations that was concerned with the reconstruction of Austria. A commercial treaty was signed in November 1925. Austro-Czechoslovak relations cooled somewhat as Fascist Italy began to meddle in Central European affairs. Mussolini, who aimed to expand Italian territory at the expense of Yugoslavia, took an increasing interest in Austria and Hungary as a potential sphere of interest and as a counterbalance to the Little Entente. Nonetheless, Czechoslovak relations with Austria remained correct if cool, even after the advent of Engelbert Dollfuss as chancellor and his imposition of a type of clerico-fascist state under Italian protection in 1934.

Despite several attempts at negotiation Czechoslovak rapprochement with Hungary proved impossible. This was not just because the majority of Hungarian nationalists remained unreconciled to territorial losses through the treaty of Trianon; it was also due to the dramatic and revolutionary political developments within the country.

In late October 1918 occurred the 'chrysanthemum' or so-called bourgeois-democratic revolution led by Count Mihaly Karolyi. This movement, while initially loyal to Karl of Habsburg as king, withdrew Hungary from the Dual Monarchy. Karolyi formed a provisional government on 31 October and a republic was proclaimed on 16 November; Karolyi became its president on 11 January 1919. The aim of Karolyi and his minister for nationalities, Oszkar

Jaszi, was to make concessions to the minorities in the form of federation or limited autonomy in return for their continued loyalty to Hungary. Quite soon, however, it became clear that Slovaks, Czechs, Ruthenes, Serbs, Croats and Romanians all wished to be united in either an existing or an altogether new motherland. This was fully in accord with the Allied principle of self-determination which would be embedded in the peace treaties.

Before the treaty of Trianon was signed, Karolyi's democratic Republic was overthrown by Hungarian Bolsheviks, and Bela Kun's Soviet Republic was proclaimed on 21 March 1919. There followed a red terror in Hungary itself as well as armed attempts to regain former possessions of Hungary such as Slovakia. The Hungarian Soviet Republic survived until 1 August, but any hope of the resumption of bourgeois democracy was killed on 16 November when Admiral Miklos Horthy marched on Budapest at the head of the national army. There followed a white terror against the left; Hungary reverted to being a kingdom; and on 1 March 1920 Horthy was elected regent for the absent king.

Such developments were naturally viewed with alarm by all the successor states who had reason to fear both Hungarian attempts at territorial revision of the peace treaties and a possible Habsburg restoration in Hungary. Austria formally renounced such an eventuality in the treaty with Czechoslovakia of December 1921. Accordingly Benes constructed the Little Entente (so-called because it reflected the Great Entente of Great Britain and France) as a means of unified defence against Hungary. Between August 1920 and June 1921 a series of agreements bound the successor states loosely together: the convention of alliance between Czechoslovakia and the Kingdom of Serbs, Croats and Slovenes; the Rumanian–Czechoslovak alliance; and the alliance of Rumania with Yugoslavia.

The Little Entente was both strengthened and extended by the two attempts of Karl of Habsburg to reclaim the Hungarian throne. On 26 March 1921 he returned to Hungary from Switzerland and began negotiations with Horthy. The Regent's reluctance to relinquish the power he enjoyed coupled with protests from the successor states and the former Allies led to Karl's withdrawal on 1 April. He was back on 20 October, secured the loyalty of part of the army and marched on Budapest. Protests by the Little Entente combined with its members' military mobilisation resulted in the threat of armed intervention by the great powers; Karl's forces were defeated by those of Horthy and the government. Karl was taken prisoner and then exiled to Madeira where he died the following April. However the Habsburg cause was kept alive by his widow Zita in the name of their young son Otto. Horthy continued to rule as regent, and Hungary never renounced its claims to any of the former lands of the crown of St Stephen.

Benes believed that the peace of Europe and the security of Czechoslovakia could be promoted, protected and policed by the League of Nations acting on the principle of collective security. In September 1923 he was one of the chief authors of the treaty of mutual assistance, and in October 1924 was largely responsible for the Geneva protocol, which was meant to strengthen the covenant of the League. However, he also saw the need for treaties or agreements with individual states. Consequently Czechoslovakia made a treaty of alliance with France in January 1924 and treaties of friendship with Italy in July 1924 and with Poland in April 1925. (There had been a Czechoslovak–Polish commercial treaty in October 1922.)

On 6 February 1924 Benes made a report on foreign policy to the Czechoslovak chamber of deputies. This speech was considered sufficiently important in propagandic terms to be published in English (and doubtless French) as well as in Czech. It outlined the principles upon which Czechoslovak policy was based, its achievements to date and its aims and objectives for the future.

Benes explained the origins of the Little Entente. Its formation had been provoked by the monarchist Kapp Putsch in Germany and by Karl's attempt to reclaim the Hungarian throne. However, it was also an answer to those who claimed that the rise of the successor states had 'balkanised' Central Europe. He spoke of the successful Czechoslovak rapprochement with the Austrian Republic, and continued negotiations with Hungary. Though these last had been interrupted by several crises within Hungary, in September 1923 Czechoslovakia, with its partners in the Little Entente, had requested the League of Nations to begin negotiations over the financial stabilisation of Hungary. A political convention had been negotiated with Poland, and though some territorial disputes were still outstanding Benes felt that the peace of the region depended on the formula 'Poland and the Little Entente'.

Benes also discussed Czechoslovak relations with the great powers. In February 1921 a treaty was signed with Italy, and Czechoslovakia later adhered to the treaty of Rapallo between Italy and Yugoslavia. Relations with Germany had been stabilised, and a commercial treaty signed. Though Bolshevik philosophy, methods and propaganda were to be abhorred, Benes declared, still it was necessary to bring Russia back into international affairs; without this, an enduring peace in Europe would be impossible. While recognising that Britain had little interest in the affairs of mainland Europe and hence no need for formal alliances, Benes hoped that Czechoslovakia would draw closer to it through its formal treaty with Britain's Entente partner. The treaty with France was signed on 25 January 1924. This declared that both countries would defend the status quo and oppose any attempted monarchical restoration in either Hungary or Germany as well as any attempt at union of Germany and Austria. There was no military convention as such, though existing cooperation in military matters would continue.

The policy of making treaties with individual powers had to be defended from the charge that this was precisely the policy of bloc building which had led to World War I. Critics at home and abroad (particularly in Britain) had called for the neutralisation of Czechoslovakia and its sole reliance on the League of Nations. Benes showed that this was not practicable. Neutrality, he observed, had not saved Belgium from invasion in 1914, and while the League possessed considerable moral force it lacked military strength. It had been unable to end the Graeco-Turkish war or to avert the Corfu crisis, when Fascist Italy had first bombarded then occupied the island in retribution for the murder of an Italian general on the border between Greece and Albania. Thus a formal treaty with France was essential for the security of Czechoslovakia. Benes' clear view of the shortcomings of the League thus absolves him of the charge of naïve credulity which has too often been levelled at him in this respect.

The complexion of international affairs changed dramatically with the Franco-German rapprochement at Locarno in October 1925. The agreements provided for the security and maintenance of Germany's Western frontiers, but not those in the East. This was largely because neither France nor Britain was eager for entanglements in Central and Eastern Europe. Though Benes could and did comfort himself with the realisation that Poland was more directly at risk than Czechoslovakia, this was an ominous development for the future. In addition, the apparent commitment of France to defence of the Rhine meant that it would be unable to render effective military assistance to its allies in the East. None the less France negotiated new treaties with both Poland and Czechoslovakia which guaranteed aid in the event of German aggression.

It is evident from their foreign policy that the loss of the region of Tesin (Cieszyn in Polish, Teschen in German) still rankled with the Poles. In the early 1930s and in face of the rise of the Nazis in Germany Benes tried, as foreign minister, to reach an accommodation with his Polish opposite number, Colonel Josef Beck. Instead, Poland signed a non-aggression pact with Nazi Germany in 1934. In 1936 the French approached Benes to ask whether Czechoslovakia would join France in the defence of Poland in the event of a German attack. Benes replied unequivocally in the affirmative, but the Poles refused the French request of a promise of reciprocal action should Czechoslovakia be under attack from Germany. As late as August 1936 Benes approached the Poles through the French, offering joint Czechoslovak–Polish military preparations against potential German aggression. Once more his proposal was rebuffed.

While the Weimar Republic remained a parliamentary democracy (on paper, at least), Czechoslovakia had little to fear from German aggression. Indeed – and despite the ambitions of Stresemann to restore German hegemony at the expense of the successor states – relations with Weimar Germany remained correct, if not exactly warm. The rise of the Nazi state, with its overtly irredentist, expansionist and pan-German ambitions, would naturally raise new fears.

As has been shown, Benes believed that Soviet Russia would have to play a part in international affairs if Europe was to enjoy peace and security. In addition, he felt that multilateral regional pacts were better than unilateral ones, which increased both the dependence of small powers upon great ones and the risk of war. As early as spring 1933 the Soviet Union had expressed its willingness to make a pact with France and the Little Entente, but nothing came of this until the following year. As a result of Poland's conclusion of the non-aggression pact with the Third Reich in January 1934 Louis Barthou, the French Foreign Minister, evolved a plan for an Eastern pact involving the Soviet Union and Czechoslovakia. Some months later Barthou was murdered in Marseilles at the side of King Alexander of Yugoslavia; the assassins were Croatian fascists in the pay of Mussolini. The plan for an Eastern pact died with him. Instead his successor, the cynical and corrupt Pierre Laval, proposed two bilateral treaties, between France and the Soviet Union and between the Soviet Union and Czechoslovakia.

The Soviet–Czechoslovak treaty of 16 May 1935 was no substitute for the multilateral pact that Benes and Barthou had envisaged. Most fatefully, it made Soviet aid to Czechoslovakia in case she were attacked by an aggressor contingent upon the French fulfilling their treaty obligations by rendering assistance first. Benes saw this provision as safeguarding Czechoslovakia's position between East and West; but time and the Munich crisis would show that he had placed too much trust in his Western ally.

Indeed, trust in the good intentions of Britain and France led Czechoslovakia to toe the Western democratic line on foreign involvement in the Spanish civil war. Initially Leon Blum, head of the French popular front government, had promised aid to the Spanish popular front government against the military revolt of the right, ultimately led by General Franco. Soon, however, he was persuaded by the British (Anthony Eden in particular) to adopt a common policy of non-intervention in Spain. In 1937 Czechoslovakia was among the signatories of the non-intervention agreement sponsored by the British and French, and its representatives participated in the discussions of the non-intervention committee in London. While 'Spain for the Spaniards' seemed a reasonable principle, in reality non-intervention crippled the republican side in the Spanish war by denying it the right to buy arms abroad except from the Soviet Union. At the same time, Hitler and Mussolini were brazenly supplying Franco's nationalists with men, materials and technical expertise.

Meanwhile Czechoslovakia's enemy, Hitler, was going about as a roaring lion, seeking how to devour the Republic. Hitler had a personal hatred of Czechoslovakia as an artificial state born out of the detested Paris peace settlement; as a barrier to his pan-Germanic ambitions of uniting all Germans in one Reich; and as an uncomfortable example of a parliamentary democracy that worked. As early as September 1934 the German Nazis were subsidising Konrad Henlein, head of the 'Sudeten' German Party, to stir up agitation and sedition among Czechoslovakia's ethnic Germans. The investment clearly paid off, since in the Czechoslovak elections of spring 1935 more than 60 per cent of the German population voted for Henlein's party.

An investigation by a British observer of relations between Czechs and Germans is particularly valuable because of its objectivity. Elizabeth Wiskemann's *Czechs and Germans: A Study of the Struggle in the Historic Provinces of Bohemia and Moravia* was published in 1938, before the Munich crisis but after Henlein's announcement of the Karlsbad programme. This is a judicious analysis of the situation which, read with other contemporary accounts and scholarly studies, helps to evaluate the situation.

Most of the Germans' complaints stemmed from the language laws and the land reform. The language law of February 1920 restricted the use of the local language in the courts of a district to those with a minority population of 20 per cent, this being the rule in pre-war Austria. The language decree of 1926 declared that court officials were to help applicants who were ignorant of the local language. Furthermore, non-residents could apply to a jurisdiction where their own language was in use; for example, a German-speaking citizen of Prague might travel to Karlovy Vary (Karlsbad in German) for a suit at law. The language decree of 1928 slightly extended the right of district councils in predominantly German areas to conduct their business solely in that language. The Germans complained, however, that both in legal matters and in education they met with unfair treatment.

The minority school law was passed by the provisional national assembly in April 1919. This stated that 40 children speaking a minority language in a district justified the opening of a lower elementary school (for those aged 6 to 10 years); 400 such children justified a higher elementary school (for those aged 11 to 14). However few German schools were opened; rather, the law was used to open Czech schools in German areas. On the other hand new

German schools were established in Slovakia, where they had not existed before World War I.

Particularly crucial in the matter of provision of schooling and of legal affairs was the nationality census of 1921, since a local minority which failed to reach the magic figure of 20 per cent of the population would not be allowed schools and courts which used its own language. Wiskemann noted that there was a great deal of confusion about nationality in the aftermath of the collapse of Austria–Hungary, but felt that 'there can be no doubt...that chauvinist [Czech] officials often exploited the gen-eral confusion in order to reduce the numbers of the minorities'.[2]

Wiskemann compared educational provision in Czechoslovakia with conditions in Nazi Germany in 1937. In German schools in Czechoslovakia there were on average 34.3 pupils per class, as against 37 in Czechoslovak schools and 40 in schools in the German Reich. Moreover, in the Reich there was one technical institute per six million head of population, while the Germans of Czechoslovakia, who numbered some three million, had two technological institutes and one university.

In secondary education Wiskemann found 'very few tangible Sudeten grievances'. Most complaints came from teachers, in that, for example, Czech language was taught in German schools by Czechs, who also taught German language in Czech schools. It is worth noting here that by the 1930s many German 'activist' parents preferred to send their children to Czechoslovak schools, where they would be safe from bullying by the children of Henleinist parents. The law of July 1919 concerning public libraries seems quite fair and reasonable. Special language libraries would be provided for communities with a minority school of 400 pupils. Where the minority was less than this but amounted to 10 per cent of the population they could share a library with the majority nationality.

Another huge source of grievance for the ethnic Germans was the Czechoslovak land reform. Naturally the great German (and Hungarian) landowners were not best pleased at losing part of their estates, but the law did not affect them alone. Both German and Czech employees on the great estates were hostile to the land reform because they feared victimisation, and Wiskemann concluded that the Germans were indeed harshly treated by all the evidence. While she dismissed the German claim that the reform was intended to denationalise the minorities she found that in practice German applicants did suffer discrimination at the hands of lower officials in the land office. Thus, for example, a German from Bohemia might be offered compensation in the form of land in inhospitable Eastern Slovakia. If he refused it, he would be judged to have forfeited his claim under the law.

Employment was yet another area where the German population claimed undue discrimination against them. Under Austria–Hungary they had dominated the state and local bureaucracy, but the general reduction of civil servants in the 1920s affected Germans more than Czechs. This was because the latter were usually bilingual, while the Germans were reluctant to learn the Czech language. The retirement of older officials naturally reduced the number of German civil servants. In 1938 the principle of proportional representation of the nationalities in the civil service became official policy, but the Munich crisis and collapse of Czechoslovakia meant that this was never implemented.

Sudeten Germans dominated the light industries of Czechoslovakia such as textiles, glass and ceramics. After World War I the internal market shrank from over fifty-one million to about thirteen and a half million consumers. Germans now had to import raw materials and pay freight charges and tariffs when exporting goods. All this did not bode well, though its implications did not become obvious for a good ten years, when light industry enjoyed a boom. However it became particularly vulnerable during the financial crises of 1931 which devastated Weimar Germany. Capital placed in banks in Germany was frozen; the Sudeten banks themselves had been heavily involved in industry and had taken grave risks; while the textile industry, long dependent on the banks, found that its foreign markets had vanished. Sudeten Germans faced unemployment, and it was easy to raise accusations of discrimination against the authorities. However, Wiskemann remarked that it was plain that the government could do no more to protect the Czech weavers of Brno than the German weavers of Reichenberg (Liberec).

Despite all the grievances alleged by the Sudeten Germans it seems highly unlikely that Czechoslovakia would have collapsed or disintegrated without the interference of the German Nazis and the well-meant but ultimately futile attempts of the Western democracies to keep the general European peace by placating Hitler. It was thus international affairs, rather than internal problems, which caused the demise of the First Czechoslovak Republic.

In the two years before Munich there were carefully orchestrated protests and demonstrations in the German language areas. Naturally enough, these heightened tensions between Czechs and Germans. The writer and journalist Milena Jesenska reported on the atmosphere of increased crisis in the 'language frontier' regions. Undoubtedly, existing antagonisms were exacerbated by the interference of the Third Reich with its encouragement of the Bohemian Germans.

Meanwhile Henlein was posing as a loyal but baffled subject of Czechoslovakia. On a visit to London in December 1935 he had long discussions with the veteran Czechophile R.W. Seton-Watson. The English professor noted Henlein's explicit rejection of Pan-Germanism and his ruling out of any form of union of the German-speaking areas of Czechoslovakia with the Third Reich; his description of the totalitarian principle as 'untenable' and prefer-ence for an 'honest democracy' in the style of T.G. Masaryk; and his utter repudiation of anti Scmitism. The two met again in Prague in January 1936. Seton-Watson recalled that they agreed on the basis of the indivisibility of the Bohemian lands; the real possibility of an agreement within the frame-work of the Czechoslovak constitution; the rejection of totalitarianism and anti-Semitism; acceptance of Masarykian democracy; and outright denial of any connection with Hitler.

All this time Henlein was being subsidised by Berlin to encourage Bohemian German separatism. The separation of the predominantly German-speaking areas would entail the dissolution of Czechoslovakia. While there was a fairly solid 'language frontier', particularly in Western Bohemia, there were also scat-tered 'linguistic islands' in different parts of the country. In addition, the ethnic populations of towns and even villages were often mixed. Thus the use of the term 'Sudeten' by the Nazis and their Bohemian cats' paws was deliberately misleading, implying as it did a unity of population. In fact, the Sudeten moun-tains formed only one of the ethnic German areas. Racial autonomy and the alleged wrongs of the Bohemian Germans were not the concern of Berlin; however, loss of the language frontier would make vulnerable the defences of the Czechoslovak state. The absorption of the so-called 'Sudetenland' became both more feasible and more desirable after the *Anschluss* of Nazi Germany with Austria in March 1938.

That same month Henlein was instructed by Hitler to keep on raising demands that the Czechoslovak government would be unable to satisfy. Accordingly on 29 April at Karlovy Vary (Karlsbad) Henlein announced a six-point programme of Bohemian German demands. These included full self-government for the German areas and the appointment there of German officials, as well as the complete reorientation of Czechoslovak foreign policy. These demands amounted to virtual autonomy for the 'Sudetenland'; but what really stuck in the throats of the democratic government was the demand to profess Nazi ideology freely and legally.

By May the French and British democracies were thoroughly apprehensive of the escalating situation. They (or rather, their heads of government and foreign ministers, respectively Neville Chamberlain and Edouard Daladier, Lord Halifax and Georges Bonnet) demanded that the Czechoslovak govern-ment accede to the demands of Henlein. Hunted but determined, President Benes and his Prime Minister Milan Hodza refused to accede to the 'Karlsbad

Programme'. On 20 May rumours reached Prague that German troops were massing on the frontier. In a matter of hours the Czechoslovak army was partially mobilised, in an impressive display of strength and efficiency. Britain and France were forced to pledge aid if German troops crossed the borders of Czechoslovakia, while for their part, the Germans had been shown how quickly the Czechoslovaks could respond to a military threat. On 28 May, in conference with his generals, Hitler avowed his 'unshakeable will' that Czechoslovakia should be destroyed. On 30 May he signed a directive for war with the beleaguered Republic.

In a move that foreshadowed the Munich conference, the British demanded that the Czechoslovak government request a mediator to assess the grievances of the 'Sudeten Germans'. Such assistance arrived in Prague on 3 August, in the unpromising form of the shipping magnate Lord Runciman, who was accompanied by his formidable and Germanophile wife. The Runciman 'mission' spent most of its time in Czechoslovakia being entertained in the castles of German-speaking nobles and listening to the grievances of those who had 'suffered' from the land reform. Repeated requests from Wenzel Jaksch, leader of the German Social Democrats, that the members of the mission should listen to the views of his constituents was ignored. Colonel Frantisek Moravec, head of Czechoslovak intelligence, was assured by members of the British party that their government was determined to appease Hitler, and that nothing that was said in the Czechoslovaks' defence would be taken into consideration. Runciman's determination in this respect was confirmed by staged demonstrations on the part of the Sudeten Germans.

Moravec's report of the attitude of the British is confirmed as veracious by Chamberlain's conversation with North American journalists, for whom he threw a private luncheon party at this time. Chamberlain declared that, for geographical reasons, neither Russia, France nor Britain could fight for Czechoslovakia. That country was not homogeneous and could not survive in its present form; thus it had better aim for the best terms possible from Hitler.

The Sudeten leaders were astonished and dismayed when, on 2 September, Benes submitted to them his 'fourth plan'. This fulfilled the 'unfulfillable' Karlsbad demands. Only a staged demonstration at Moravska Ostrava on 7 September gave them the excuse to break off negotiations. Plainly, they were hoping to take direction from Hitler's speech at the Nuremberg rally on 12 September.

This speech, while vilifying Benes in particular and the Czechoslovaks in general, did not declare war on the Republic but only threatened it. Two days previously the violence in the 'Sudetenland' had been carefully escalated.

This set the scene for the direct entrance into Czechoslovak affairs of an unlikely knight errant, Neville Chamberlain.

The British Prime Minister was undoubtedly well-meaning and courageous, but all attempts to clear him of the charge of 'senile vanity' (as Jan Masaryk, Czechoslovak minister in London termed it) fall on the obstacle of his own family letters. In these missives Chamberlain boasted to his sisters frequently of the brilliance of his exploits and the excellent reception accorded to his views and speeches. It should be emphasised here that Britain had no reason to become involved in the affairs of Central Europe. It is true that France, Britain's ally, was bound by treaty to assist Czechoslovakia if she were the subject of aggression. Britain, however, had no such obligation. It was just that Chamberlain thought that he was the man to deal with Hitler personally; accordingly on 13 September he proposed a meeting with the German leader. Audience was granted for 15 September, at Berchtesgaden. Chamberlain, then aged 76, got into an aeroplane for the first time in his life. He did not bother either to inform or to consult with Benes.

At Berchtesgaden Hitler demanded the 'return' of the Sudetenland to Germany; a somewhat odd request, as Bohemia and Moravia had never formed part of either Bismarck's or Kaiser Wilhelm's Second Reich. Chamberlain took Hitler's proposals home with him, and discussed them on 17 September with his own cabinet and with Daladier and Bonnet. The Czechoslovak government was then presented with the demand that areas with at least 50 per cent German population should be transferred immediately to the Third Reich. Naturally Benes and his government rejected this proposal. However, this refusal was followed by an ultimatum. The Czechoslovak Republic would have to accept the Anglo-French plan, or face invasion; the French would not stand by their guarantee in the treaty of 1935, and if they did not assist Czechoslovakia then neither would the Soviet Union. Faced with international isolation on account of the French betrayal, the Czechoslovak authorities had no choice but to accept Hitler's terms, which they did on 21 September.

Despite the fact that the plausible and perfidious Henlein had fled to Nazi Germany on 14 September, Chamberlain chose to repose his hopes in the fair-mindedness of the Fuehrer, whom he met at Godesberg on 22 September. There he was dismayed to find that the latest concessions were not enough. Hitler demanded German occupation of the 'Sudetenland' by 28 September, and also wanted the claims of Hungary and Poland on behalf of their minorities in Czechoslovakia to be met. Moreover, all military installations and industrial, commercial and agricultural enterprises were to be left intact. Despite the blatant injustice of Hitler's shifting demands neither the French nor the British were prepared to go to war in defence of Czechoslovakia. After some hard bargaining Hitler changed the date of secession of the 'Sudetenland' to 1 October.

In London trenches were dug in the parks and gas masks were issued to civilians. Clearly a 'war in sight' panic was being encouraged. In a well-known speech on 27 September Chamberlain declaimed that it was 'horrible' and 'fantastic' that the British should be 'digging trenches and trying on gas masks here' in the cause of 'a quarrel in a faraway country between people of whom we know nothing'. This speech was in stark contrast to the one made the day before by Hitler at the Berlin Sportpalast. In this apparently hysterical tirade he savagely attacked Benes personally for atrocities against the Bohemian Germans. Benes was a purveyor of terror; Hitler was 'a decent German soldier'. Jan Masaryk, as Czechoslovak minister in London, presented his government's response to the Godesberg memorandum. This he rejected as the type of ultimatum usually presented to a vanquished power, not to a sovereign state. The Prague government could not accept such outrageous demands; in a famous call to history he declared, 'The nation of St Wenceslas, John Hus and Thomas Masaryk will not be a nation of slaves.'

Quite incredibly, Chamberlain instructed the British ambassador in Berlin to reassure Hitler that the demands of the Godesberg memorandum would be fulfilled. On 28 September both Bonnet and Chamberlain asked for Hitler's arbitration in the matter, while the British also begged for Mussolini's mediation.

The upshot of all this febrile diplomatic activity was the infamous conference at Munich, on 29–30 September. The negotiators were Hitler, Daladier, Bonnet, Chamberlain and Halifax; Mussolini played the role of honest broker, while the Czechoslovaks were not invited at all.

The Munich *Diktat* went far beyond the demands of Godesberg. The participants in the conference decided that the 'Sudetenland' would be occupied by Nazi Germany in five stages between 1 and 10 October. Altogether, about 11,000 square miles of Czechoslovak territory with a population of more than 800,000 – 719,000 of them being Czechs rather than ethnic Germans – was to be handed over to the Third Reich. (In addition, on 22 November the Germans awarded themselves a sixth zone which had not been mentioned at Munich, and which gave them at least 60,000 further Czech subjects.) The ceded territory contained more than 80 per cent of Czechoslovakia's chemical, textile and glass industries, and more than 70 per cent of its iron and steel works, and accounted for at least one-third of the Republic's total exports. In addition, 93 per cent of Czechoslovak lignite production was lost to Nazi Germany, as well as 55 per cent of black coal output and 46 per cent of electrical energy.

It was agreed that all matters pertaining to the 'Sudetenland' would be decided by an international commission. This principle was a dead letter before the Munich agreement was even signed, as the Czechoslovaks had to surrender their fortifications and military secrets as soon as the territory was occupied. Indeed, when Hitler later went to inspect the frontier defences he was quite awed that he had managed to acquire these without a single shot being fired. Britain and France promised to guarantee the new frontiers of Czechoslovakia against unprovoked aggression; Germany and Italy did not.

In the early hours of 30 September the Czechoslovak representatives in Munich were summoned by Chamberlain who, announcing that he was 'pleasantly tired', yawned uncontrollably (or was it contemptuously?) as he informed them of the fate of their country. No response was expected from the Czechoslovak government. Chamberlain went home to a rapturous reception, taking with him (as he modestly said), 'peace with honour' and 'peace for our time'. The Czechoslovak delegates went home with the news that their country had been sold over their heads. After some debate on the possibility of armed resistance and a futile appeal to the Soviet Union for support, the Czechoslovak President and government capitulated.

In contrast to his British colleague, Daladier seemed ashamed and embarrassed when the German ultimatum was presented to the Czechoslovak representatives. Presumably this is why, in his memoirs published in 1946, he stated quite mendaciously that Benes and the Czechoslovak government had actually requested the Anglo-French ultimatum in order to justify their acceptance of the Munich agreement. This calumny was repeated by Bonnet. The French also spread the story that Benes himself had suggested the surrender of the 'Sudetenland' to Hitler as a means of resolving the crisis.

Thus (in the words of Churchill's famous speech during the Munich debate in the British parliament) 'All is over. Silent, mournful, abandoned, broken, Czechoslovakia recedes into the darkness.' Churchill went on to prophesy, quite accurately, that the state was now indefensible and would be swallowed up by Nazi Germany. He also described the Munich agreement as 'a total and unmitigated defeat'; but this was not the popular view in Britain, and he was howled down.

One European power besides the Third Reich scored a notable victory at Munich, namely, Stalin's Soviet Union. Both Stalin himself and the native Czechoslovak Communists were able to capitalise on the fact that the Soviet Union had not participated in the Munich conference. Indeed, by the terms of the Soviet–Czechoslovak treaty the Soviet Union was bound to render military assistance to Czechoslovakia – but only if the French first went to the aid of the threatened country. Thus the Kremlin was able to stand aloof from the 'betrayal' of Czechoslovakia by the 'capitalist' powers.

Much later, Klement Gottwald, leader of the Czechoslovak Communist Party and eventually president of the country, claimed that Stalin had offered the Czechoslovaks unilateral military assistance. Benes, ran the Communist version of events, had refused this in order to save capitalism and the Czechoslovak bourgeoisie, and because he feared the consequences of a Soviet victory. Therefore he had preferred to sacrifice Czechoslovakia and leave its people to endure the Nazi occupation. That such an offer was made seems highly unlikely. After World War II Benes revealed that three times he had asked the chief Soviet representative in Prague, Sergei Alexandrovsky, what aid could be hoped for from Moscow, and that he failed utterly to get an answer. For his part, Alexandrovsky telegraphed Benes' request for information to the Kremlin, but shortly afterwards sent another message stating that Benes no longer required an answer, as Czechoslovakia had accepted the Munich agreement.

That the Soviet Union had no intention of rendering assistance to the Czechoslovaks is revealed by Litvinov's devious speech at a meeting of the political committee of the League of Nations on 23 September. The Soviet Union, he stated, was not bound to aid Czechoslovakia in the absence of French action, but it might do so voluntarily or as the result of a decision of the League. Such intervention, however, could not be insisted upon as a duty.

All the same the Soviet leadership, possibly with post-war considerations in mind, continued to maintain the fiction of its willingness to help Czechoslovakia at the time of Munich. At an official banquet in the Kremlin in December 1943 Stalin bluntly asked Benes why he had not fought in 1938. Later that evening he showed Benes a newsreel of Soviet troops, and told him reproachfully that the red army had been at Czechoslovakia's disposal in 1938.

Benes himself has been held accountable for the Munich debacle. He has been criticised variously for choosing untrustworthy allies, for putting too much faith in the system of collective security, and for refusing to use the military option against Nazi Germany. It is quite possible that military action, for instance, would have led to a short, sharp localised war in Central Europe rather than a global conflagration; but this can never be known for certain.

Estimates of Benes' diplomatic abilities vary considerably. Several British diplomats thought him to be too 'busy', devious, and quite possibly dishonest. In 1940 William Strang of the Foreign Office acknowledged him to be resourceful and active, but felt that he had to be watched continually. Robert Bruce Lockhart, who knew him well, described Benes as self-reliant and self-confident, guided by fixed moral principles, fortified by strict self-discipline, and having clear aims. At the same time he admitted that these qualities were unattractive if admirable. The British historian of the League of Nations, who had the opportunity to see him at work at Geneva, thought Benes 'the cleverest, the best-informed, and for many years the most successful of European ministers.'[3]

Benes defended himself against his critics after Munich. He pointed out that during the crisis the Czechoslovak cabinet virtually abdicated its responsibility, leaving him to make difficult decisions alone. He also rejected the post-Munich criticism that he should have tried to establish personal contact with Hitler; after all, this was precisely what Chamberlain, in his naivete, had done.

For 20 years Czechoslovakia had maintained the model of a working parliamentary democracy, alone among the states of Central and Eastern Europe. In part, it is true, it had been betrayed from within, by the Nazified element of the ethnic German minority, but largely it had been sacrificed by the Western democracies. It should have come as no surprise that Hitler broke the Munich agreement the following March by invading the Czech lands and dismembering the sorry Second Czecho–Slovak Republic. What no one could have predicted, however, was that the Czechoslovaks at home and abroad would wage an unremitting battle against national extinction.

## Notes

[1] Edvard Benes, *Five Years of Czechoslovak Foreign Policy* (Prague, 1924), p. 9.
[2] Elizabeth Wiskemann, *Czechs and Germans: A Study of the Struggle in the Historic Provinces of Bohemia and Moravia* (2nd ed., London and New York, 1967), p. 124.
[3] F.P. Walters, *A History of the League of Nations* (Oxford, 1960), p. 116.

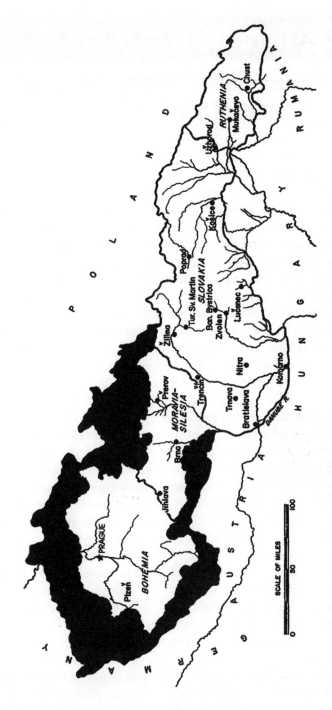

Map 2  *Czechoslovakia after Munich, 1938–1939.*

# 4 World War II

## Resistance, Propaganda and National Survival

The Munich agreement left Czechoslovakia in a truly indefensible state, and in a very short time its neighbours cynically helped themselves to its territory. Meanwhile Edvard Benes succumbed to Nazi pressure and resigned the presidency. He left the country, also at Nazi insistence, travelling to London as a private person though, oddly enough, on a diplomatic passport. It seems highly unlikely that Benes intended to abandon his country to its fate, though in the current circumstances he was unable to do anything to help it. Later, both he and the Czechoslovak government in exile would declare that, for Czechoslovakia, the war with Germany had begun in September 1938.

Munich destroyed the First Czechoslovak Republic by altering the frontiers of the state, and in its place a Second Republic was proclaimed under the hyphenated name of Czecho-Slovakia; the legality of this entity was dubious at the time, and was certainly challenged later. In its work of mutilating Czechoslovakia Nazi Germany was aided and abetted by that country's neighbours. On 30 September 1938, the very day the Munich agreement was signed, Colonel Josef Beck demanded that Tesin, that old bone of contention, be ceded to Poland. By 10 October the Polish army had occupied the area in question, and in November they went on to take additional territory in Slovakia and in Czech Silesia. In terms of population this new 'Polish' territory contained 132,000 Czechs, 77,000 Poles, and 20,000 Germans. In addition, Poland was one of the first countries to accord recognition to the Slovak state (thus participating further in the dismemberment of Czechoslovakia), and later encouraged an anti-Benes group of exiles who claimed leadership of the Czechoslovak liberation movement.

Not to be outdone by Poland, Hungary hastened to lay claim to most of Slovakia and parts of Sub-Carpathian Ruthenia. By the first Vienna award of 2 November 1938, which was arbitrated by Nazi Germany and Fascist Italy, Hungary gained substantial and strategic territory in both Slovakia and Ruthenia. It would swallow the whole of Ruthenia after Hitler's occupation of the Czech lands some four months later. Altogether some 1,150,000

Czechoslovaks were transferred to Hungary, Poland and Germany by the awards and agreements of 1938–39.

On the night of 14–15 March 1939 the Third Reich completed its work of destruction by invading and occupying the Czech lands as a German 'Protectorate', having persuaded the not wholly unwilling Slovaks that it was in their best interests to declare independence from the Czechs. The clerico-fascist Slovak state which emerged was nothing more nor less than a puppet-satellite of Nazi Germany.

The British and French governments protested formally to the Nazi German authorities on 18 March at the annexation of the remainder of the Czech lands. This they condemned as an outright breach of the Munich agreement, and therefore of no legal validity. They proceeded to issue guarantees to Poland, Rumania and Greece in the event of German aggression. Quite clearly they felt that Czechoslovakia was past praying for. Indeed, in a speech to the House of Commons on 15 March Chamberlain had declared that, because of Czechoslovakia's 'disintegration' through 'internal disruption', Britain was no longer obliged to guarantee its frontiers.

Certainly the British government seems to have looked the other way when, later that same month, the Bank of England handed over to its German counterpart 23,000 kilograms of Czechoslovak gold. This had been deposited in the English bank for safekeeping by the Bank of International Settlements. That summer de facto diplomatic recognition was accorded both to the German Protectorate of Bohemia and Moravia and to the puppet Slovak state.

All this might lead to the assumption that Czechoslovakia was not only knocked out of World War II before that war even began but had actually ceased to exist. In fact, a struggle for national survival in the face of apathy and occupation began. When considering Czechoslovakia in World War II a number of areas of concern spring to mind: Slovak separatism and the occupation of the Czech lands; the question of patriotic resistance in both these regions of the former Czechoslovakia; and the work of the Czechoslovak action abroad, in political, propagandic and military terms, to avert the strong possibility of national extinction.

The fate of the Czech lands will be considered first. Hitler's complaint that the compliant Chamberlain had spoiled his triumphant entry into Prague was ominous. Indeed, given the Nazis' quest for living space, their pan-Germanic claim that Bohemia and Moravia were 'German spaces', and the attraction of the mineral, industrial and agricultural resources of the region, the survival of the 'Second Czecho–Slovak Republic' seemed in doubt.

On 14 March the Slovak Diet made a unilateral declaration of independence. True, Slovakian separatism had a well-documented history, and negotiations between Bratislava and Prague had broken down over the question of finance for the poorer part of Czecho-Slovakia. However, the previous day the Nazi leadership had summoned to Berlin Father Jozef Tiso, head of the new Slovak government and leader of the Hlinka Party. There he received an ultimatum; either the Slovaks could take independence under the benign protection of the Reich, or Slovakia would be thrown to the Hungarians and other friendly neighbours.

Benes had been succeeded as president of Czechoslovakia (or rather, Czecho-Slovakia) by Emil Hacha, a highly respected elderly judge with no political experience whatsoever. On 14 March he was summoned to Berlin along with the foreign minister Frantisek Chvalkovsky. Hacha was presented with a 'request' for German protection of the Czech lands which he was required to sign. The two Czechs were quite literally chased round the table by the Nazis and subjected to threats of various kinds. Hacha resisted for several hours; at one point he suffered some sort of seizure, possibly a minor heart attack, and had to be revived with an injection from a Nazi doctor. This intense physical and psychological pressure combined with the information that hundreds of German bombers were poised to strike at Czechoslovakia at last induced Hacha to sign. (In fact, German troops had already crossed the Czechoslovak frontiers.) He would do so only after telephoning to the government in Prague.

Hitler finally got his triumphant entry into Prague, and a painting, later reproduced on a postage stamp, showed him leaning out of a window of the castle and looking down on the conquered city. The Czech lands became the Protectorate of Bohemia–Moravia and, unlike Slovakia, were subject to direct military occupation. The former diplomat Constantin von Neurath was appointed as Reich Protector, with the notorious Sudeten Nazi Karl Hermann Frank as State Secretary. Frank, who had a pathological hatred of the Czechs, was described by Seton-Watson as 'mocking, negative and intransigent'. Curiously, Konrad Henlein seems to have been marginalised from the start, possibly because, having fulfilled his limited purpose, he was found to be insufficiently gifted to play a part in the government of the Protectorate.

This new state was seen first and foremost as a source of booty, for Nazi Germany, the occupying forces and the native Bohemian Germans. Huge quantities of metals, minerals and agricultural products were exported directly to the German Reich, which also gained control of the gigantic Skoda armaments works. On a more mundane level the occupying troops threw themselves on the resources of Prague and the Czech countryside with gusto, eating and drinking themselves into a state of oblivion; more than one account exists of German soldiers being hospitalised by their own gluttony.

For the first few months the Czech population bore the occupation pacifically enough. They were not unsympathetic to the plight of President Hacha and the government, which was led by the respected General Alois Elias. (The Nazis chose not to make use of Czech fascists, obviously recognising their inherent uselessness, but preferred to get established politicians to form the administration. In any case, General Gajda's Fascist League refused to collaborate with the German occupiers.) Even so, resistance was expressed through a 'policy of pinpricks'. Such apparently petty torments as changing the destination boards on trams or politely giving the Germans wrong directions did much to annoy and unsettle the occupiers; it is said that the entire railway system ground to a halt by the use of the Czech phrase meaning 'I do not understand German' (*Nerozumim nemecky*). A petty kind of harassment which particularly grated on the Germans was the 'v for victory' campaign, which had originated in Belgium and soon spread throughout occupied Europe. The letter v was chalked on trees, painted on walls and even traced in the snow throughout the Protectorate. The Germans tried to counter this by claiming that the v stood for 'Viktoria', an old German word for victory; but no one was fooled.

Falsification of production figures was not uncommon, and as late as May 1941 an official newspaper complained at 'national differentiation' between German cows, which produced 4.5 litres of milk per day on average, and their Czech sisters, who could only manage 2.5 litres. One of President Benes' exiled propagandists, Jiri Hronek, remarked that the Germans' lack of humour made them particularly vulnerable to this sort of petty persecution.

Be that as it may, certainly the Germans were unnerved by the Czechs' polite hostility. The Czechs were promised good treatment in exchange for cooperation and acceptance of their fate as a subaltern people. (Bohemian Germans automatically became Reich citizens; Czechs and, of course, Jews, were merely Reich subjects.) Nonetheless, a violent incident in the industrial town of Kladno triggered brutal persecution by the Nazis in June 1939. The discovery of the body of a German policeman on the street led to the arrest and execution of over 200 Czechs and the imposition of a huge fine and a curfew. Kladno apart, the Czechs' simmering resentment culminated in violent confrontation in the autumn of 1939.

The first German action against the Czechs was the taking of some thousands of hostages on 1 September (the gifted artist Josef Capek was among them); these were taken mostly to Dachau, and were to guarantee the good behaviour of the Czech population after the invasion of Poland. Tensions mounted with the approach of Czechoslovak national day (28 October). Peaceful demonstrations in the cities were brutally broken up, and in Prague a student, Jan Opletal, was so badly beaten he later died of his injuries. At his funeral on 17 November the students of Prague staged a peaceful protest marked by a few instances of aggression from the German forces of order. Student demonstrations also took place in other cities such as Brno. These protests furnished the pretext for a horrific attack that night on the student body all over Prague and elsewhere in Czechoslovakia. Some hundreds were beaten, tortured, shot or hanged outright; some thousands were hauled off to slave camps in the Reich. As punishment for their rebellion it was announced that all universities and institutes of higher education would be closed for three years; in the event, they were to stay closed for the duration of the war.

'Resistance by pin-pricks' as well as outright acts of sabotage were constantly recurring. So recalcitrant did the Czechs prove even in the face of brutal retaliation that in the autumn of 1941 von Neurath was recalled and replaced by Reinhard Heydrich, up to now known as 'the blond beast' and soon to be called 'the hangman of Prague' as well as to become one of the chief architects of the Holocaust.

Like their brothers and sisters throughout occupied Europe, the Jews of the Czech lands were the special object of the Nazis' murderous intentions. In the Protectorate, however, a cynical refinement to Nazi methods was added, in the shape of Terezin or Theresienstadt.

This citadel had been built in the eighteenth century by Maria Theresia, ironically as one of three fortresses pointing towards the enemy, Prussia. Here the Nazis claimed to have set up an independent Jewish town, with its own government and even its own post office and postage stamps. Quite brazenly they invited the Red Cross to inspect this showpiece in 1944. Film taken at the time shows the inmates enjoying musical events, sports facilities and health care. There was even film of a concert given by the children of Terezin.

The reality of life in Terezin is shown graphically in the reminiscences and novels of Ivan Klima, who spent most of his childhood there. Terezin was a concentration camp like any other, its inhabitants starved and used as slave labour. (Most of the happy 'inmates' in the Red Cross film were, of course, hired actors.) Besides its propagandic purpose, Terezin's chief function was as a transit camp for the extermination camps in the east, and Jews were transported there from Germany, Austria and the Netherlands. Several thousand perished at Terezin itself; many more passed through there on their way to the gas chambers.

Meanwhile the Slovaks were finding their coveted independence more than a little hollow. The declaration of Slovak independence of 14 March 1939 was nothing more nor less than the result of Hitler's determination to destroy Czechoslovakia. Nonetheless it was supported by all the Slovak Catholic clergy, while the bulk of the population at least acquiesced in the apparent vindication of the Slovak cause. However the falsity of independence soon became evident.

Indeed, the treaty of protection between Slovakia and the Third Reich of 23 March 1939 stated that Germany could station troops and build fortifications on Slovak soil, and thus effectively control Slovakia's defence and foreign policy. Although Slovakia was regarded as Nazi Germany's 'calling card' to Eastern and South-Eastern Europe (in as much as Slovakia demonstrated the benefits of co-operation with the Nazis), the Reich Germans viewed the resources of Slovakia much as they did those of the Protectorate, and forced requisition of timber, industrial goods and foodstuffs was not infrequent. (Although, as in the Czech lands, there was a pretence of paying for these products, in reality the Slovaks, like the Czechs, made a loss rather than a profit.) As a satellite of the Third Reich Slovakia was obliged (in terms of almost pathetic bravado) to declare war on the Allies, rather than (as had been hoped) to preserve neutrality. Any attempt at an independent policy was swiftly stifled by the threat of concession of further Slovak territory by the Germans to Hungary.

Nor was political life less than stormy. The conservative and clerical majority of the ruling Hlinka Party led by Jozef Tiso was largely inimical to Germany because of the Nazis' treatment of the Catholic Church in the Reich and also because of reservations about Nazi racial ideology. In March 1939 Tiso became the first (and last) president of the 'independent' wartime Slovak state; but the cabinet was dominated by the extreme wing of the Hlinka Party led by Vojtech (or Bela) Tuka, Sano Mach and Ferdinand Durciansky. This radical faction had been in existence since the 1920s, and blatantly admired both Italian Fascism and German Nazism. In October 1938 the extremists had founded the Hlinka Guard as the Slovak equivalent of the Fascist *squadristi* (blackshirts) and the Nazi *Sturm Abteilung* (brownshirts). Perhaps it was fortunate for them that the party's founder Andrej Hlinka had died in the previous August, having affirmed in his political testament that the future of the Slovaks lay in a common home with the Czechs.

The radicals repeatedly tried to inflame the population against the resident Czechs (most of who, not unnaturally, emigrated), the Jews, and the Czechoslovak action abroad. It was widely believed that politicians such as Mach and Tuka would be happy to sell Slovakia to Hungary in exchange for power for themselves. Indeed, there are indications that these people were willing to push Slovakia further towards overt fascism. A government decree of September 1939 made all male Slovaks between the ages of six and 60 eligible for service in the Hlinka youth or Hlinka guard. In autumn 1940 the guard was plotting some kind of coup, which was aborted by the army in January 1941.

The radicals did not have it all their own way, however. The Slovak constitution of 21 July 1939 was far from merely echoing German National Socialism. Rather, it showed the influence of the Austrian corporative and clerico-fascist state under Dollfuss and his successor Schuschnigg; of the authoritarian, Catholic regime of Salazar in Portugal; and of papal encyclicals on social teaching. In December 1939 the Slovak government tried to introduce corporatism on the Austrian model, with the population being organised into six 'social estates'. This was too close to home for the Nazi Germans, who denounced the scheme and in retaliation seized control of the Slovak armaments industry. Slovak vasselage to the Third Reich was confirmed by the Salzburg conference of July 1940, where the Germans dictated personnel changes in government and party.

The following month, on German orders, Tiso signed the decree which deported about 70,000 Slovak Jews to the Reich, most of whom were exterminated. This was one of the crimes for which Tiso would be executed after the war. That Slovak Catholic consciences were not at ease over this matter is shown by two pieces of evidence. One is the sizeable number of reports from Slovakia to the Czechoslovak government in exile in London which recounted assistance given to Jews by Catholic clergy (largely, as in the Reich itself, in the form of forged baptismal certificates). The second is a law of May 1944 which halted the 'resettlement' of Slovak Jews in Germany and instead interned them in relatively more humane camps in Slovakia. Unfortunately these Jews were to be murdered by the German forces which occupied Slovakia following the failure of the national uprising of August 1944.

In practical terms the pre-war Czechoslovak state had vanished; that it was (more or less) reconstituted after the war was largely due to the Czechoslovak action abroad which ultimately came under the recognised leadership of Edvard Benes. The position of the Czechoslovak emigration was fraught with difficulty as well as with internal dissension. Not the least of its troubles was the dubiety of its legal standing as representative of the Czechoslovak nation. Official recognition of a government in exile and other organs was essential if 'Czechoslovakia' were to be treated by the Allies as a co-belligerent and thus given some voice in both wartime and post-war policy making.

To add to the difficulties, there was Benes' famous 'Munich complex'. This was quite understandable; he had seen both himself and his country sacrificed by his ally, France, and by Great Britain. He never fully recovered from a strong feeling of betrayal, both personal and national. Edward Taborsky, his wartime private secretary and future biographer, believed that it was this as much as his long-established view of Czechoslovakia as a bridge between East and West, which led him to repose too much confidence in Stalin and the

Soviet Union. Certainly British diplomatic activity during and after the war tended to reinforce the 'Munich complex' rather than otherwise.

Be that as it may, after a brief sojourn in London Benes made his way to North America, where he gave academic lectures as a professor at Toronto and elsewhere. (His lectures would form the basis of his book *Democracy Today and Tomorrow.*) More crucially for dismembered and occupied Czechoslovakia, he worked hard to make contact with American government agencies, to gather support from the highly influential Czech and Slovak émigré organisations, and to make propaganda for the Czechoslovak cause.

The Czechoslovak emigration was well aware of events in Europe, and reacted accordingly. During the 'May scare' of 1938, when the Czechoslovak armed forces mobilised against a reported massing of German troops on the frontiers, the Czech National Alliance of America was revived and a corresponding Slovak National Alliance was formed. A huge rally was organised at the Chicago stadium on 26 September, during the crisis which led to the Munich conference. Another took place on 15 March 1939, the day of the Nazi invasion of the Czech lands, in Pilsen park in Chicago, the chief speaker being Jan Masaryk. At another mass meeting in the same city on 18 April the chief American Czech and Slovak émigré organisations offered Edvard Benes the leadership of the Czechoslovak action abroad.

Benes held informal and unofficial talks with Franklin D. Roosevelt in May 1939, in the course of which the American president allegedly promised recognition of a future Czechoslovak government in exile. Sensing the approach of war, Benes returned to London in July 1939, as a private citizen who was obliged by the British authorities not to engage in political activity. Eventually, however, the British came to recognise that he was the only man capable of uniting and leading the Czechoslovak action abroad.

Not that Benes was without rivals, or even enemies. The French government, whether from personal dislike or guilt over Munich, tried to exclude him from negotiations to form a Czechoslovak national committee in Paris in autumn 1939. They preferred to work with the Slovaks Stefan Osusky and Milan Hodza, who actually formed their own committee independently of Benes'. It must be stressed that Hodza and Osusky did not stand for a 'Slovak' as opposed to a 'Czechoslovak' cause; rather, they were motivated by personal ambition and financial considerations in their intrigues to exclude Benes. The British authorities, however, had realised that Benes was the only man of sufficient stature to represent the Czechoslovak nation, and advised against his exclusion.

There were other complications. First, after the Nazi invasion of 14–15 March 1939 Czechoslovak legations in various capitals (among them London,

Paris and Washington) had refused to acknowledge the legality of the Protectorate or to hand over their premises to the Germans. These legations and their staff were recognised by the host governments as representatives of the hyphenated Czecho-Slovak Second Republic, despite the claim by Benes and his followers that the continued existence of the legations was proof of the juridical continuity of the First Czechoslovak Republic. Second, though official recognition of any sort was denied by foreign powers to the Protectorate, the Slovak state had been accorded *de facto* (though not *de jure*) recognition, largely for reasons of trade and in hopes of its neutrality in any conflict with Germany.

Finally, Benes had unnecessarily complicated his own position as president (as he claimed) of the pre-war First Republic which still existed. While it could be argued that the Nazi occupation of the Czech lands was illegal because it broke the terms of the Munich agreement; while there might be some justice in the claim that Benes' resignation as president was invalid because made under duress; there was still no escaping the fact that Benes had sent a message of congratulation to his successor Hacha, a fact which seemed to signify acceptance of the status quo. All this, together with the European Allies' patent lack of interest in the Czechoslovak cause, created a huge task for Benes and his supporters.

Indeed, relations with the Czech home front were an exceedingly complex and delicate matter. Benes and his supporters abroad felt, probably rightly, that it was better to have a puppet government of Czechs than direct rule from Berlin. Thus while the Tiso state could be denounced as treasonable and illegal, in messages home (initially, at least) the Czechoslovak emigration emphasised loyalty and obedience to the Prague government on the part of the Czech population; the official line of the exiled Czechoslovaks was that the Prague government was a government in captivity. Moreover, like Hacha and his administration Benes and his supporters were against any violent manifestation of opposition to the occupiers, fearing a bloodbath. Instead they advocated passive resistance and continuation of the policy of pinpricks. While all this was desirable and even necessary in terms of 'our people at home' (as Benes frequently called them), it could only serve to obscure the legal position of the emigration when it came to official recognition by foreign powers.

As has been seen, both the French and British authorities were willing to recognise a Czechoslovak National Committee, though not a government in exile, largely for reasons of authority over Czechoslovak servicemen who had escaped to France and hoped to fight for the Allies. Benes' struggle for recognition of a government, with himself as president of the Republic and a national council to act as a parliament in exile, was long and arduous. Matters were eventually simplified by the fall of France in 1940, which concentrated most Czechoslovak political figures and fighting men in Britain.

On the outbreak of war between the Allies and Germany on 3 September 1939 Benes and the Czechoslovak exiles were in an ambivalent position. On the one hand, they had no official standing; on the other, the British government appointed Robert Bruce Lockhart as liaison officer between itself and the Benes camp. Moreover, the European service of the BBC invited Jan Masaryk, son of the President-Liberator and former Czechoslovak minister in London, to make weekly broadcasts in the Czech language; he first did so on 8 September.

Official recognition from the Allies came with painful slowness and after tortuous negotiations. The Czechoslovak National Committee in Paris was recognised by the French on 14 November 1939 and by the British on 20 December. In July 1940, after the fall of France, the British accorded recognition to a provisional government, to be based in London. This led Jan Masaryk to ask Bruce Lockhart whether the Czechoslovak airmen who had died fighting with the Allies were only provisionally dead. Indeed, use of the term 'provisional' was only one of three flaws the Czechoslovaks found in the British recognition. The other two were the fact that the British government would not grant recognition or support to any future boundaries in Central Europe; and that the legal and juridical continuity of Czechoslovakia before and after Munich was not recognised by the British.

Full, *de jure* recognition of a government in exile only came in July 1941, some four hours after the Soviet Union, newly entered into the war by virtue of the German invasion of its territory, had accorded the same recognition to the Czechoslovaks. Benes as president officially declared war on the Axis powers on 16 December 1941. The Czechoslovak government in exile was to exercise authority and make policy decisions on behalf of the home population. Besides the cabinet, there was a national council which exercised the functions of a parliament.

Jan Masaryk was to prove an able propagandist, not only to the Czechoslovaks at home but also to the Allies. He, together with Benes, Dr Hubert Ripka and a host of less eminent speakers and writers became adept at publicising the Czechoslovak cause. Their propaganda had a number of emphases. These may be analysed under the following headings: the call to history; the juridical continuity of the First Republic despite Munich, dismemberment and occupation; the Czechoslovak contribution to the war effort; Czechoslovakia's role as a bridge between East and West; and the solution of the Sudeten German question.

The 'call to history' particularly concerned the Czech lands, and was important to counter German propaganda, which claimed that Bohemia and Moravia historically constituted a 'German space'. This assertion, which had met with notable sympathy from the Western appeasers at the time of Munich, was reiterated throughout the war. Therefore the Czechoslovak action abroad emphasised that the First Republic (or at least, its Czech lands) was a continuation of the medieval kingdom of Bohemia. This view is epitomised by a post-war book by J.V. Polisensky, *History of Czechoslovakia in Outline*, based on lectures he gave in London in 1946. This survey of 'Czechoslovak' history begins before the arrival of the Slavs in Central Europe, proceeds through the medieval and early modern periods to the national awakening of the nineteenth century, the First Republic and the German occupation before ending with the liberation of 1945. This seamless view of history was no mere academic whimsy; right up to the end of the war the Czechoslovaks feared that in the peace settlement Czechoslovakia might be reduced in territory, or simply not reconstituted at all. Therefore this aspect of propaganda in particular was concerned with the question of national survival.

Equally, Czechoslovak concern that the state might disappear in the post war settlement was the motive of the second strand of propaganda; the juridical continuity of the First Republic. This was no idle fear, as even in the British Foreign Office the opinion was voiced that Czechoslovakia had been an ill-conceived failure, and ought not to be revived. At the same time Otto von Habsburg, son of the last emperor, was busy trying to persuade the Western democracies that the surest safeguard against Communism in Central Europe would be to turn the region into a federation with himself as president. It must be said that there were many in Western governments, bureaucracies and legislatures who would not have been averse to the restoration of the old Austro-Hungarian monarchy. The Czechoslovaks at home as well as abroad were also concerned that article 2 of the Atlantic Charter, which criticised territorial changes made against the wishes of the population, might be used to prevent the return of Czechoslovak territory which had been seized by the Germans, Poles and Hungarians.

For all these reasons the Czechoslovak propaganda stressed both that Benes' resignation of the presidency was illegal, since forced from him by Nazi pressure, and that the Munich agreement had no validity in international law, not least because it had been signed over the Czechoslovaks' heads and without the consent of the national assembly in Prague. This was a little too much for the British to swallow, and they argued that, as the agreement was now in the statute book, it formed part of British law. Eventually, however, they conceded that Munich had been nullified by Hitler's invasion and occupation of the Czech lands. Even so, the British authorities would not bind themselves to recognition of any post-war frontiers.

The third strand of propaganda emphasised Czechoslovakia's standing as a co-belligerent. This was proved by resistance on the home front as well as by the presence of Czechs and Slovaks in the British armed forces. Jiri Hronek's book *Volcano Under Hitler* described the courage of the Czech population in pursuing the 'policy of pinpricks' in the face of fearsome reprisals. Even in Slovakia there was covert resistance to the Tiso regime and its German masters, while Slovakian soldiers took every opportunity to desert to their Russian brothers. Czech troops had fought in France, Britain and elsewhere, while Czech airmen in the RAF had carried out about 500 bombing raids over enemy territory and had shot down at least 205 enemy aircraft. An official publication of 1943, *Four Fighting Years*, proudly recorded that, between them, Czechoslovak airmen had been awarded one KCB, one DSO, 25 Flying Medals and eight other British decorations. Although the Czechoslovak war effort was hardly decisive in the Allied victory, it did at least show willingness to participate fully in the war.

In the matter of co-belligerency there was the difficulty of the position of the Protectorate government. This was also an anomaly with regard to Benes' own claim of juridical continuity as president of the Republic. For humane and practical reasons Benes felt that it was better to have a Czech government in Prague, however compromised, than direct rule from Berlin. His attitude changed, however, with the entry of the Soviet Union into the war, feeling it would be better if President Hacha and Prime Minister Elias should resign their posts. He instructed them to do so by secret messages sent through the Czech underground. Both men hesitated, however, and Elias was arrested in September 1941 for his secret contacts with Benes. After the arrival of Heydrich and the intensification of the reign of terror against the Czechs the tone of the exile propaganda changed to one that was critical of and even hostile to the Hacha regime.

The strand of propaganda which was probably most significant in terms of Czechoslovakia's future was that which stressed its historic role as a bridge between East and West. In political and cultural terms it was stressed that this had been as true of the medieval kingdom of Bohemia as for the modern Czechoslovak state. Benes had always been convinced that the chief reason for the failure of diplomacy between the wars had been the exclusion of the Soviet Union from international affairs. Particularly after 1941, when the Soviet Union perforce had to enter the war, he and Ripka stated repeatedly that there could be no secure and lasting peace without Soviet participation in the affairs of the continent once Germany was defeated.

It would be facile to say that this played directly into the hands of Stalin, who took every chance to proclaim his virtue in not having recognised the Munich pact. In truth Czechoslovakia, which was a direct neighbour of the Soviet Union, had little choice in the matter. In addition, the Czechoslovak Communists were growing in popularity and strength. In any case, it soon became clear that neither the British nor the Americans felt any commitment to Central Europe, and were unlikely to intervene in its affairs once the war was over. Even Jan Masaryk, who was suspicious and fearful of Soviet intentions, told Bruce Lockhart more than once that he would rather go to bed with Stalin than kiss Hitler's behind.

Since the time of Munich Soviet dealings with Benes and his colleagues had been far from straightforward. On 23 August 1939, the day the Nazi-Soviet non-aggression pact was signed, the Soviet ambassador in London, the duplicitous Ivan Maisky, told Benes that the agreement was a reprisal for the anti-Soviet attitude of Britain and France at the time of Munich. In September 1939 Maisky lied outright to Benes when he said that the Soviet invasion and occupation of Eastern Poland had not been prearranged with the Germans. That same month the Soviet Union gave official recognition to the Slovak state (thus acquiescing in the dismemberment of Czechoslovakia and contradicting its stance of March 1939), and ordered the closure of the Czechoslovak legation in Moscow. Meanwhile the Czechoslovak Communists safe in Moscow conducted a vicious and slanderous propaganda campaign against the Czechoslovak action abroad, refused cooperation with the Czech and Slovak underground at home, and denounced the war as an imperialist conflict. Maisky explained all this to Benes by saying that the Soviet Union was still committed to the liberation of Czechoslovakia, but that for reasons of tactics it had to appear to 'zigzag'.

Benes' appraisal of the international situation, however, convinced him that, sooner rather than later, the Soviet Union would enter the war against Nazi Germany, and therefore there was no point at all in taking offence at this powerful neighbour and future ally. His wisdom in this matter was confirmed when Soviet Russia was precipitated into the war by Operation Barbarossa, the German invasion of June 1941. Soon after this the Soviet Union hastened to regulate its diplomatic relations with Benes and the government in exile, and to promise forthrightly that it had no intention of interfering in Czechoslovakia's internal affairs.

Benes appears to have believed this assertion; nonetheless he was realist enough to recognise the ambitions of the Czechoslovak Communists and their strength in terms of both domestic support and the backing of Moscow. He realised that after the war they would have to participate in government, though he hoped that the democratic traditions of Czechoslovakia would prevent them from monopolising power. In a codicil to his will written before he left for his visit to the Soviet Union Benes recommended that two cabinet posts be given to Communists.

So much for the Eastern end of the bridge. As for the West, Benes appraised the situation and the post-war needs of Europe quite accurately. He estimated correctly that Great Britain was more concerned with its empire than with the European mainland, and therefore he saw the necessity of reviving France as a great power after the war. He respected Charles de Gaulle as the leader of the Free French and saw in him a post-war national leader. Interestingly enough, the Soviet leadership disagreed. Molotov told Benes in 1943 that the French were a nation of weaklings, and that the entire political establishment which was rotten to the core had colluded with the Nazis. Accordingly France should be punished for its appeasement and collaboration. The victim of that policy of appeasement was more inclined to be merciful and positive.

The final strand of Czechoslovak propaganda concerned the Sudeten German question. The German population was seen as the one disruptive element in the First Republic; moreover, it had directly betrayed its homeland to the Nazi Germans of the Reich. From his very first negotiations with the British authorities Benes emphasised that, for the sake of the future security of Czechoslovakia, there would have to be some post-war transfer of the German population. 'Transfer', of course, meant 'expulsion'. Churchill professed his approval of this policy in April 1943. In May Benes was careful also to secure President Roosevelt's agreement to the transfer, and later in the year obtained the approval of the Soviet authorities.

Contrary to the Czechoslovak propaganda which stressed the inviolability of Czechoslovakia's frontiers, Benes showed himself willing to consider some exchange of territory with Germany so that the areas with the highest concentration of Bohemian Germans could be incorporated into Germany proper. Meanwhile a spate of publications for the popular English-speaking market described the treachery and cruelty of the Bohemian Germans: Hronek's *They Betrayed Czechoslovakia* (1938); Franz Koegler's *Oppressed Minority?* (c.1943); Bohumil Bilek's *Fifth Column at Work* (1945); and Karel Sedivy's *Why We Want to Transfer the Germans* (1946). Hubert Ripka's more sober official pamphlet, *The Future of the Czechoslovak Germans* of 1944, was no less ominous for the 'nazified' part of the 'Sudeten' population.

Although propaganda might have understandably exaggerated the degree of resistance to the Nazis in the Czech lands, true it is that in autumn 1941 there was an almost universal boycott of the press there, at the orders of the Czechoslovak provisional government broadcasting on the London radio.

Whether or not this proved to be the last straw for the Nazis, in September von Neurath was suddenly recalled to Berlin and replaced by Reinhard Heydrich. Immediately a reign of terror was unleashed on the Czechs. According to German sources, 6000 were arrested in the first week of Heydrich's tenure of office and 414 executed by the end of the year. The Czechoslovaks in London thought the real figures were much higher. In an official publication, *On the Reign of Terror in Bohemia and Moravia under the regime of Reinhard Heydrich*, they showed by way of comparison that, while during the troubles of autumn 1939 the Germans stated that only 12 people had been executed, in reality it was about 150; while those killed on the streets or by the Gestapo probably numbered more than a thousand.

Heydrich was nothing if not thorough in his methods. The former prime minister Alois Elias was tried and convicted of treason, having been accused of maintaining secret contact with Benes and the Czechoslovak government in exile. Particular targets were the Czechoslovak legionaries (veterans of World War I) and the patriotic gymnastic association, Sokol. Persecution of the Jews naturally intensified (Heydrich had already been hard at work preparing the 'final solution' of the European 'Jewish problem'). However, Heydrich did not rely on terror alone, but employed what the veteran Communist revolutionary Karl Radek had called the 'whip and sugar stick'. Rations of meat and fats were increased, and the message that collaboration and submission would be rewarded was clear.

Just who took the decision to assassinate Heydrich, who authorised it, and when, must remain unclear. Certain it is that among the groups of Czechoslovak fighters parachuted into the Protectorate from Britain during 1941–42 was one which bore the code name 'Anthropoid'. Its members landed in the Protectorate in December 1941 but did not attempt to kill Heydrich until May of the following year. Much speculation surrounds the matter. It has been posited that the initial target was not Heydrich but Emanuel Moravec, the 'quisling' in the Prague government who preached defeatism and acceptance of German superiority.

The mystery is intensified by the fact that the operation seems to have been bungled from the first, and that the assassins, betrayed by a fellowpartisan, were killed in a shoot-out in a Prague church. Whatever the origins of the plan, and regardless of whether Benes authorised it or even knew of it, certain it is that on 27 May 1942 Heydrich was attacked as he drove through a Prague suburb by Jan Kubis, a Czech, and Jozef Gabcik, a Slovak. Gabcik's sten gun jammed as he tried to shoot Heydrich, and a grenade thrown by Kubis hit Heydrich's car seat, not his body. Nonetheless the 'Hangman of Prague' died of septicaemia some days later.

Even before he died the reprisals for the attempt started. Undoubtedly the Germans were seriously shaken that one of their chiefs could be attacked so impudently by members of a subaltern nation; nonetheless the savagery of their revenge shocked world opinion. According to figures published by the Czechoslovak government in London, 1960 Czechs were killed in retaliation for Heydrich's death by the end of 1942. Kurt Daluege, Heydrich's successor as deputy *Reichsprotektor* in Prague, admitted in his trial after the war that 1331 people, including 201 women, were executed in retaliation for Heydrich's death. Another source claimed that 3000 Jews were taken from the concentration camp at Terezin and summarily executed. Frantisek Moravec, chief of Czechoslovak intelligence abroad, estimated that perhaps 6000 Czechs were slaughtered. Among the more prominent victims was General Elias, who was executed the day after Heydrich's assassins were killed.

Particularly repulsive was the destruction of the villages of Lidice near Prague and Lezaky near Pardubice, both singled out because of alleged contacts with the parachutists. At Lidice all the men and some women were shot (the Germans actually had themselves filmed committing this atrocity); the rest of the women were sent to Ravensbruck concentration camp in Germany, and the children taken away. A handful of these were found suitable for 'aryanisation' and sent to live with German families; the rest disappeared, apparently starved to death at Lodz in Poland. At Lezaky the entire adult population was taken to Pardubice castle and beheaded; the fate of the children is unknown.

Whatever the terrible cost to the home population, the assassination of Heydrich and consequent reprisals won a great deal of sympathy and admiration for the Czechoslovak cause. In July 1942 the British government finally repudiated Munich, on the grounds that it had been broken by the Nazi invasion of 15 March 1939. In spring and winter of the following year President Benes visited both Washington and Moscow. He was received in the American capital with all honour, something that made a good propaganda point for the people at home. His second journey to Moscow resulted in the signing of the Soviet–Czechoslovak treaty of 23 December 1943. Though the British had expressed displeasure and opposition to the treaty, it signalled that Czechoslovakia was now fully acknowledged by Stalin as an ally. Furthermore, there was provision for other small states of Eastern and Central Europe to join the alliance.

The Czechoslovaks had been in serious negotiation with the Poles about some sort of post-war federation or confederation since October 1940. The prime minister of the Polish government in exile, General Wladislaw Sikorski, had been an opponent of the authoritarian regime of Pilsudki and his successors, Smigly-Rydz and Beck, and was quite willing to seek some accommodation with the Czechoslovak neighbour. Each partner in the union would keep its sovereignty, with its own head of state, government, parliament and armed forces. There would, however, be a common economic and foreign policy, with close political and military cooperation. These plans were interrupted by the untimely and unexpected death of Sikorski in an air crash, but finally and fatally stumbled on the obstacle of the opposition of the Soviet Union. The provision for other states to join the Czechoslovak–Soviet alliance was the most that Benes could salvage for the Poles.

Meanwhile in Slovakia resistance to the clerico-fascist state and its Nazi 'protectors' had been steadily growing. According to reports from Slovakia received both by Benes in London and the press reading bureau in neutral Stockholm, the Slovaks were imitating the 'pinpricks' policy of their Czech neighbours and also committing acts of sabotage. Textile mills, ironworks and power stations were among the industrial concerns damaged, while in the summer of 1942 the authorities had had to post fire guards to protect the crops in the fields, particularly in the Vah valley. Of even greater nuisance value against the authorities and the Germans were the groups of partisans who infested the mountains and carried out acts of serious sabotage. Resistance culminated in August 1944, with the Slovak national uprising.

This had been planned in the previous December, when the 'Slovak National Council' was formed following negotiations between democratic and Communist representatives in the underground resistance movement. (The Communists, ever obedient to Stalin, had changed their attitude to both the war and the home resistance after June 1941.) The partisans who staged the uprising were made up of all sorts and conditions of men, from Slovak army officers to Communists. After the war, and particularly after the coup of February 1948, the Communists naturally exaggerated their role in the resistance. Even so, this was considerable. However, if they expected help from either the party leadership uneasily ensconced in Moscow or from the Soviet Union itself, they were to be disappointed.

It is well known that Stalin disliked revolutions and other movements over which he himself did not exercise direct control. Moreover, he despised foreign Communists as 'peasant politicians' (contemptuously, he described the Czechoslovak Communists to Benes as simple and unlearned folk), and terrorised those leaders who had sought sanctuary in the Soviet Union. The Czechoslovaks in Moscow, under the leadership of Klement Gottwald, were abjectly obedient to Stalin's wishes. Their comrades in exile in London, while outwardly on good terms with Benes and the exiled government, also followed Moscow's orders.

The Slovak national uprising met with some initial military success, as it seems to have caught both the Slovak authorities and the Germans unawares, although both Benes and the British Foreign Office had prior knowledge of the preparations. The Slovak National Council assumed the role of a provisional government to administer the liberated areas. Ultimate victory, however, depended on military aid from abroad, and this was not forthcoming.

While Stalin promised assistance in negotiations with Benes and the Czechoslovak government in exile he cynically delayed sending troops and materials. The rising lasted for ten weeks, but the Soviet troops, a mere 60 or so miles away, made no attempt to come to the aid of the Slovak insurgents. In early September 1944 Fierlinger, the Czechoslovak minister in Moscow, was informed orally by a member of the commissariat for foreign affairs that the Soviet authorities were satisfied that this was a truly national uprising. He was also led to believe that a red army offensive would be launched to assist the Slovak insurgents. Belatedly, the Soviets began to drop weapons and ammunition by air, and promised to send the Czechoslovak parachutists and airmen who were based on Soviet soil. The promised aid, however, was too little, too late. General Rudolf Viest was sent by Benes to take command of the insurgents; he reported that the Slovaks had only six tanks, very few anti-tank weapons, and no barbed wire or mine-throwers. None of the aid promised by the red army had materialised.

Moreover, Moscow let it be inferred in both London and Washington that the Soviet Union would take an unfavourable view of Allied aid to the Slovaks. Accordingly, although the Allied command in southern Italy was willing to help, and managed to deliver 24 tonnes of weapons, ammunition and medical supplies on 17 September and 7 October, the order was given to cease assisting the rebels. Both the Americans and British had decided that, since Slovakia was in the Soviet sphere of operations, and since Moscow had not replied to the Allied requests for approval of aid to Slovakia, they would not interfere.

This was all the more disappointing to Benes and the exiled government because, like Masaryk in World War I, they were anxious not to play the Russian card alone. The Czechoslovaks asked the British directly and repeatedly for military assistance and medical supplies, and seemed anxious lest Soviet aid might turn into interference. The British authorities, however, delayed committing themselves until they had learned of the attitude of the Soviets.

The uprising was brutally crushed by the Germans and the usual vicious reprisals followed. However, a delegation from the Slovak National Council managed to reach London by December and conducted negotiations with the

Benes government. While the Slovaks expressed themselves in favour of a Czechoslovak state after the war, this was to be decentralised to some extent, with Slovakia being granted a large measure of autonomy.

As the war drew to its conclusion arrangements had to be made for the liberation of Czechoslovakia and the restoration of the state. Benes had been satisfied with his negotiations in Moscow in 1943 and with the apparently close and harmonious relations between Czechoslovakia and the Soviet Union; but he had been obliged to make concessions to the Czechoslovak Communists or rather, to their master Stalin. Benes and the government would return to Czechoslovakia, not directly from the West but by way of Moscow. The government was to be reconstituted, and to contain some Communist members. This was not as humiliating or crippling as Stalin's treatment of the Poles, who had been forced to disavow their own London government and accept Stalin's 'Lublin committee' which was dominated by the Communists; but it still showed where the whip hand lay.

In addition, Benes had to accept the loss of Sub-Carpathian Ruthenia in the course of the 'liberation'. This province had certainly benefited from 20 years of Czechoslovak rule, though Benes was willing to cede it to the Ukraine if the Soviet Union so wished. Repeatedly, however, Soviet officials and politicians, including Stalin himself, had asserted that Ruthenia would be returned to Czechoslovakia and the pre-Munich borders of the Republic would remain intact. What changed the Soviet mind on the matter is not known, but on 7 November 1944, the anniversary of the Bolshevik revolution of 1917, Soviet radio broadcast a message to Stalin which spoke of the 'eternal dream' of the Sub-Carpathian Ruthenians to be united in one family with their Ukrainian brothers.

Stalin's agents had, of course, manufactured a nationalist agitation which allegedly demanded unification of Ruthenia with the Ukraine. Village mayors were presented with a unification petition ready for them to sign; Ruthenians were press-ganged into the red army; and the representative of Benes' London government, Frantisek Nemec, was terrorised and even robbed while red army officers looked on. While the Soviet-inspired access of Ruthenian nationalism was transparently artificial, there was no crossing the will of Stalin.

Accordingly, after a sojourn In Moscow, the London exiles would set up headquarters in Kosice, in Slovakia, as the red army rolled westwards on its task of liberation. Benes was in a sombre and worried mood, not helped by the stroke he suffered just before his departure. His chief concerns were the intentions of the Soviet policy makers, and the activities of the Czechoslovak Communists at home.

Benes and the government left Britain in March 1945, and held discussions with the Soviet leadership and, as in 1943, with the leading Czechoslovak Communists. There were particularly difficult negotiations between Benes, the Communists and the other parties over the formation of the new 'Kosice government', which was actually established in Moscow. By and large the Communists got their own way, gaining all the major ministries with the exception of that of justice. They claimed quite accurately that they would be the largest party in post-war Czechoslovakia, and therefore deserved to obtain the ministries of the interior, information and education, and agriculture.

Most virtuously, the Communists did not claim the premiership for one of their own. This seeming generosity was, of course, quite spurious, as the new prime minister was Zdenek Fierlinger, the Czechoslovak diplomatic representative in Moscow. Officially a Social Democrat, Fierlinger was quite probably a crypto-Communist; certainly he followed Moscow's orders with abject devotion. Equally the Communists did not insist on the ministry of defence, since this was filled by another fellow traveller, the 'non-party expert' General Ludvik Svoboda, who had distinguished himself fighting alongside the red army on the eastern front. Finally, Vladimir Clementis was made deputy minister of foreign affairs in order to keep Jan Masaryk, his chief, under surveillance; and Gottwald and Viliam Siroky, respectively heads of the Czech and Slovak Communist parties, became deputy premiers.

Why did Benes agree to such a marked Communist predominance in the Kosice government? His private secretary Edward Taborsky offered some explanations. In the first place, and as a democratic president, Benes felt that he should stay above the parties. He also thought that the Communists might be tamed by the responsibility of governmental office, and that they could be restrained by the democratic forces in politics. Finally, Benes was in a hurry to leave Moscow for Czechoslovak territory. He knew quite well that the home Communists were busy establishing themselves in the localities, backed by the might of the red army and the presence of Beria's sinister Soviet security force, the NKVD. He felt that his own presence would boost the morale of the democratic elements in Czechoslovakia.

In early April Bratislava was liberated by the Red Army, the following month Tiso, who had fled to Austria, signed a document of surrender to the Allies. In May Prague rose up in revolt against the Germans; much blood was shed, though comparatively little material damage done to the city. The question of which of the Allies would liberate the capital became pressing; true, the Soviets were coming from the east, driving all before them, but the Americans under General Eisenhower were coming from the west and had already liberated Plzen. Indeed, they came within some 15 miles of Prague, where they halted. Similarly, General Patton and his forces had crossed into Czechoslovakia from Bavaria on 17 April, but at Soviet insistence stopped their march eastwards. With the hindsight of the cold war this seems like a capital mistake, given the propaganda opportunities it afforded the Soviets. However, and in plain terms, General Eisenhower was not willing to risk incurring American casualties for purely political, as opposed to military reasons. Thus it was the red army which liberated Bohemia's ancient capital.

In the event the liberators proved to be quite as rapacious as the German oppressors had been; indeed, possibly more so. Before leaving Moscow Benes had reached an agreement with Molotov on the question of Soviet war booty, since the red army had been seizing all industrial concerns, products and raw materials which had been administered by the occupying Germans. After some forceful discussion Molotov agreed that only German enterprises transferred from the Reich or constructed during the occupation would be classed as war plunder.

Even so, the ordinary Soviet soldier was quite capable of a little plunder on his own account. Eyewitness accounts speak of theft on the large and small scale, of drunkenness, and sheer greed for material goods. Fortunately for the Czechoslovak population all Soviet troops had been withdrawn by the end of 1945.

On 3 April Benes stood once more on Czechoslovak soil. It had been decided to travel to Prague by train and by car, so as to enter as many towns and villages as possible and to cheer the forces of democracy. On 8 May the presidential entourage left Kosice, passing through Banska Bystrica (the centre of the Slovak national uprising), Bratislava, Brno, and many smaller places besides. In every place Benes received a rapturous and emotional reception from the vast crowds which engulfed his car.

In May President Benes returned to Prague in triumph, greeted by the acclamations of the crowds who lined the streets. It was a moment of victory to be savoured sweetly, as none knew better than Benes that immense problems would lie ahead. For the moment, though, it seemed that the motto of the First Republic had proved its veracity: 'Truth Prevails'.

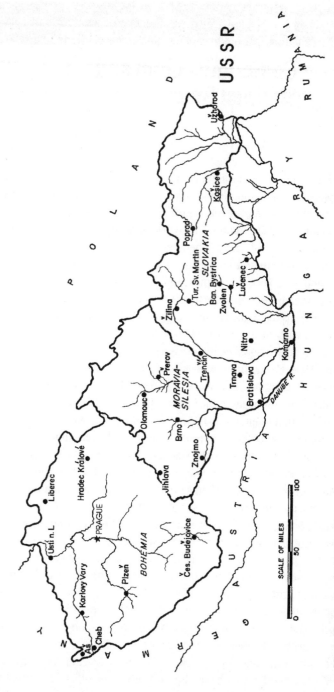

Map 3 *Czechoslovakia, 1945–1992.*

# Communist Coup and Stalinist Rule

The triumphal return of President Benes to Prague in May 1945 was greeted with euphoric acclamation. Nonetheless, Benes was not blind to the difficulties he would face in reconstructing the state as a democracy. If truth were indeed to prevail, the Communist Party would need careful handling. There was also the problem of relations between Czechs and Slovaks, and the position of the national minorities.

The composition of the first, provisional government which would return to Czechoslovakia from Moscow reflected both the Communists' strengths and their devious methods. The distribution of cabinet posts appeared to be equitable, as each of the four Czech and two Slovak parties all had three seats each. In reality, however, there was a majority of Communists and their fellow travellers. The Communist parties of the Czech lands and Slovakia had separate representation; and two of the Social Democrats, Fierlinger and Lausman, were subservient to the Communists, as was General Svoboda the so-called 'non-party expert' who had fought in the Soviet Union and who now became Minister of Defence. Indeed Fierlinger had been appointed prime minister at the Communists' own request, and so pliant was he to their purposes that he was later termed 'Quislinger'. The only genuine non-partisan minister was Jan Masaryk, in charge of foreign affairs. The Communists and Social Democrats, however, held the Ministries of Information, Education, Social Welfare, Agriculture and the Interior. This last position gave them control of the police, security and intelligence services.

One of the most pressing issues facing the new government was that of the German minority. The 'German problem' was dealt with swiftly and, in many cases, brutally. During the war the Allies had been persuaded that a substantial proportion of the German population would have to be transferred from Czechoslovakia in order to preserve the stability of the state. However, before the government could organise an orderly transfer of the German population a wave of 'wild' expulsions took place, as well as localised massacres, individual murders and other acts of retribution. This made official action by the authorities imperative if further violence were to be avoided. In July 1945 the government requested the Allies to put the question of transfer of the German population on the agenda of the Potsdam conference. This became article XII of the Potsdam declaration, which also concerned Germans in Poland and Hungary. On 2 August Benes issued a presidential decree to regularise the situation. All 'Sudetens' had become German Reich citizens during the war, and now they had to demonstrate their loyalty to the state when reapplying for Czechoslovak citizenship. Special courts would prosecute active supporters of the Nazi regime. Additional decrees ordered the confiscation of all German property. The only exception to these harsh measures was to be the active German anti-fascists who could demonstrate their resistance to the Nazi Protectorate.

The transfer began on 25 January 1946. The Bohemian Germans were to be moved out of Czechoslovakia in heated railway carriages – something of a contrast to the cattle trucks which had carried the Czechoslovak Jews to deportation. Each could take away a small amount of personal property (weighing 30 to 50 kilograms) and an allowance of 1000 Reichsmarks. Families were not to be separated, and the Czechoslovak government would provide rations for the journey and three further days. Nearly 800,000 persons were transferred in this way, while about 30,000 transferred themselves voluntarily. Another 16,000 or so were transferred by agreement with the West German authorities, so that they could be reunited with relatives. From a pre-war population of over two million, only about 165,000 ethnic Germans remained in Czechoslovakia.

The deportation of the Germans suited the Communists admirably. As many areas of the country were now seriously under-populated, they were able to agitate for a distribution of German land and other property to their natural constituents, the urban working classes and poorer country people. (As they had successfully campaigned to have the Agrarian Party outlawed, they were able to gain a great deal of peasant support.) More than six million acres of land confiscated from the Germans was available for reallocation, and it should not be forgotten that the Ministry of Agriculture was controlled by the Communists. By spring 1948 a million and a half Czechoslovaks had moved into the border regions lately populated by the Germans. These people were quite vulnerable to Communist propaganda, as they now had a personal stake in the future of the state. Thus to a general, national fear of a revanchist Germany could be added the prospect of dispossessed Bohemian Germans returning to reclaim their property from its new owners.

Indeed, the Communists were able to take advantage of social and political tensions in all areas of Czechoslovak life. They were able to infiltrate every organisation which would be potentially useful to them, from rival political parties to mass movements of organised workers. There is no doubt that they aimed at a seizure of power even before the war had ended. The timing of the takeover would, of course, depend on both internal and international factors.

The internal factors were manipulated by the Communists long before the returning government touched its native soil. In accordance with Stalin's general strategy in Eastern and Central Europe, the tactic of setting up a national front and a coalition government was adopted. Thus the Communists were guaranteed a role in the overt politics of the state. In discussions with Benes in Moscow in 1943 they had declared that, as the entire administrative apparatus was compromised by collaboration with the occupying Germans, it should be replaced by 'people's committees' at every level. This was done in 1945, under the aegis of the red army and of Beria's NKVD, the Soviet secret police.

After the liberation they set about what Josef Korbel has correctly called 'the Communist subversion of Czechoslovakia'. They demanded and organised the formation of working-class mass movements, an overall trade union organisation, factory councils and a workers' militia. This last was dissolved in 1946, but secretly reactivated and rearmed by the Communists for the coup of 1948. All these organisations were swiftly infiltrated by the party.

The treasonable plans of the Communists were actually assisted by the *ad hoc* post-war arrangements for the governance of Czechoslovakia. The President was endowed with the power to rule by decree, and a provisional assembly (similar to that which obtained immediately after World War I) merely confirmed these decrees, 98 of which were issued between May and October 1945. Among these presidential laws were the nationalisation decrees. These were really quite moderate, in that they affected only 17.4 per cent of businesses and 57.7 per cent of the work force, with most smaller factories remaining as private enterprises; even so, Benes only signed them under pressure from the Communists. Gottwald and his comrades were anxious to keep Benes as president, given the elder statesman's prestige and popularity. For the rest, time and cunning were on their side.

The first post-war elections were held in May 1946; the Communists polled 37.9 per cent of the votes cast. In the Czech lands they obtained 40.1 per cent of the vote, well ahead of their nearest rivals the National Socialists, who polled 23.5 per cent. In Slovakia, however, with only 30.3 per cent of the total vote, the Communists lost out heavily to the National Democratic Party, who scored a resounding 62 per cent. Analysis of the results showed that the Communists had benefited from the votes of the peasants (doubtless anticipating a radical land reform in their favour) as well as those of the young (the voting aged had been lowered from 21 to 18). Meanwhile the threat of armed intervention by the Soviet Union was more than implicit. The liberators of the red army had all left Czechoslovak soil by the end of 1945, However on 22 May it was announced (rather than requested) that Soviet troops would cross Czechoslovakia from Hungary and Austria to the Soviet zone of Germany. Although the intervention of Jan Masaryk prevented this from occurring, the red army presence so close to the country can only have assisted the Communists in the elections.

Yet it has to be said that one fatal event determined the greater part of the Czechoslovak electorate to vote Communist, namely, Munich. The Czechoslovak Communist Party, like the Soviet Union itself, had never accepted the Munich agreement, and thus it could use its propaganda to emphasise the treachery of France and Britain in 1938 and the weakness and tendency to compromise of the democratic system as a whole. In 1946 Shiela Grant Duff visited Czechoslovakia as a member of a Fabian Society delegation, and heard time and again the single word uttered as an accusation; 'Munich'. Thus Communism could seem like a viable alternative to the system which had delivered Czechoslovakia to the Third Reich and (it was said) would not hesitate to give her over to a revengeful German government in the future. In addition, the Communists could manipulate both social discontent and idealism by depicting the shortcomings of the capitalist or democratic system in general and of the First Republic in particular.

Naturally the Communists were pleased with the election results, which gave them several key cabinet posts and enabled them to replace as premier the fellow-traveller Fierlinger with the party leader Gottwald. However in January 1947 Gottwald announced that in the next elections the Communists must gain 51 per cent of the vote, and thus destroy democracy by its own means. A number of strategies were undertaken in the following months to prepare for a Communist seizure of power either through the ballot box or, failing a respectable electoral majority, by extra-parliamentary means.

The democratic politicians of post-war Czechoslovakia have been criti-cised for weakness of will and mistaken tactics when dealing with the Communists. Josef Korbel felt that Benes was wrong, as president, to stand aloof from party-political struggles. Indeed it is true that, on 23 February 1948, at the crisis-point of the Communist coup, Benes told the government minis-ter Hubert Ripka that the democrats would have to defend themselves; as president, he would have to remain above the conflict, above the parties. The historian Karel Kaplan, himself an enthusiastic recruit to the Communist party in 1948, criticised the democrats for adhering to constitutional proced-ures and not resorting to extra-parliamentary tactics like their undemocratic opponents. In their defence it must be said that the non-Communist ministers and other politicians saw the national front as a genuine attempt to reconcile socialism with democracy. In addition, and given the lively interest of the Soviet Union in Czechoslovak developments, as well as the electoral strength of the Communists, there was little they could have done. Finally, both Benes and Jan Masaryk were seriously ill during the various crises of 1947–48.

The international situation, too, was propitious for the Czechoslovak Communists. Czechoslovakia had been unique among the states of Central and Eastern Europe in being prepared to accept Marshall aid and to send a delegation to the Paris conference which would discuss it. The democratic Czechoslovak politicians, still attempting to depict their country as a bridge between West and East, were also planning a treaty with France which would balance their alliance with the Soviet Union. However Stalin summoned Gottwald, Masaryk and other ministers to Moscow, and invoked the Czechoslovak–Soviet treaty of 1943. This had explicitly forbidden each signatory to join in any coalition organised against the other. The Marshall plan, asserted Stalin, was just such an anti-Soviet coalition. On the return of the Czechoslovak ministers it was announced that Marshall aid – a tactic plainly inimical to the Soviet Union – would not be accepted. Jan Masaryk famously remarked on his return to Prague: 'I left for Moscow as Minister of Foreign Affairs of a sovereign state. I am returning as Stalin's stooge.'

The exact role of Stalin and the Soviet Union in the actual planning and execution of the Communist seizure of power is in fact far from clear. In September 1947 the Communist Information Bureau (Cominform) was founded as a successor to the Comintern and an answer to Marshall aid. Its purpose as proclaimed at the founding meeting was to remove all 'reactionary' (that is, democratic) elements from the national fronts in various states and to make a more overt bid for power. It seemed as though Stalin were giving the green light to the Czechoslovak Communists.

This might have been wishful thinking, but certainly the leading Czechoslovak Communists – men like Gottwald, Clementis, Zapotocky and Slansky – were slavish followers of Stalin. Gottwald had been chosen by the great man as the first Czechoslovak member of the executive committee of the Comintern in 1928; the following year he was again selected by Stalin to be general secretary of the Czechoslovak party. These people were known as 'Muscovite' Communists because of their place of residence during the war years. They seem to have been hypnotised by the Soviet leader, who they had followed blindly in the pre-war years when he ordered a suicidal policy of non-cooperation with other parties against the menace of Nazism and fascism. This is all the more astonishing in view of Stalin's contempt for and terrorisation of the 'peasant politicians' from Central and Eastern Europe who took refuge in the motherland of socialism. The Yugoslav Milovan Djilas has left a graphic record of Stalin's routine humiliation of foreign Communists. The Rumanian Ana Pauker remained Stalin's devoted handmaiden despite his order for the execution of her husband. Perhaps even more surprising is the fact that Stalin's disciples were undeterred by the fate of those German Communist and Social Democratic refugees who Stalin handed back to the Nazi authorities before the outbreak of the Great Patriotic War in 1941. Whether acting on Stalin's direct orders or merely hoping to please him, the Czechoslovak Communists embarked on an accelerated campaign of intrigue and intimidation from autumn 1947.

Their chief target was Slovakia, where they had done badly in the polls compared with their performance in the Czech lands. Slovak separatist nationalism was always a worry for the Communists, and this was why they managed the trial and condemnation of Jozef Tiso, who was executed in March 1947 despite the efforts of the non-Communist Slovak politicians to have the death sentence commuted to one of life imprisonment. In November of that year they used the secret police which was controlled by the Communist Minister of the Interior, Vaclav Nosek, to foment and then expose the so-called 'conspiracy in Slovakia'. This was designed to discredit the majority Democratic Party, which was accused of treasonable activities. However the Communists were unmasked after an inquiry by the democratic Minister of Justice, Prokop Drtina.

Even so, the Communists managed to create a crisis which was orchestrated with the trade union organisation and the peasant union to clip the wings of the Democratic Party. Accusations of corruption and incompetence aimed at the board of trustees (the regional government of Slovakia) led to the well-timed resignation of Husak, four other Communist trustees and a fellow traveller. Husak declared that the board was thereby dissolved, and against the protestations of the Democrats entered into negotiations to form a new one. This was announced on 18 November; although the Democrats were still represented on it, their majority had been swamped by the Communists and their allies from the inconsequential Freedom and Labour Parties. This tactic of using ministerial resignations to force a governmental crisis would be used again in the Prague coup of February 1948.

Meanwhile on 11 September a shocking incident had occurred in Prague, when three democratic ministers – Masaryk, Drtina and Zenkl – were sent parcel bombs disguised as perfume bottles. Fortunately none of them was killed or even injured, but an inquiry revealed that the Communists had organised the affair, possibly to cause panic and as a signal for the Communist coup to begin.

In November the Communists received a temporary setback to their plans when their puppet Fierlinger ('Quislinger') was voted out of the leadership of the Social Democratic Party. Quite ominously the Soviet Union expressed its displeasure at this independent gesture by a political party of a sovereign state. In the event Fierlinger was succeeded by Lausman, a well-known political trimmer who would prove to be compliant to the Communists' plans.

In January 1948 the Communists found an urgent and concrete reason for speeding up their preparations for a putsch. Research into public opinion showed that the party would gain fewer rather than more votes in the coming elections. As the path of legalism was apparently now closed to them, the Communists resorted to force.

The actual crisis of February 1948 was precipitated by a constitutional issue. Nosek as Minister of the Interior had ignored a government decree of 13 February which ordered him to reinstate eight high-ranking non-Communist police officials who he had dismissed the previous day. As a result of this 12 democratic government ministers resigned on February 20. President Benes was at first reluctant to accept the resignations, but eventually did so on 24 February. The democratic ministers had calculated that their resignations would cause the government to fall and elections to be called immediately. In fact, as only a minority of ministers had resigned, Gottwald was able to form a new cabinet on 25 February. The Communists had seized control of Czechoslovakia.

In retrospect both the democratic ministers and the President have been blamed for acting unwisely and playing into the Communists' hands. Certainly Benes, recovering from two recent strokes, was badly advised to accept the resignations. However, it is debatable whether constitutional measures could have been taken, given the Communists' determination to seize power. The investigation into the 'perfume bombs' affair had revealed three huge caches of Communist weapons; Nosek had deployed heavily armed police troops around Prague; and the Communists had armed the workers' militia. Its deputy commander Josef Smrkovsky informed the party leadership that a state of battle readiness would be announced, and that 7000 of the militia in Prague would receive 200 cartridges each. Svoboda as Minister for Defence had ordered the armed forces not to interfere in 'internal affairs' and had promised loyalty to the Soviet Union. Mass demonstrations of workers were organised in Prague in order to intimidate the democrats. The only counter-manifestation was a demonstration of loyalty to Benes by students on 24 February. Their numbers have been estimated variously at 10,000 and 25,000. What is indisputable is that the students were met with police brutality, and a number of demonstrators were injured and killed.

Indeed, it was not simply a matter of accepting resignations and naming a new government. Between 20 and 25 February panic and chaos were promoted on the streets. The trade union organisation convened a mass meeting of the factory councils in Prague for 22 February; plainly this was meant to intimidate the democratic ministers, and was a repeat of the tactics used in Slovakia in November. At noon on 24 November two and a half million workers held a one-hour strike as a demonstration of the strength of the proletariat. 'Action Committees' were secretly organised by the Communists in factories and in local and national government agencies; these were then purged of 'reactionary' elements.

The leaders and officials of the democratic parties were forcibly prevented from entering their offices and even subjected to physical assault. Former Justice Minister Prokop Drtina suffered the traditional Czech fate of defenestration; though this was a suicide attempt, rather than attempted murder, in January Gottwald had threatened him with 'a bad end'. Drtina had tried to kill himself in protest at Benes' broken promise not to accept the democratic ministers' resignations and at the President's refusal to see him to give an explanation of his conduct. The moderate Social Democratic leadership was forcibly deposed and replaced by the Communist fellow traveller Fierlinger. (The opportunist Lausman managed to keep his position temporarily.)

In Slovakia the Communists used both cunning and brute force to accomplish their coup. Bratislava, the capital, was less in the international eye than was Prague, and so events there proceeded rather more smoothly. On 21 February Husak informed the democratic members of the board of trustees that the resignations of the ministers from the central government also bound them; consequently they were expelled from the board. Armed police were posted at the offices of these trustees in case they tried to remain in possession. The Communists took eight out of the 15 seats on the board for themselves, giving the rest to members of compliant parties and representatives of the Communist-controlled mass organisations.

The part played by the Soviet Union in the actual execution of the coup is not entirely clear. Certainly Valerian Zorin, former Soviet ambassador to Czechoslovakia, arrived unexpected and unannounced in Prague on 19 February and left immediately after the new government was formed. It is said that Stalin offered to help Gottwald by sending the red army as reinforcements and that Gottwald refused; but this seems unlikely, given Gottwald's usually abject attitude to his master.

On the afternoon of 25 February Gottwald announced the new government from a balcony in Wenceslas Square. He was wearing a Russian bearskin hat, a hat which, it later transpired, actually belonged to Clementis. Gottwald was visibly drunk. There seemed little hope for democracy, or even civilised governance. True, there were two democratic ministers left in the government, the loyal Slovak Vavro Srobar and Jan Masaryk. But the last vestiges of the legacy of the elder Masaryk would soon vanish.

The Communist party arrogated all power to itself. Parliament's role was reduced to mere endorsement of government legislation. Parliamentary deputies could be nominated or recalled without reference to the electorate. The government itself, while technically responsible to parliament, was really only answerable to the party. The national front became farcical, with the partner parties of the Communists compliant to their wishes.

On the morning of 10 March the latest defenestration of Prague was found to have occurred. Jan Masaryk's body was discovered in a courtyard of the Ministry for Foreign Affairs, beneath an open bathroom window. The evidence for murder or suicide is ambiguous. True, Masaryk was depressed, and his British friend Bruce Lockhart had thought some time before this that he might take his own life. On the other hand, this sincere democrat and patriot, a man above party and solely in the service of his country, the son of the President Liberator, was a mighty embarrassment to the Communists. Whether he was pushed or whether he jumped is actually immaterial; what is certain is that the Communists killed him.

Other democratic ministers, party leaders and officials managed to escape from Czechoslovakia: the long-serving National Socialist Hubert Ripka; the Social Democrat Vilem Bernard; the diplomat Josef Korbel; officials in Benes' service such as Edward Taborsky and Jaroslav Smutny. Henceforward the Communists would exercise a 'leading role' in politics; this was merely a euphemism for their monopoly of power. The façade of the national front alone remained as a mockery of democracy. On 7 June Benes relinquished the presidency, on grounds of ill health; on 14 September he died. In February he had told the Communists of 'my deep democratic conviction. I cannot but remain faithful to it at this moment as in my opinion democracy is the only solid and permanent basis for human life and honesty and dignity'. Just before he died he told his secretary Taborsky: 'My greatest mistake was that I refused to believe to the very last that even Stalin lied to me cynically both in 1935 and later, and that his assurances to me and to Masaryk were an intentional deceit.'[1] These two statements summarise both Benes' personal tragedy and the historical dilemma of Czechoslovakia itself.

Benes was to be the last democratic president of Czechoslovakia until December 1989. His funeral was the occasion of anti-Communist demonstrations, as was the annual gymnastic display by the Sokol, who had last used the occasion politically as an anti-Nazi and patriotic demonstration in 1938.

Once the President was buried,·however, the Communists hurried through a formidable body of legislation designed to end democratic and even civic freedom in the country.

Not all the democrats escaped abroad, and what they could expect at the hands of the triumphant Communists was demonstrated by the shocking fate of Milada Horakova and those tried with her. Active in the National Socialist Party during the First Republic, and particularly concerned with the rights of women and the welfare of children, Horakova had joined the underground resistance to the Nazi occupation. She was imprisoned three times, in Pankrac (Prague), Terezin and Munich. After the war she became a deputy in the new national assembly and held important positions on several committees. She was a doctor at law, and also President of the Council of Czechoslovak Women and a member of the International Council of Women. However she resigned her parliamentary mandate after the Communists seized power, and as punishment she was given a show trial on outrageously fabricated charges.

The 'crimes' of which she was accused, and to which under intolerable pressure she confessed, would have been merely the exercise of political choice in a free democracy. Naturally the prosecution introduced a sinister twist to perfectly legitimate actions while, in the nightmare world of Stalinism, a spurious and backdated legality was given to their own proceedings. Thus, according to the prosecutor's indictment, 'even before' February 1948, that is, when a democratic regime still obtained in Czechoslovakia, Horakova had taken part in meetings and discussions at Hubert Ripka's house. These activities were translated by the Stalinists into secret conferences, where the orders of imperialist ambassadors (especially those of France and the United States) were received and followed. The prosecutor also stated that she had been deprived of her parliamentary mandate, when in fact she had resigned it, after which she committed herself to 'criminal illegality' in working for cooperation between the right wing of the Social Democratic Party and Roman Catholic 'reaction'.

Between August 1948 and September 1949 Horakova had organised the illegal (in Communist terms) leadership of the Nationalist Socialist group, which she confessed to building up as a 'fifth column' in the event of imperialist aggression against Czechoslovakia. Furthermore, she had helped Ripka to escape abroad, and had maintained contact with him and other political èmigrès. Despite an international outcry and pleas for mercy from many quarters, Horakova was hanged with three other 'traitors' – Jan Buchal, Oldrich Pecl and Zavis Kalandra – on 27 June 1950. This blameless woman had survived the Nazi tyranny, only to be killed by her fellow countrymen.

The trial of the 'Horakova group' demonstrated the need of the Communist regime to rid itself of intelligent opponents who, moreover, were in a position to offer an alternative view of recent events to that put forward by the Communists themselves. Most of the defendants had been active politically before and after the war, and had spent time in Nazi prisons or concentration camps. Two examples, those of the other women convicted with Horakova, will suffice. Frantiska Zeminova, aged 69, was a former deputy to the national assembly and deputy chairman of the National Socialist Party. After enduring the rigours of confinement and interrogation she was sentenced to 20 years' imprisonment; as an especially nasty twist, on the anniversary of her conviction she was to have a 'hard bed' and be put in solitary confinement. Her younger colleague Antonie Kleinerova was also a former parliamentary deputy, who had been imprisoned by the Nazis for four years. Moreover, she was the leading representative of the Society of Friends in Czechoslovakia. Probably it was this last detail, which would offend against the party's anti-religious convictions and also perhaps reveal the bogus nature of the Communist 'peace camp', that determined a life sentence for her. Of the 13 members of the 'Horakova group', four were hanged, four received life sentences, while the remaining five were given sentences of between 15 and 28 years.

Once in power the Communists set about dealing with their ideological enemies, chiefly the bourgeoisie and the churches. (Punishing both of these would, of course, release material assets which could be subsumed into the command economy.) The Communists had made it clear even before seizing power that they meant to foment class war in Czechoslovakia by promoting the politics of envy. As has been shown, they used the transfer of the Germans to transfer German property to their own natural constituents, the urban and rural poor. In August and September 1947 they had tried to introduce the so-called 'millionaires' tax' as a means of relieving poor farmers afflicted by the drought of that year. In economic terms this was nonsense, given the weakness of the Czechoslovak crown (one million crowns were worth only 20,000 American dollars) and the scarcity of even crown millionaires; relatively small revenues would be generated by such a levy. However the measure was meant to be socially and politically divisive. It was successfully opposed by the non-Communist ministers, but the names of these dissenters were immediately published by the Communists so as to depict them as aiders and abettors of those callous wealthy people who ground the faces of the poor.

The real onslaught on the bourgeoisie came in October 1949, with Action B ('class warfare'). Within six weeks about 10,000 people had been arrested without explanation and sent to forced labour camps, including the horrendous uranium mines at Jachymov and Pribram. (The uranium was being exploited for the benefit of the Soviet Union.) In June 1951 *Prehled* ('View'), the organ of the information service of the exiled Council of Free

Czechoslovakia published an incomplete list of 29 known labour camps. Among these Ruzyne near Prague held 6500 prisoners, Pribram 7000, Jachymov XIV 2800 and Vitmanov u Jachymova 23,000. Altogether, about 90,400 people were detained in these camps, of whom over 9000 were women and 3600 were juveniles. By 1952 it was estimated that about 120,000 people were being held in 40 to 50 labour camps, which were administered by the Ministry of the Interior.

The property of those arrested was confiscated, while other measures were taken against the 'class oppressors'. They were moved from the cities such as Prague, Brno and Plzen (Pilsen) and rehoused in places where it was difficult to find work; or they were reduced to one or two rooms in their former apartments. Naturally the professions were purged of 'unreliable elements', and the children of bourgeois parents were not allowed to study at university or even beyond elementary school level. Vaclav Havel recalled how he had to leave school at fifteen, initially denied access to higher education simply because of his class origins, and how, as victims of 'Action B', his family was assigned a cottage in a hamlet in a remote area in the border regions. (Fortunately for the Havels, the cumbersome nature of the bureaucracy resulted in the retention of two small rooms in the Prague flat which the family had originally owned.)

This social engineering – replacing the perceived old elites with new ones composed of the party and proletarian faithful – was a direct imitation of Soviet policy. Yet the Communist Zdenek Mlynar, employed as a young lawyer in the public prosecutor's office, found the system to be bogus and corrupt. Flats and houses were 'expropriated 'in 'the public interest', and their former denizens were sent to repopulate the former Sudeten German regions, living for the most part in wretched, dilapidated cottages. This entirely illegal process was justified as war against the class enemy and as being in the interests of the state, the public and the working class.

In practice, as Mlynar discovered, not a single unit of expropriated housing was actually given to workers in need of accommodation. Instead they were allotted to officers in the security and armed forces and to functionaries of the Communist party and its various political or administrative bodies. Most of the former owners were not, strictly speaking, of the bourgeoisie (that is, owners of factories or other business enterprises or people possessed of 'unearned income'); rather, they were professionals such as doctors and lawyers, or white-collar workers. Moreover, they were not chosen as victims of expropriation on the basis of class, but according to the value of their property. As a sop to the proletariat, which did not benefit from this transfer of property, food rationing was introduced according to social class. Naturally the working class got bigger rations than those from the former 'exploiting classes'.

The terror against the bourgeoisie ran parallel to the campaign against the churches ('Action K'), particularly the Roman Catholic Church. Christianity was a rival ideology to Marxism, and one that provided an alternative or independent focus of loyalty within the state. From the beginning the Communists kept up the pretence that freedom of worship was guaranteed; what concerned the new regime was merely the Church's interference in public spheres, particularly that of education. All the same, a large number of priests and prelates were arrested and tried on fabricated charges of treasonable activity.

Church and state were in conflict over four main issues. The government demanded that the clergy take an oath of loyalty to the Communist regime, and that the hierarchy withdraw its prohibition on clergy taking political office. For its part the Church wanted the freedom of Catholic schools, associations and the press to be restored, and demanded compensation for property it had lost through nationalisation and land reform.

The protests of the hierarchy led by Josef Beran, Archbishop of Prague, led the Communists to found the so-called Catholic Action. This was a movement which aimed to divide the lower clergy and laity from the bishops. Beran condemned this organisation as un-Catholic and schismatic; he was first placed under surveillance and then under house arrest. An order went out that pastoral letters and other communications from the hierarchy could only be read or published by the clergy if they had obtained prior permission from the Ministry of Education; permission that was hardly likely to be granted. Priests who defied the order faced imprisonment or at the least fines. Meanwhile the façade of religious freedom was maintained by the continued existence of the People's Party as one of the partners of the Communists in the national front. This, however, was a spurious partnership, and for 20 years the People's Party was dominated by the collaborator-priest, Josef Plojhar, who was also a Soviet agent.

In July 1949 the papacy reacted to the growing threat of world Communism by excommunicating all Communists and their supporters, including Catholics who read or distributed Communist literature. The Czechoslovak regime retaliated by declaring that any priest who exercised excommunication would be guilty of high treason.

Besides this frontal and brutal attack, the Communists sought to undermine the Church from within. New legislation in July made the clergy the salaried servants of the Communist state. The salaries, along with pensions and insurance benefits, were generous. On the other hand, forced labour camps were set up for both priests and nuns who did not conform to the Communists' notions of loyalty.

Early in 1950 the Communists went to quite ludicrous lengths to discredit the Catholic faith. A crucifix in the church of the remote Bohemian village of Cihost was said to have bowed several times and then leaned towards the west; this was depicted as pro-American propaganda, and the parish priest and church warden were both arrested and interrogated. Even more ludicrous was the accusation that enemies of the state had manufactured a vision of the Virgin, who appeared in the sky among American troops brandishing the flag of the United States. This ridiculous claim was on a par with the accusation that the US air force had deliberately dropped Colorado beetle over Czechoslovakia so as to wreck the harvest.

While the pro-American Madonna was palpable nonsense, a more concrete blow was struck at the Catholic Church by the expulsion of the last Vatican diplomat in March 1950; henceforward the Czechoslovak hierarchy had no official means of communication with Rome. In May 1950 another potential source of resistance was dealt with; the religious orders were dissolved, their property, apart from a very few monasteries, confiscated by the state. The pretext for this was accusations of anti-state activity by some of the most eminent heads of the orders and religious houses, who had been given a show trial the previous month. Other priests and religious were not even put on trial. On 13 April 1950 the Benedictine abbey of Rajhrad in Moravia was invaded by members of the Communist-controlled state security police and people's militia. The monks were sent to various internment camps, the library seized.

With the power of the hierarchy and the religious orders broken, priests who wished to continue serving their flocks had no choice but to take the oath of loyalty to the Communist state. (Though a small number of clergy went underground, continuing to exercise their ministry clandestinely.) This both compromised the clergy morally, and damaged the morale of the Church. The non-Catholic churches were swiftly cowed by government action against the Roman Church, and quickly though on the whole reluctantly fell into line.

Despite this persecution many Christians, particularly Catholics in Moravia, stubbornly continued to practise their faith. At the pilgrimage church of the Name of Mary at Krtiny, for example, there is an 'image of grace' of the Virgin known variously as the 'shield' or 'jewel' of Moravia. Votive paintings offered by various parishes are still displayed there; they bear dates ranging from 1920 to 1989, with some coming from 1948, 1956 and 1960.

Having crippled all potential sources of opposition in the country, the Communists turned on each other. The purges and show trials of leading party members in the 1940s and 1950s were not peculiar to Czechoslovakia; they were widespread throughout the Soviet bloc. Indeed, the trigger for the general European purge was the arrest of Laszlo Rajk in Hungary in June 1949. The causes of this development are quite complex, and still not entirely clear. Certainly, the Czechoslovak leadership shared both the cynicism and the paranoia of Stalin himself, though it appears that they were under pressure from both the Soviet Union and other satellite states.

Gottwald had succeeded Benes as President, while Rudolf Slansky remained Party Secretary, Zapotocky became premier and Clementis followed Jan Masaryk as Foreign Minister. Clementis was dismissed from his post in March 1950, and arrested in January 1951. In November 1950 came the arrest of Otto Sling, regional party secretary for Moravia. In January 1951 it was the turn of Artur London, under-secretary for foreign affairs, and Osvald Zavodsky, Minister of State Security. In February they were followed into prison by Karel Svab, under-secretary of national security. In September Slansky lost the post of General Secretary of the party and was made Deputy Premier as a consolation prize; he was arrested in November.

The causes and course of the purges are complicated, and their roots seem to lie in the international Communist paranoia which followed the expulsion of Yugoslavia from the Cominform in June 1948. Henceforward there was a frantic search for 'Titoists' and foreign agents in all the Soviet satellite countries. A key though unwitting figure in the absurd conspiracy theory that evolved was the American journalist Noel Field. After World War II Field had been active as a charity worker for the Unitarian Service Committee. In March 1949 he and his wife were lured to Prague from Switzerland, kidnapped and taken to prison in Hungary; in August his brother Hermann disappeared from Warsaw airport into a Polish prison.

Noel Field was a vital element in the 'Rajk trial' which took place in Budapest in September 1949. Lazlo Rajk, former foreign minister, and seven other defendants all pleaded guilty to charges of Titoism, Trotskyism, bourgeois nationalism and espionage for the West. In particular they had worked for Field, head of American espionage and an agent of Allen Dulles. The ludicrous nature of the charges did not prevent the execution of Rajk and two others.

Czechoslovakia could not be immune from the hysteria and suspicion sweeping the socialist world. Pressure was put on Gottwald by Matyas Rakosi of Hungary and Boleslav Bierut of Poland to unmask the 'Czechoslovak Rajk'. Rakosi actually told Gottwald of his lack of confidence in Clementis and in Vaclav Nosek, Minister of the Interior, and helpfully supplied the Czechoslovaks with a list of suspects to arrest. Stalin, too, was in the last stages of paranoia, and, together with the leaders of the other satellite states, seems to have manufactured the theory that Czechoslovakia was the weakest link in the socialist bloc and therefore must be the centre of an international conspiracy. Both the political leadership of the Soviet Union and the staff of the red army expressed lack of confidence in the Czechoslovak army command and in particular in General Ludvik Svoboda, Minister of Defence. Accordingly Svoboda was investigated, and after the Slansky trial was stripped of all his posts and sent to work as an accountant on a collective farm.

Eager to please their Soviet masters, Gottwald and Slansky requested Russian 'advisers' from the Kremlin in September 1949. These creatures of Beria, Stalin's notorious secret policeman, were responsible to him rather than to the Czechoslovak authorities. They provided the Czechoslovaks with accounts of the interrogations and show trials of the 1930s in the Soviet Union; evidently these were to serve as a template for what followed. Indeed, at the Slansky trial Minister for State Security Ladislav Kopriva would compare the accused Czechoslovaks explicitly with Trotsky, Zinoviev, Bukharin and other 'disruptive elements' who had infiltrated the Soviet party.

The testimony of Artur London shows that the interrogators were unsure of the identity of the 'Czechoslovak Rajk' and were also uncertain as to what kind of treason they were searching for. Initially, much was made of the 'Trotskyism' of those Communists, like London and Sling, who had served in the international brigades during the Spanish civil war. Doubtless Stalin feared that they might reveal his cynical manipulation of the Spanish left during the conflict. Later in the questioning Spain became less important, as it seemed likely that Slansky himself might fill the role of arch-traitor.

The actual indictment at the trial in November 1952 accused Slansky and his 'co-conspirators' of being 'Trotskyist, Titoist, Zionist, bourgeois-nationalist traitors and enemies of the Czechoslovak people'. In the service of American imperialism they had formed an 'anti-state conspiratorial centre', and among other nefarious activities had 'undermined the people's democratic constitution, sabotaged the building of socialism, damaged the national economy, committed acts of espionage'.[2] Twelve of the 14 accused were described (in many cases untruthfully) as being of bourgeois origin. Eleven of them were 'of Jewish origin'.

Indeed, there was more than a hint of anti-Semitism in the trial. Slansky himself (who was red-haired) was described in more than one newspaper article as 'Judas'. Besides native nastiness, this anti-Semitism was rooted in the foreign policy of the Soviet Union and its satellites, which was inimical to Israel and favoured the Arab states; and in Stalin's own paranoid hatred of Jews, which had recently resulted in the uncovering of the murderous 'doctors' plot' in Moscow.

All the accused pleaded guilty as charged. Eleven of them, including Slansky, Clementis, Sling and Svab, were sentenced to death, while three, including London, were given life sentences. The executions were carried out in a matter of days. The ashes of the dead men were put in a sack, driven into the country and sprinkled on a slippery cart-road. The chauffeur of the car later joked grotesquely that never before had he driven 14 people in a Tatraplan, three of them alive and 11 in a sack.

Why did these men have to die? Possibly Gottwald feared them as rivals and, like Stalin before him, wished to write them out of history so as to glorify his own role in events. *The Book of Laughter and Forgetting* by Milan Kundera opens famously with an ironic summary of the fate of Clementis. The scene is the snowy balcony in Prague from which the drunken Gottwald is proclaiming the Communist victory in February 1948. As it is snowing, Clementis considerately gives his leader his own fur (Russian bearskin) hat. After the elimination of Clementis by Gottwald he is airbrushed from the historic photograph; so that all that is left of him and his role, remarks Kundera, is his hat.

Slansky was obviously a potential rival to Gottwald, and his persecution of non-Communists had revealed him to be utterly ruthless. Certainly Gottwald's fellow 'Muscovites' had to be purged; at the same time history had to be rewritten to show that only the Soviet Union and its faithful Czechoslovak followers had been responsible for the liberation of the country from Nazi tyranny. Thus Otto Sling, the Communist dictator of Moravia who was tried and executed with Slansky, was accused of being a British spy because he had spent the war in London and had married an English wife. The implication was that all such 'Londoners' had been corrupted by the British to work for the downfall of Czechoslovakia.

The more illustrious the victim's past, the more the need to eliminate them from public life. Thus Marie Svermova, widow of the Communist Slovak partisan hero Jan Sverma who had died during the Slovak national uprising of 1944, sister of Karel Svab, and herself a Communist since the party's foundation in 1921, was sentenced to life imprisonment in 1954 for alleged anti-state conspiracy with the late Otto Sling. She did not receive the death sentence, and as she in fact only served two years of her sentence, Svermova got off lightly compared with the fate of other victims of the show trials.

Immediately after its liberation in 1945 the governance of Slovakia had been entrusted to a board of trustees and the Slovak National Council; these were composed of both Communists and democrats. (The Communists had originally called for the proclamation of Slovakia as a Soviet republic, but on Stalin's instructions this was quickly dropped, as were plans for a loose federation of Slovakia and the Czech lands.) This system endured for a time as the 'asymmetrical model', since there were no corresponding governmental bodies for the Czech lands, only the central government and national assembly in

Prague. The Slovak Communists would be natural targets of Gottwald and his allies for a number of reasons. First, socialism demanded that both politics and the economy be rigidly centralised. Second, the Slovak national uprising gave the Slovaks some claim to the direction of their own affairs, since they had at least tried to overthrow the Tiso state. Finally, Slovak politicians like Gustav Husak knew of the negative role played by the Soviet Union (and the exiled Czechoslovak Communist leadership) in that rising.

As early as June 1948 the 'problem' of Slovak 'petit-bourgeois nationalism' was mentioned at a meeting of the presidium of the Czechoslovak Communist party. Indeed, long before the trial of Husak, Novomesky and other leading Slovak Communists on the charge of 'bourgeois nationalism', there were two legalistic attacks on Slovaks. First, between 30 August and 2 September 1950 sixteen Czechoslovak and Yugoslav citizens were tried in Bratislava. They were accused of 'Titoism', espionage centred on the Yugoslav embassy and involving the British and Americans, and Slovak 'bourgeois nationalism'. Second, a group of Slovak partisans was tried in Bratislava between 18 and 20 October 1950. This case was a blatant attempt to discredit the Slovak national uprising of August 1944; five out of the eight defendants were Communists.

In April 1954 the trial of the chief 'Slovak bourgeois nationalists' was staged in Bratislava. Most ominously, the old story of the Slovak request for direct incorporation into the Soviet Union had been repeated with embellishments. In March 1951 the secretary of the Israeli legation, himself a Czechoslovak by birth, had told a British diplomat that the Slovak Communists had made this request in 1945 at the time that the programme of the Kosice government was being formulated, then again in 1948 at the time of the Communist coup, and even more recently.

The main defendant in the trial was Gustav Husak. A lawyer and long-serving Communist, Husak had served on the illegal central committee of the Slovak party in 1943–44 under the clerico-fascist state; he had been notable in the Slovak national uprising in 1944; he had been one of the original Slovak board of trustees on liberation in 1945 and had served as its chairman in the years 1946 to 1950. He was in direct rivalry with Viliam Siroky, Gottwald's spokesman for Slovak affairs, who favoured Prague centralism as opposed to the Slovak autonomy promised in the Kosice programme. Husak was arrested in 1951, and at the trial in 1954 he received a life sentence, despite the fact that he refuted the preposterous charges against him both during interrogation and before the court itself. The other four defendants received sentences of between ten and 22 years.

Why did the victims confess so readily to the most preposterous crimes, which in some cases it would have been physically impossible for them to commit? Again, this is a complex matter. Certainly they were put to physical and psychological torture. Husak, for example, recalled being dressed in thin clothes and put into a freezing room, then being given winter clothing and transferred to a hot and airless one. Artur London spoke of torture by sleep deprivation and of being forced to walk constantly in his cell. Fear for their families also played a part in their compliance, and humiliation at the hands of the interrogators undoubtedly helped in undermining morale. Strangest of all, like religious martyrs, they came to be persuaded that they had to die for the good of the party. The interrogators distinguished between 'subjective' and 'objective' guilt; this meant that though the accused might be personally innocent, the very fact that crimes or errors had been committed made them guilty by association. The show trials themselves were farcical, in that the answers to 'impromptu' questions had been learned by heart, and on one occasion the accused gave the answer to a different question.

The purges had a ripple effect, widening to include all ranks of Communists who the accused were persuaded to name as accomplices or sympathisers. The victims were buried in unmarked graves or cremated, their ashes being scattered to the winds. Their families, who did not escape persecution either, were often ordered to change their surnames. In a particularly heartless and cynical move, Slansky's widow was accused of developing an inveterate hatred of the Soviet Union because her infant daughter had been abducted from a Moscow park during the war. Josefa Slanska, like Sling's widow, was held in detention but not brought to trial.

How could Communists themselves accept the preposterous charges against former comrades, even close friends and relatives by blood or by marriage? Zdenek Mlynar, who remained a Communist (albeit of the reform variety) even after his expulsion from the party has some instructive observations on this point. The faith of Communists, he observed, is quite as irrational as the faith of religious believers, and the party functionaries correspond to the pope (at this time Stalin), cardinals and other prelates. Although these might be fallible and sinful, still they and their followers would have implicit faith in their god, the 'objective law of history', which would lead to fulfilment of the 'interests of the working class', 'and to human progress, as understood by the Communist faith'. Mlynar also uses the image of a squirrel caught in a drum to show the alienation of Communists from other people and systems.

> As long as a Communist who possesses this kind of ideo-
> logical faith remains inside his system of logic and values,
> his ideas have no more meaning for the rest of the world
> than a squirrel running inside a revolving drum has for the

world outside the drum. And of course the reverse is also
true: the outside world scarcely influences the squirrel, for
the only solid ground he knows is the revolving drum
itself.[3]

Gottwald died in his bed in spring 1953, and there is a certain poetic justice
to his death. He caught a cold at Stalin's funeral and, his constitution weak-
ened by years of alcoholic abuse, expired of pneumonia three days later. Thus
the faithful slave followed his master to the grave. Gottwald's body was mum-
mified and laid to rest in a mausoleum inside the national monument on
Zizka Hill in Prague. Stalin was honoured by a colossal statue weighing 14,000
tonnes which stared out over the city from Letna Hill. This monstrosity was
officially unveiled on May Day 1955.

Gottwald was succeeded as president by Antonin Zapotocky and as party
leader by Antonin Novotny. Three years later the Czechoslovak Communists
experienced the double shock of Khrushchev's secret speech denouncing
Stalin, and the Hungarian uprising. Khrushchev's criticism of the Soviet show
trials of the 1930s found an unpleasant echo with those who had participated
in the more recent Czechoslovak political trials. This was the chief reason
for the rehabilitation commission, which finally sat in 1963 but did not fully
rehabilitate all the victims of the purges. The previous year the Stalin monument on Letna had been systematically demolished by high explosives.
According to Zdenek Mlynar the Hungarian uprising chiefly frightened the
Czechoslovak party because Communists were being lynched and shot on the
streets of Budapest. As is well known, Khrushchev forcibly restored order in
Hungary, and the spectre of mob rule on the streets of Prague receded.

In 1957 Novotny became president as well as first secretary of the party,
and settled down to enjoy a decade of dull dictatorship. He inherited a host of
problems from the Gottwald era which he did little to remedy. Moreover, until
1963 he consistently blocked attempts fully to rehabilitate the victims of the
show trials, despite the fact that most of the charges against them no longer
held. Tito had been welcomed back into the international socialist family by
Khrushchev; the 'Moscow doctors' had been exonerated of all charges and
rehabilitated; and the Field brothers had been released and rehabilitated by
the Hungarian and Polish governments. Only General Svoboda achieved full
rehabilitation at an early date (1954), and this was at the personal request of
Khrushchev.

The most pressing problem facing Novotny was that of the economy. As
previous chapters have shown, Czechoslovakia was rich in some natural
resources, and had an excellent industrial infrastructure. It had built up an

armaments and an automobile industry. Moreover, a long tradition of crafts-manship had resulted in the development of light industries such as textiles, glass, ceramics, shoemaking and beer brewing. In October 1945 Benes issued presidential decrees which nationalised heavy industry, the banks and insur-ance companies and which placed more than 60 per cent of the industrial labour force in the nationalised sector. This was not due solely to Communist pressure, but was a genuine attempt to reconcile socialism with democracy (or free enterprise) in the economic sphere.

However, between 1949 and 1953 the economy was remodelled on the Stalinist, Soviet line, complete with inappropriate five-year plans. Although the first of these plans brought about fast economic growth it also resulted in fluctuations in 1953–54. There was an unnecessary stress on heavy industry, particularly armaments, and this, together with the disastrous currency reform of 1953, meant acute shortages of consumer goods and a drastic fall in the standard of living of ordinary Czechoslovaks.

Agriculture did not fare any better than industry under the Communists. The latter fully supported the post-war land reform law which, as a pendant to that of 1919, provided for the confiscation and redistribution of the remaining large estates. In the build-up to the 1946 elections, Communist propaganda more than implied that land would be held individually by small and middle-sized holders, and that collectivisation was far from the party's plans. In fact, Soviet Russia once more provided the inappropriate model for Czechoslovakia. The state farm and the unified cooperative were little differ-ent from the *sovkholz* and *kolkhoz* which obtained in the motherland of socialism. Naturally the peasants were averse to both types of collective and to the threat they posed to their traditional way of life, and in 1953 there was a mass exodus of farmers from the collectives. Production, particularly of cer-eals, declined in the years following the coup of 1948.

Scapegoats were sought and found for the parlous state of the economy. In August 1954 a group of economists was tried and found guilty of 'sabotage of socialist reconstruction'. All 11 of the accused received heavy prison sen-tences. The trial had a deadly effect on the economy; it stifled initiative on the part of managers and technical experts, discouraged independent attempts to increase production, and set Czechoslovakia even more firmly in the jaws of the pernicious 'command economy'.

In political terms the monopoly of power was held by Novotny and a nar-row band of cronies; indeed, in the 1960s playing cards with Novotny was well known to be the sure path to office and influence. Novotny's belief in central-ized government coincided with his contempt for the Slovaks, and he ensured that even their limited autonomy was so whittled away as to become meaningless. In 1960 the Czechoslovak constitution had to be emended as Novotny intended to change the name of the country to 'Czechoslovak Socialist Republic', and he took the opportunity to abolish the 'asymmetric model'. His dislike of the Slovaks led him to resist the call for the rehabilitation of Gustav Husak, Laco Novomesky and other Slovaks accused of 'bourgeois nationalism'. (This group had actually been condemned after the death of Gottwald, so Novotny himself, as party leader, could be held responsible for their fate.) In 1963 their rehabilitation was pushed through despite his opposition; but this was only a partial rehabilitation, and the victims were forbidden from re-entering politics. Equally, in the previous year Novotny failed to prevent the establishment of a commission to examine the cases of other Czechoslovak Communists purged in the 1950s, but again, these people were pardoned rather than exonerated and were not considered fit to re-enter public life.

In foreign policy Czechoslovakia was indistinguishable from the rest of the Soviet bloc. It supported the Soviet Union on the German question, and followed the pro-Arab, anti-Israeli Middle Eastern line dictated by Moscow. So subservient was the Prague government to the Kremlin that there was even a joke doing the rounds about Vaclav David, Minister for Foreign Affairs; other foreign ministers were multilingual, but David spoke only one language – Russian.

In cultural terms the 1950s formed a fairly stagnant decade, at least as far as official culture was concerned. Novotny disliked and distrusted intellectuals, and worked successfully to depict them to the working classes as idle drones. As in other spheres of Czechoslovak life the example of the Soviet Union was followed to a slavish degree. Books, films, plays and music were directly imported from the USSR, and artists of all kinds were instructed to work in the arid and unreal style of socialist realism.

Even so, there were stirrings of original activity from both Communist and non-Communist intellectuals. From the early 1960s the official writers' union came to be dominated by reform Communists, whom Vaclav Havel has described as 'anti-dogmatics'. At the same time non-Communist writers and other artists were growing in confidence, and producing experimental film and theatre, for example. It would be the writers' union congress in June 1967 which would first air criticism of the regime's policy.

By the mid-1960s it was plain that economic change was imperative. It was also clear that this could not take place without political change. The stultifying atmosphere around Novotny made this seem unlikely, but though the neo-Stalinist winter he had manufactured was harsh, it would eventually be followed by a startling and remarkable spring.

## Notes

1 Quoted in Josef Korbel, *The Communist Subversion of Czechoslovakia 1938–1948* (Oxford, 1959), pp. 233, 87.
2 Printed in Josefa Slanska, *Report on My Husband* (London, 1969), p. 35.
3 Zdenek Mlynar, *Night Frost in Prague: The End of Humane Socialism* (London, 1980), pp. 31, 36.

# Prague Spring and the Soviet Invasion

In 1968 spring began in Czechoslovakia in January, with Novotny's replacement as first secretary by Alexander Dubcek. 'Prague Spring' is the term given to the reform movement that followed this brief tussle for power. The name was probably inspired by the Prague Spring music festival, first held in 1946, before the Communist coup. Attempts have been made to depict the Prague Spring of 1968 as simply a quarrel between Communists rather than a struggle for democracy. The reality is, of course, much more complex. True, the process of change was initiated by an inner-party power struggle; but this was both preceded and accompanied by popular protest and demands for reform.

The dead hand of Novotny was particularly heavy on the economy. Combined with his accumulation of offices, his arrogance, and his contempt especially for the Slovaks, this indicated to Communists and non-Communists alike that change was vital. Economic reform was the priority; and soon it became evident that this could only be accomplished if there were also political reform.

The economy had reached its crisis in 1962, thanks largely to the stranglehold of the command structure. This was over-centralised (just like politics in Czechoslovakia), and it stifled both local and national initiative. Radical reform was proposed by Ota Sik, an economics professor and a member of the central committee of the party. He suggested drastic decentralisation of the economy, with minimal government intervention. Prices should correspond to market forces of supply and demand. Factory managers should be given a wide scope for individual initiative, and there should be incentives for both management and work force. Sik even asserted that there was a place for private enterprise in a socialist economy. Naturally such sensible proposals, the antithesis of Stalinism, were resisted by the Novotny regime. By early 1967, however, the economic crisis had become so acute that Sik's reforms were adopted over Novotny's objections.

Zdenek Mlynar, in his memoir *Night Frost in Prague*, gave an insider's view of the ideological and political struggles within the party during

Novotny's last years in power. In particular he charts the development of 'reform Communism', of which he was himself a proponent. This was based on two fundamental principles: that decisions concerning the economy and society should be based on qualified expertise; and that society itself should be able to express opinions on what its true interests were. Thus specialists and technical experts, rather than ideologically acceptable party functionaries, should be employed, while freedom of expression of the various interest groups in society should be guaranteed by law. The 'leading role' of the party should not be taken for granted, as it had to be earned and re-earned through tackling changed conditions. Moreover, the party should remember that it was the conductor, not the orchestra, and should not try to usurp the powers of the state and social organisations. According to Mlynar, only the fact that these ideas and principles were circulating among party members and functionaries in the years before 1968 made the Prague Spring possible; though he did also admit the role played by popular protest.

Perhaps there is an element of special pleading in all this. Certainly, Mlynar denied that Novotny was an outright Stalinist, but rather depicted him as a supporter of Khrushchev. Novotny in this view was a 'genuine leftover from the Stalinist period', an old guard Communist rather than a follower of Stalin. Nor was his period in power the bleak Stalinist night which Western commentators have depicted. It must be realised, though, that Mlynar was quite bitterly comparing the Novotny era with the 'black light' of the Husak period of 'normalisation' which followed the experiment of 1968. Yet he was right to identify reform Communism as one of the two motors of Prague Spring. Without the willingness of the party leadership to consider reform, no such reform would have been possible.

Political as well as cultural discontent surfaced in June 1967, when the writers' union held its congress. Speakers here made unprecedented attacks on Novotny's policies at home and abroad; a particular target was the censorship. The authorities responded with some expulsions from the union and from the editorial board of its journal, *Literarni Listy* ('Literary Leaves'). The paper itself was banned that autumn. Plainly, Novotny believed that this minor purge would be enough to stifle any future dissent. At the end of October, however, came a student demonstration in the Strahov district of Prague. Ostensibly this was to protest at the inadequate electricity supplies in the hostels, and the students marched holding lighted candles. The symbolism of their demand for light was not lost on the authorities, and the peaceful protest was broken up brutally by riot police. The significance of this violent incident in the prelude to Prague Spring is shown by the fact that, early in 1968, both the chief of police and the Minister of the Interior made public apologies to the students. Thus from the beginning the reform movement was propelled by popular discontent as well as by elite politics.

In the highest echelons of the Czechoslovak Communist Party a deadly struggle took place from October 1967 to January 1968. Its seriousness can be gauged from the fact that Novotny accused his future supplanter Dubcek of 'bourgeois [Slovak] nationalism'; a charge which, as has been seen, could result at the least in a long prison sentence. The Novotnyites were opposed by a disparate group of 'liberals', made up of economists and other experts as well as disaffected Slovaks. These had political grievances, as well as resentment at the continued economic backwardness of Slovakia. In 1960 the board of trustees, set up in 1945, had been dissolved. A few token individual trustees remained, but these had few independent powers and were answerable in any case to the Slovak national council. This body had now no more than a formal existence, with no legislative powers. In short, everything was subordinated to the over-centralised government in Prague. Meanwhile some Slovaks were calling for a return to the post-war 'asymmetric model', with the national council as a legislative body, a reinstated board of trustees, and also representation in the national government and assembly in Prague. Increasingly, though, there were calls for some sort of federation.

Novotny evidently hoped to invoke the might of the Kremlin in the struggle with his opponents, and in December 1967 Leonid Brezhnev visited Prague at his invitation. Brezhnev was actually preoccupied with his own power struggle within the Soviet politburo; moreover, he seems to have suspected Novotny of favouring other Soviet figures and factions than his own. At any rate, he declined to intervene in the conflict within the Czechoslovak party with the famous words, 'it's your business'. Thus he publicly abandoned the man who was so thought to be a subservient tool of the Soviets that a popular rhyme went, 'I'm Antonin Novotny, I'll do what you want of me'.

Indeed, Mlynar believed that this was more than just simple desertion. Rather, Brezhnev was happy to sacrifice Novotny so long as there was a strong pro-Soviet faction within the Czechoslovak leadership. Indeed, Mlynar discerns Brezhnev's hand behind the promotion within the party and the government of such unlikely 'reform Communists' as Alois Indra, Vasil Bilak, Milos Jakes and Oldrich Pavlovsky. In effect, these former Novotnyites were to be the wolves within the sheepfold. Certainly, all were active in the August plot in 1968 to replace the reform Communist leaders with a revolutionary government and tribunal.

There were several heated meetings of the presidium of the central committee; on 19 December, for example, uproar broke out when Ota Sik announced that the economy was in crisis and called for Novotny's resignation. Novotny was persuaded to resign as first secretary in January 1968; he would be relieved of the presidency in March. The old guard was not about to let go of power easily, however. It emerged in February that Generals Janko and Sejna had actively plotted a military coup in December to keep Novotny in both his offices. Largely because he feared he would face charges of financial corruption, Sejna fled to Italy and, with the aid of the CIA, defected to the United States on his patron's resignation of the more important of his two posts. Janko committed suicide.

The presidency would be entrusted to the apparently safe hands of the elderly General Ludvik Svoboda, the 'non-party' minister of defence from 1945 to 1950, when he was purged from the government. In view of developments in 1968 it is most interesting that his surname means 'freedom' in Czech. Certainly, the Communists were looking for a neutral, elder-statesman type of president, and one, moreover, who would be acceptable to both Czechs and Slovaks. Most Czechs favoured Josef Smrkovsky, while Cestmir Cisar was the darling of the Czech students. The Slovaks preferred either Husak or his co-defendant in the trial of 'Slovak bourgeois nationalists', the poet Ladislav Novomesky. Obviously a candidate acceptable to both Czechs and Slovaks was necessary, and Svoboda was the choice. It is perhaps significant that immediately after his election Svoboda laid a wreath on the grave of Tomas Garrigue Masaryk, the President Liberator. Such a gesture had not been made since the Communist seizure of power.

The question of who would be first secretary was even more problematic. After intense negotiations within the party a compromise candidate, Alexander Dubcek, was chosen. He was reluctant to take up the post, but he was the only candidate who could achieve the necessary majority of votes in the central committee. His right-hand men were Drahomir Kolder, the highly conservative secretary to the central committee, and Oldrich Cernik, a reform-minded economist who was soon to be prime minister. Dubcek's appointment was approved by Leonid Brezhnev in a telephone call, and later that month the new Czechoslovak leader visited Moscow to receive the Communist equivalent of a papal blessing. For his part, Dubcek took the opportunity to reassure the Soviet leadership of Czechoslovakia's adherence to socialism and loyalty to the Soviet Union.

Ominously in view of later events, both the Soviet Union and the Warsaw pact neighbours demanded repeated reassurance. At a Warsaw pact summit in early March concern was expressed at the appearance of 'anti-socialist' elements in Czechoslovakia. At the Dresden summit later that month, Dubcek and the other Czechoslovak leaders faced trenchant criticism of their policy from Brezhnev, Ulbricht and other neighbourly politicians. Their fear was that the Czechoslovak Communists were losing control of the situation, and this fear, shared by some elements of the Czechoslovak party leadership, would culminate in the invasion of August.

But this is to anticipate events. What was the character and background of the new first secretary who emerged in January 1968? Dubcek was a Slovak, unusually young for such high Communist office (46), and with surprisingly clean hands. Born and bred a Communist, he had spent his childhood in the Soviet Union where his idealistic parents had volunteered to join a 'help project'. Dubcek himself became a Communist party member in 1939 and later joined the partisans. In 1944 he participated in the Slovak national uprising against the Nazis and the Tiso puppet-state. He was wounded twice; his brother Julius was killed. In the 1950s Dubcek trained at the party higher school in Moscow, and thereafter rose unspectacularly through the ranks of the Slovak party.

When considering the causes and consequences of Prague Spring it is essential not to underestimate Dubcek's sincere commitment to Communism and to the Soviet Union. He was, it is true, profoundly shocked and grief-stricken by the atrocities uncovered by investigations into the purges and show trials; but what appalled him was the fact that Communists, of all people, should have been guilty of such crimes. As is shown by the action programme of April 1968 which is associated with his name, he and his allies did not envisage a pluralistic democracy for Czechoslovakia; indeed, the superiority of democratic socialism over its bourgeois or liberal counterpart was asserted more than once. Morally convinced that Communism was the best of all possible systems, he acknowledged the errors of the past and sought reform of the party as well as the state.

Dubcek was the first and last genuinely popular Communist leader of Czechoslovakia. The slogan 'socialism with a human face' was coined for him by Radovan Richta, a researcher and speech writer in the party apparatus. Yet his ready smile made it easy to identify Dubcek with the concept. Mlynar was of the opinion that Dubcek's popularity was largely based on the fact that he believed in his own words and policies, and accordingly the people trusted him for his sincerity.

The spirit of change passed swiftly beyond the walls of party and government offices. On 14 February 1968 the first public political discussion since the Communist seizure of power took place in Prague. Also in that month Novotny's ban on the writers' union newspaper was lifted; this was the beginning of the end of censorship. In March there was a student demonstration at the grave of Jan Masaryk, who was popularly regarded as a martyr for democracy. This took place on the twentieth anniversary of his demise, and in April student demands led to the establishment of a commission of inquiry into

Masaryk's death. Cautious steps were taken towards first the relaxation, then the suspension, of the censorship; it was formally outlawed in June. In March the Deputy Minister of the Interior, fearful of what past misdemeanours might come to light, committed suicide. The hitherto tame national assembly demanded the rehabilitation of former political prisoners, living and dead; those surviving formed Klub 231 to press for justice. This organisation revealed that some 62,000 people had been wrongfully prosecuted and punished from 1948 to 1968; statistics which caused no small amount of shock and grief to Dubcek.

Each month of spring brought fresh, previously unimaginable developments. In April a commission was formed to investigate the show trials of the 1950s, and the widows of two of the most prominent victims, Rudolf Slansky and Otto Sling, prepared to write and publish accounts of their husbands' and their own ordeals. An even earlier victim of the Communist distortion of history was also allowed, posthumously, to speak for himself. Edvard Benes' account of the crisis of 1938 was finally published in Prague as *The Days of Munich.*

Also in April the first mass meeting of students and workers took place (thus overturning Novotny's policy of dividing the intelligentsia from the proletariat, the better to rule them both); and the club of independent writers and the discussion group KAN (for committed non-party members) were founded. Such developments, however, were not to every Communist's liking, and concern was expressed at demands for political pluralism. The intellectuals Vaclav Havel and Ivan Svitak argued respectively for the formation of an opposition party and for a three-party system. It was feared that popular demands for reform would soon outstrip what the Communist Party was willing or even able to concede. Under pressure from conservatives like Indra and Kolder restrictions were placed on the formation of new organisations, and revival of the Sokol gymnastic movement was forbidden.

On the political front a new government dominated by reform Communists was formed on 6 April, with Oldrich Cernik as Prime Minister, Ota Sik and Gustav Husak as deputy premiers, and Josef Pavel as Minister of the Interior. It is possible to discern three trends in political thinking among the party leadership. First, there were radicals like Sik and Frantisek Kriegel, appointed chairman of the national front. Second, there were conservatives such as Bilak, Kolder and Indra who favoured some limited reform that would set the economy to rights and consolidate their own positions. Finally, there were the moderate reformers, led by Dubcek and including Cernik, Mlynar, Spacek and Smrkovsky.

Meanwhile the immensely popular Smrkovsky became chairman (speaker) of the national assembly. Smrkovsky's life forms a kind of summary of the history of idealistic Communism in Czechoslovakia. He joined the party in 1933, was active in the underground resistance in World War II and was one of the leaders of the Prague uprising of May 1945. During the Communist coup of February 1948 he was most effective in organising the workers' militia. After holding several party and governmental posts he was suddenly arrested in 1951 and illegally sentenced to life imprisonment. Conditionally released in 1955, he was a forestry worker until his rehabilitation in 1963.

Even more momentous for the political future of the country than the placing of reform Communists in high office was the publication of the action programme and its approval by the central committee of the party on 5 April. This plan was the work of a team of reform Communists and technical experts. Among these were Zdenek Mlynar, Radovan Richta, Bohumil Simon, Ota Sik and other economists, as well as the historian Karel Kaplan, who was also active on the commission formed to investigate the show trials. A speech which Dubcek made to the plenary session of the central committee on 1 April shows that it has been rightly identified with his name and intended policies.

While expressing his commitment to Communism Dubcek emphasised that this should be a humane form of socialism, respecting the rights and dignity of the working people and gaining their cooperation in all spheres of activity. He wanted to create a system which would combine socialism with democracy in order to solve the problems of the economy and society. He boasted that freedom of speech and of the press were no longer demands, but realities. However free discussion between Communists and non-Communists was not the same as democratic pluralism; there were to be no new political parties, and no contested elections.

Turning to the action programme itself, it was clear that it addressed both the troubled Communist past and the economic, social, political and ethnic problems of the present. The cult of personality imposed by Gottwald and Novotny was denounced. Four current characteristics of the Czechoslovak state were described. These were a lack of antagonism based on class (thus class warfare was now redundant); an outdated economic system in need of reform; the need to prepare to join the scientific and technological revolution; and a broad opportunity for social initiative, free discussion and democratisation of the social and economic system. The command economy with its inefficiency and inequity was condemned outright; there would be an end to centralised decision-making. There was also to be a de-levelling of wages and salaries in order to encourage initiative, competition and increased performance. The rights of the national minorities were asserted, and the problems faced by women were viewed sympathetically.

Unequivocally, the Communist party would not renounce its 'leading role' (or more accurately, monopoly of power), but it would seek to reassess this. The party should serve society rather than rule it, and should win the voluntary support of the population by its efforts. Freedom of association, assembly and expression were to be safeguarded. Victims of past political injustice were to have their cases reopened, and the Ministry of the Interior and the secret police were to be reformed and to have their powers curtailed. There were to be reforms in the fields of social welfare, education, housing and the health service. All these, together with improvements to agriculture, industry and trade, would enhance the quality of life of the ordinary Czechoslovak and increase the country's international standing. This regenerated economy and society would serve as both a reproach and a stimulus to bourgeois democracy abroad, which was limited in comparison with Czechoslovak socialist democracy. Indeed, an Austrian commentator had remarked that the Czechoslovak experiment posed more of an ideological threat to the West than to the Communist bloc.

Two final points are of significance. First, the constitution would be redrafted to redress the grievances of the Slovaks by introducing a federal arrangement. Decentralisation was to be the key here, too; the Slovak national council would become a legislative body, and the Slovak council of ministers would become an executive one. Control of the Slovak budget would pass to Slovak national organisations; there would be no possibility in a political or a constitutional sense of the Slovak nation being outvoted by the Czech, and the principle of equal rights of the two nations was asserted. Finally, in terms of foreign policy the existing alignment of Czechoslovakia within the Warsaw treaty organisation and the ComEcon (Committee for Mutual Economic Assistance) was confirmed. Though peaceful coexistence with capitalist states was desired, loyalty to the Soviet Union was quite literally underlined in the typescript of the action programme.

Despite such protestations the action programme met with a mixed reception in the Soviet politburo. While some members found it unobjectionable Brezhnev denounced it violently, saying that it could lead to the restoration of capitalism in Czechoslovakia. It was natural although ominous that the Soviet leadership should take a close interest in developments in Czechoslovakia. In late May Kosygin went to Karlovy Vary (Karlsbad), ostensibly to take the water cure at the spa on a private visit. However Dubcek was summoned to see him, and an agreement of sorts was negotiated. It was confirmed that the Communist party would retain its 'leading role', but that the economic reforms would proceed; that Warsaw Pact manoeuvres would be held in Czechoslovakia, but that an extraordinary party congress (necessary in view of Dubcek's many opponents in the party presidium and apparatus) could be held.

The month of May 1968 seemed to show the leadership, party and people in hopeful unison. The spontaneous rally of youth at the Jan Hus monument in Prague's Old Town Square seemed to be a prelude to the astounding spectacle of the May Day parade. Traditionally this was a stony, solemn and well-orchestrated affair. In 1968 legionaries from World War I and veterans of the Spanish civil war – both previously victims of Communist persecution – joined the procession. In contrast to his grim-faced predecessors mechanically reviewing the achievements of actually existing socialism, Dubcek smiled and waved at the marchers and onlookers who reciprocated quite spontaneously. On that day Dubcek seemed to embody his own slogan of 'socialism with a human face'.

All seemed well on the surface, but both before and after the euphoria of May Day popular demands and expressions of feeling often outstripped what Dubcek and the government and party leadership might grant with safety, or even desire to grant. The philosopher Ivan Svitak drew the contrast between democracy and mere democratisation. Surveys of public opinion in the press reveal a variety of political responses. In July the Socialist Party newspaper *Svobodne Slovo* ('Word of Freedom') revealed that nine out of ten readers questioned favoured the creation of a strong, independent opposition party rather than the continued existence of the cosmetic national front. (Earlier, in March, this journal had published an open letter to Dubcek demanding that a multiparty democracy be established.) The Prague evening paper revealed that 87 per cent of those surveyed were happy with the present government, though only 53 per cent thought they were more confident in the government than in January; and that 89 per cent wanted to continue on the path of 'socialism with a human face', while just 5 per cent wanted a return to capitalism.

On 27 June the manifesto *2000 Words* was published. Its author was the novelist Ludvik Vaculik, and it was signed by 70 writers and other public figures. The manifesto condemned the Communists for their past monopoly of power and corruption. However, it also stated that construction of a democratic system would be impossible without the participation of the reform Communists, and expressed support for the Dubcek leadership. It also alluded to the possibility of foreign intervention in Czechoslovakia, and it was this as much as its criticism of past errors which probably made it offensive to the Soviet and Eastern European authorities. The official Czechoslovak party central committee's resolution on Vaculik's manifesto thus stressed that all Communists must be united behind the action programme; *2000 Words* was not to be an alternative policy document.

Indeed, Dubcek himself was afraid that democratisation was evolving at too fast a rate, particularly for the neighbours in the Soviet bloc. In May and June he held meetings with journalists where he begged them to behave with moderation so as not to jeopardise the achievements of Prague Spring. He was visibly and audibly distressed when he discovered that many of them wanted to go further in the direction of reform than did the reform Communists. Yet independent opinion polls conducted in the spring and early summer revealed that 70 per cent of the population expressed support for the Communist Party's policies, about 25 per cent of them without reservation.

The Czechoslovak government and party were moving with caution and moderation, but even so, alarm bells were ringing in most of the Warsaw pact capitals. The socialist neighbours were afraid that Dubcek was losing control of the situation and of public opinion, and that this could spell the end of the party's 'leading role'. In addition, foreign leaders like Wladislaw Gomulka of Poland, Todor Zhivkov of Bulgaria and 'Frozen Walter' Ulbricht of East Germany were concerned that the Czechoslovaks' taste of freedom might unsettle their own subjects and lead to similar demands being voiced. Not that they had any intention of satisfying any such demands. Mlynar, who had the chance to observe them at close quarters, characterised Ulbricht and Gomulka as vain, self-satisfied, hostile and senile, and as quite intoxicated with their own power; Zhivkov he thought to be merely incredibly stupid. Be that as it may, it is unquestionable that these politicians believed that the Czechoslovaks must be brought into line lest the cataleptic calm of the Soviet bloc be disturbed.

At the end of May the commanders of the Warsaw pact armed forces arrived in Czechoslovakia to prepare for military manoeuvres. Although the Czechoslovaks had agreed to this there was more than an implied threat in the heavy military presence on Czechoslovak soil. Unease was increased when the visitors showed no hurry to leave; indeed, the last of the Soviet troops left on 3 August, long after the manoeuvres were over.

Unease also pervaded the highest echelons of Communist power abroad. The leaders of the Soviet Union, Poland, East Germany, Bulgaria and Hungary met in summit in Warsaw, whence on 15 July they despatched the 'Warsaw letter' to Prague. (The Czechoslovak leadership had been invited to the meeting, but Dubcek had prevaricated.) The letter contained a stiff rebuke to Dubcek, and the demand that he halt the reforms of Prague Spring. Dubcek's response was to appear on national television to ask the Czechoslovak population for its support, and to send a moderate though unrepentant reply to the Warsaw missive.

This statement of the presidium of the central committee of the Czechoslovak party affirmed the leading role of the party and Czechoslovakia's foreign policy orientation within the Soviet bloc. It denied the charge of counter-revolution and defended the abolition of the censorship. It complained that Czechoslovakia, a fraternal nation, had been judged and condemned without being represented at the summit, and demanded bilateral talks with its critical allies. Czechoslovakia, it stated, would continue on the road to democratic socialism.

Bilateral talks (that is, discussions between the Czechoslovaks and all the Warsaw pact leaders) were the last thing that the Soviet Union wanted. Accordingly, at the end of July the Soviet leadership arrived in the border town of Cierna nad Tisou for negotiations with its Czechoslovak counterpart. The tension of the atmosphere was heightened by the mundane fact that Soviet trains ran on different gauges to Czechoslovak ones, so that each night Brezhnev and his entourage marched out of Czechoslovak territory, apparently in displeasure and suspicion. The negotiations were indeed difficult, and only concluded in Bratislava on 3 August with a summit meeting between the Czechoslovak leaders and the five powers who had signed the Warsaw letter. Nonetheless, all seemed well when Brezhnev publicly embraced Dubcek. In reality, this was the kiss of Judas.

While Dubcek and the reform leadership enjoyed widespread public support, many of the conservative Communists on the central committee had reservations about the reforms of Prague Spring. More dangerously, there was a small band of old guard Communists who deeply disapproved. The chief malcontents were the Czechs Drahomir Kolder, Alois Indra and Milos Jakes and the leader of the Slovak Communist Party, Vasil Bilak. These happily lent themselves to intrigue with the Kremlin. The plot was to depose the current government and party leadership and replace it with a puppet administration, a 'revolutionary government of workers and peasants', to be led by themselves. A 'revolutionary tribunal' would also be established, to try and condemn the Dubcek leadership. The coup would take place under cover of an invasion, and thus be reinforced by troops from the Soviet Union, and from the fraternal allied states whose leaders had signed the 'Warsaw letter'.

The pretext for both coup and invasion would be the charge that the Czechoslovak Socialist Republic was being threatened with 'counter-revolution'. Indeed, some time later Bilak mendaciously told the West German newspaper *Der Spiegel* that he, together with Dubcek, Smrkovsky and others, had signed a 'letter of invitation' to the fraternal allies. This was alleged to have occurred at the Bratislava summit on 3 August 1968, and the letter was supposed to have stated that Czechoslovakia was threatened with a counter-revolutionary coup. Although Dubcek later denied having signed the letter, and it is unthinkable that Smrkovsky would have done so, it is perfectly possible that Bilak and his allies did put their signatures to such a document to ask the Soviet Union for assistance on the pretext of counter-revolution.

Accordingly on the night of 20–21 August 1968 men and tanks from the Soviet Union, Bulgaria, Poland, East Germany and Hungary poured over the Czechoslovak frontiers. The presidium of the central committee was in session. Its chief business was to discuss the projected extraordinary party congress. However, the plotters were meant to force a divided vote in that body over a critical report on the state of the country by Kolder and Indra. The lack of unanimous support for the government and party leadership could then be used to justify the armed 'fraternal assistance' from the Warsaw pact five. First Secretary Dubcek and premier Cernik were arrested at gunpoint, as were Josef Smrkovsky, speaker of the national assembly, and three reforming members of the presidium, Frantisek Kriegel, Josef Spacek and Bohumil Simon. They were spirited away to an unknown destination, and it seems that there were plans to execute them immediately. According to Dubcek's later account they were taken to Poland, then to Sub-Carpathian Ruthenia (formerly part of Czechoslovakia, now in the Soviet Union). It seemed to Dubcek that his captors were uncertain how to treat him. By 23 August he and the rest of the kidnapped Czechoslovak leaders were in Moscow. The plot had somehow gone wrong. Indeed, armed intervention and native treachery had been thwarted by the unexpected resistance of the Czechoslovak people.

The authorities appealed for calm and the avoidance of armed resistance. On the whole this was respected, and the Czechoslovak armed forces were not put on alert. This would later give rise to the popular lament that 'three times we had an excellent army, three times we were not allowed to use it: 1938, 1948, 1968'. More than 20 years later Dubcek would repeatedly justify this passivity on the not unreasonable grounds that it was the only way to avoid a blood bath. This was the view of the whole reform leadership, who had practical military matters to consider.

Of first importance was the fact that the Czechoslovak army was far from independent. Like all the Warsaw pact armies it was ultimately under Soviet control, since red army officers occupied key positions in the command and its codes and communications systems were well known to them. In addition, the loyalty of many Czechoslovak officers was suspect, and it was by no means uncertain that they would defect to the Soviet side should there be a confrontation. Finally, armed resistance by the civilian population would lend colour to the accusations of counter-revolution and evoke the memory of the Hungarian uprising of 1956. For all these reasons, as well as the moral one of not inflicting violence on the aggressors, passive resistance was the only type permitted to the Czechoslovaks.

None the less the Czechoslovak public did not submit passively to the occupation. During Prague Spring the term *hydepark* had been coined, meaning an informal open-air meeting for discussion. Now in Prague and other towns dozens if not hundreds of *hydeparky* would congregate round the tanks of the invaders. These last were bewildered. Some of them had believed that they were rendering 'fraternal assistance' against 'counter-revolution', and had expected to be welcomed as liberators. Others thought they were on manoeuvres. None or at least few of them seem to have realised they were in Czechoslovakia; some thought that they were in Israel; and one group of Ukrainian troops had even been told that they were going to Nazi Germany!

Besides serious argument from the students and other members of the Czechoslovak public who gathered round their tanks, the bewildered invaders met with hostile and derisory graffiti; much of this has been recorded by Alan Levy in his eyewitness account of Prague Spring and the invasion, *So Many Heroes*. Some of these were purely insulting: 'RUSSIAN CIRCUS IN TOWN! DO NOT FEED THE ANIMALS'; 'THE BIGGER THE TANK THE SMALLER THE BRAIN'. Another invoked the famous heart surgeon: 'CALLING DR BARNARD! HELP!! DR BREZHNEV HAS TRANSPLANTED THE HEART OF EUROPE INTO THE BEHIND OF RUSSIA.' Others were more serious, demanding the return of Dubcek and the withdrawal of foreign troops. Still others were tactical: 'DO NOT HARM ONE HAIR ON THEIR HEADS, BUT DO NOT GIVE THEM ONE DROP OF WATER.' Indeed, the invaders found it hard to get water in any part of the country.

One piece of graffiti recorded by Levy was a bitterly ironic comment on the 'revolutionary government of workers and peasants' which the renegades hoped to set up. 'HELP WANTED: ONE PUPPET PRIME MINISTER, ONE NATIONAL ASSEMBLY SPEAKER, ONE FIRST SECRETARY, ONE NATIONAL FRONT CHAIRMAN. ONLY TRAITORS NEED APPLY. CONTACT SOVIET EMBASSY.' Thus there was general awareness of the traitors in the camp, and general contempt for them. Indeed, the announcement on 22 August that Dubcek's post of first secretary would be held jointly by Kolder, Indra and Bilak met with such loud and widespread derision that it was never repeated.

Despite the invaders' best efforts a free press was still functioning. The newspaper *Lidove Noviny* (People's News) published a number of cartoons during or immediately after the crisis. One such was a grotesque caricature of Ulbricht as the barebreasted figure of Marianne from Delacroix's famous painting of *Liberty Leading the People*. This bizarre creature promised the Czechoslovaks '*Liberte! Egalite! Freundschaft!*' The omission of *Fraternite* was a bitter comment on the 'fraternal assistance' so generously offered by Ulbricht and his colleagues. Another cartoon depicts Brezhnev in the guise of a gigantic Baroque statue of St Florian. This saint was traditionally invoked against fire, and was shown dressed as a Roman legionary and pouring water from a bucket onto a burning house. In this version a diminutive Dubcek stands by the house and shouts up at the huge Brezhnev, 'But there is no fire!'

The invaders were finding little evidence of counter-revolution, so they resorted to provocations. One of these was the 'discovery' of a cache of 'American' weapons in Western Bohemia. Another was a demonstration in the centre of Prague in support of a petition demanding that the people's militia be disbanded. Had this been genuine it would have constituted evidence of anti-Communist activity; but a later investigation found that more than 50 security police were among the protesting crowd.

Besides their general call for passive rather than armed resistance, the legal Czechoslovak authorities were not idle in organising a response to the invasion and to the renegades who had plotted with the Soviets. The emergency session of the presidium of the central committee continued to sit until the early hours of 21 August, when it was rudely interrupted by news of the invasion. Before their arrest and kidnapping the leaders managed to compose and to smuggle out to the radio station a refutation of the invaders' and traitors' claims that 'fraternal assistance' against 'counter-revolution' had been requested by the party leadership and government of Czechoslovakia. Troops of the 'five' had crossed the borders of the country without the knowledge of President Svoboda, Speaker Smrkovsky, Prime Minister Cernik or First Secretary Dubcek.

As this statement was being read out on the radio all the transmitters suddenly went dead. This was the result of a plot by powerful Soviet sympathisers: Karel Hoffman, Minister of communications; Viliam Salgovic, head of the Soviet network in the state security police; and Josef Sulek, head of the Czechoslovak news agency. The statement was finally broadcast thanks to action by Smrkovsky and the initiative of the radio operators, who arranged for alternative means of transmission.

This statement was broadcast some hours before one by TASS, the Soviet news agency, which declared the absolute opposite to be true. The population, however, was not fooled, and even Dubcek's conservative opponents on the central committee demanded an account from the traitors and in particular the names of those who had presumed to request 'fraternal assistance'.

One incident reveals both popular revulsion against those who had invited the invaders in, and the fear the culprits had of popular vengeance. On the morning of 22 August members of the remaining party leadership were summoned to the Soviet embassy in Prague. Unlike the rest of their colleagues, Indra and Bilak had accepted the offer of transport in a Soviet armoured car.

This vehicle crossed the river over a bridge on which lay a tram which had collided with some Soviet military vehicles. The armoured car was unable to move either backwards or forwards. An interested crowd gathered, and Bilak and Indra were so terrified of being recognised that they endured the sweltering heat of their armour-plated prison for nearly an hour before it could move again.

The chief item on the agenda of that meeting of the remnants of the party presidium was the convention of the fourteenth party congress, scheduled for 9 September. This was something that the occupiers and their collaborators were anxious to prevent. Once more, however, their objective was foiled by the solidarity of party and nation behind the reformist leadership. The congress actually convened secretly on 22 August at the giant CKD engineering works in the Vysocany district of Prague. ('Dummy' or decoy congresses were set up in other areas in order to fool the invaders.) Despite the unavoidable absence of Dubcek, Smrkovsky and other members of the leadership, and despite the fact that the majority of the Slovak delegates were forcibly prevented from reaching Prague, the congress was extremely active. An open letter of unequivocal support was sent to Dubcek, who was also confirmed as first secretary. A new central committee and a new presidium were elected. The traitors were excluded, while liberals and reformers were promoted. The congress protested at the detention of the country's and party's leaders, and threatened a general strike.

Control of the mass media by loyal Czechoslovaks was also a vital ingredient in the failure of the Soviets and their native stooges to present their view of events. Both radio and television managed to keep broadcasting for almost a week by dint of moving from one clandestine studio to another every few hours. While the occupiers and their collaborators produced an 'official' edition of the party paper *Rude Pravo* ('Red Right') every day, the loyal staff of the real newspaper produced and distributed their own versions.

Similarly, the invaders had taken over the Prague radio station building immediately. The people of Prague had set up a barricade of buses and lorries in front of the entrance to the building; the tanks of the invaders simply drove through them and into the crowd. This horror infuriated rather than cowed the population, and for the week of the invasion clandestine radio stations operated throughout the country.

The tactics of the populations of Prague and other towns in face of the occupiers constituted a return to the 'policy of pin-pricks' employed during the Nazi occupation. (Indeed, in graffiti the two middle initials of the USSR were often rendered as the lightning flashes of the Nazi SS, while the hammer and sickle symbol was turned into a swastika.) Street signs and direction posts were altered or put in the wrong places. People politely gave the wrong directions to the invaders, and helpfully warned troops seeking water that wells or stand-pipes had been poisoned by the 'counter-revolutionaries'. By and large the Czechoslovaks were obedient to the government order not to offer armed resistance; but some of the invaders were either nervous or trigger-happy, and it is estimated that 77 civilians were killed and about 1000 wounded. One of the most emotive symbols of the invasion was the sight of people carrying flags dipped in the blood of the martyred.

Meanwhile in Moscow the 'negotiations' between the Soviet leaders and their Czechoslovak captives were not going smoothly; in truth, their plot having been foiled, the former had no idea what to do with the latter. Dubcek and the other leaders were adamant in their refusal to abandon the reforms of Prague Spring. Stalemate seemed to have been reached even before President Svoboda's arrival in Moscow with what remained of the Czechoslovak party leadership on 23 August.

Svoboda had not exactly been invited to the talks, but while he intended that his personal intervention would save his government and party leadership the Soviets for their part were hopeful that he could persuade the prisoners to see reason. The depth of the Soviets' desperation can be seen in Brezhnev's threat to Svoboda, that if the Czechoslovaks did not cooperate then their country would once more be dismantled. Bohemia and Moravia would become a protectorate, this time under Soviet rather than German auspices, while Slovakia would become a republic of the Soviet Union. Svoboda is said to have threatened Brezhnev with the dissolution of the Czechoslovak Communist Party in the event of the leaders' not returning home.

Svoboda's position was not that of a reform Communist, but was rather more straightforward. He was, first and foremost, a soldier and a patriot. His concern was to get his country's political leaders home unscathed and then deal with the crisis in Czechoslovakia. Because of this attitude, he helped the Soviets to persuade the Czechoslovak delegation to sign the Moscow protocol.
⁻ The Czechoslovaks were put under immense psychological and physical pressure, were isolated from news of outside events and even from each other. Dubcek was under sedation for much of the time, his colleagues alternately bullied and cosseted. Eventually, and not without heated discussion and protest, Dubcek and the rest of the delegation signed the Moscow protocol on 26 August.

The only Czechoslovak who refused utterly to sign was Frantisek Kriegel, allegedly abused by Kosygin as a 'filthy little Galician Jew'. Brezhnev planned to keep him in Moscow, virtually as a hostage. He would not have been able to return to Czechoslovakia but for the fact that his colleagues refused to board their plane without him. This was one of the last acts of courageous solidarity achieved by the founders of Prague Spring.

In the Moscow protocol the Czechoslovaks had to make a number of concessions. The fourteenth party congress at Vysocany was declared invalid. The traitors who had colluded with the Soviets were to be protected from reprisals, while members of the government who had made protests abroad during the invasion would have their activities reviewed. A degree of censorship of the media would have to be reimposed, though Dubcek and some of his colleagues were privately optimistic that this could be both retarded and limited. This optimism was misplaced, as was their trust in the declaration that a phased withdrawal of all occupying troops would begin as soon as the 'threat to socialism' in Czechoslovakia had disappeared.

What can have induced the reform Communists in the delegation to put their signatures to a document which Mlynar (who signed it) later described as the 'death sentence' of the Prague Spring? They wavered from day to day, even hour to hour, about whether or not to sign; but ultimately the psychological pressure exerted on them persuaded the Czechoslovaks that acceptance of the Moscow protocol was their only hope of salvaging some of the reforms. All of them but Dubcek, who had been kept in isolation, had reached this position by 26 August. Most dramatically, at the last moment Dubcek refused to sign, but was persuaded by his colleagues that this was the only way. In retrospect, Mlynar admitted that this was 'Dubcek's most clear-headed moment'; but the majority opinion prevailed, and he appended his signature to the rest.

What was most sinister in the Moscow protocol was the use of the word 'normalisation'. This was a piece of Soviet jargon, meaning reimposition of Communist control and of Soviet influence. Ultimately, it would mean nothing less than the complete negation of Prague Spring. Although its full significance as a term would only become apparent in the following months and years, many in Czechoslovakia were already aware of the danger and absurdity of the term. Indeed, the clandestine Catholic newspaper *Lidove Demokracie* ('People's Democracy') entitled an article, 'Normalisation? Kafka Lives!'

On his return to Prague a highly emotional Dubcek explained matters to the Czechoslovak population on television, once more requesting the public's understanding and cooperation. His own immense popularity and the almost universal contempt in which Kolder, Bilak and Indra were held meant that he would not be disposed of immediately; indeed, the Moscow protocol had confirmed him in office as first secretary. Yet it was not mercy, but rather a finely calculated piece of cruelty that determined that Dubcek should preside over the beginning of the end of Prague Spring.

This started with the Moscow treaty of October 1968, signed for the Czechoslovaks by Dubcek, Cernik and Husak. Contrary to the promise of the Moscow protocol, this accepted the presence of about 100,000 Soviet troops on Czechoslovak soil for an unspecified period. (The occupation was in fact to last until May1991.) It also noted the Soviet view of the action programme as incorrect, and agreed to postpone the calling of a Czechoslovak party congress, again for an indefinite period.

The significance of the Czechoslovak experiment for the whole of Eastern Europe was, in the immediate future at least, negative. The Brezhnev doctrine, first announced to the Poles in November 1968, was merely a reiteration of the mendacious TASS statement of 21 August; spelt out simply, it meant that any attempt at independent policy in any sovereign state would meet with armed intervention from the fraternal neighbours. While for the most part these same neighbours settled back in the sleep of the dead, Czechoslovakia woke from its brief dream of relative freedom to the long grey day of normalisation.

# 7 Normalisation and Dissent

## 1968–1988

More than 20 years after Prague Spring and its appalling repression Alexander Dubcek's autobiography would be published posthumously under the title *Hope Dies Last*. This summed up his philosophy in the face of adversity. However, in the winter of 1968–69 there seemed little reason for hope. True, Dubcek himself remained as first secretary until 17 April 1969, when he was succeeded in that post by the veteran Slovak Communist, Gustav Husak. As a sop which deceived no one, he was accorded the meaningless title of chairman of the new federal assembly; meaningless, because the assembly had no freedom to vote, and the position was largely a ceremonial one. In January 1970 he was demoted to be ambassador to Turkey. In Ankara he was blatantly and contemptuously under the eye of the Czechoslovak and Soviet secret police, and on his recall within a few months he was ejected from the party. Before that, in a particularly vicious twist to the Kremlin's policy, he was forced to preside over the abortion of his own reform movement.

Piece by piece, the reforms of Prague Spring were removed, and all the old repressions were put back in place. The decisions of the Vysocany congress of August were declared null and void. Largely at the behest of the Soviets organisations like K 231 and KAN were outlawed, thus putting an end to any form of political pluralism. Informal and unofficial pressure on individual publications was followed by the repeal of the law abolishing censorship in September 1969. Naturally the Czechoslovak population did not simply acquiesce in the destruction of freedoms so recently won; but there were hard lessons to be learned by those who dissented.

On 16 January 1969 a most shocking demonstration took place in Prague; Jan Palach, a student at Charles University, set himself on fire in Wenceslas Square in protest at the process of normalisation. He died in agony some days later, and was widely regarded as a martyr for Prague Spring. Indeed, almost immediately he was compared with the medieval Czech hero Jan Hus. Huge demonstrations followed his self-sacrifice. The authorities were able to prevent equal publicity for a second victim of self-immolation, Jan Zajic. Perhaps it was Communist efficiency; on the other hand it may be that, just as with Nazi atrocities in wartime Czechoslovakia the village of Lidice is remembered but that of Lezaky largely forgotten, so it was that Palach rather than Zajic came to symbolise protest at normalisation.

In March came the famous 'ice hockey riots'. The Czechoslovak national side won two resounding victories over the Soviet team at the world ice hockey championships in Stockholm. The first match, on 21 March, resulted in a score of 2–0. Czechoslovak spectators in Stockholm could be heard chanting Dubcek's name, while in Prague the crowd poured onto the streets. There were spontaneous demonstrations of joy in Wenceslas Square, and the offending score was daubed on the windows of the Soviet airline offices. Clearly, the population was delighted that, though humiliated in politics, it was unbeaten in sport. The return match on 28 March produced a score of 4–3, and clearly incited the Czechoslovaks. This time the Soviet airline offices were reduced to rubble by the mob, and mayhem generally ruled for a few hours. The whole incident was used by both the Soviet authorities and hard-liners among the Czechoslovak Communists to suggest that Dubcek was losing control of the country. His resignation as first secretary the following month was not unconnected with the ice hockey demonstrations.

The first anniversary of the August invasion was bound to be an emotional one, and it was used by the Husak regime to provoke and crush 'counter-revolutionary riots'. From the night of 19 August tear gas and police charges were used against peaceful demonstrators in Prague. On 21 August 1969 – the exact anniversary of the Warsaw Pact invasion – the population marked its grief by a boycott of public transport and places of entertainment. Thousands of Czechoslovaks simply walked to work. Such a mild and dignified form of protest unnerved the native Communists and their Soviet masters, and violent suppression was used once more against unarmed civilians. The violence inflicted by the Czechoslovak authorities themselves was used as the pretext to pass emergency laws. These draconian measures carried severe penalties of imprisonment or removal from Prague for anyone who protested.

Individuals, too, suffered for actions deemed to be displeasing to Moscow. Take the case of Marta Kubisova, the pop singer retrospectively known as 'the voice of 1968'. In August she recorded 'Marta's Prayer', actually a version of the famous prayer for Czech freedom composed by Jan Amos Komensky (Comenius) in his enforced exile after the battle of White Mountain in the seventeenth century. This version of the prayer was particularly pointed and poignant in view of the August invasion:

> May there be peace in this land;
> May malice, envy, fear, and conflict go away;
> May the direction of your affairs be returned
> Into thy hands again, O Czech people![1]

Such seventeenth-century subversion probably would have been enough to make Kubisova a target for the post-August regime and its Soviet masters; but she offended them further.

She waited to meet Dubcek – still a party dignitary though no longer first secretary – as he arrived for an official meeting. So overwhelmed was she at seeing him that she impulsively kissed him as she handed over a small personal gift. Her punishment was that she was forbidden to work in the music industry and instead was consigned to employment in a factory which made polythene bags. Naturally, she was forbidden to sing in public. This prohibition was to endure until the velvet revolution of 1989.

Manual labour was, in fact, usually the sentence for those students and intellectuals who had been vocal or visible either during Prague Spring or during the Warsaw pact occupation. The universities, research institutes and the professions were thoroughly purged of those who had been active in Prague Spring or who had even shown sympathy with the reforms. A total of 21 academic institutions were closed, and 900 university teachers lost their posts. Students were prevented from completing their studies, and quite often their own children were barred from higher education. University professors became tram drivers; eminent lawyers went to work as stokers.

The two years from the end of Prague Spring in August 1968 were officially designated as a period of 'normalisation'; this dreary term can actually be applied to the following two decades. In their study of the velvet revolution Bernard Wheaton and Zdenek Kavan identify three bases of normalisation. The first was a purge of all major economic and political organisations, including the Communist party itself. Indeed, half a million Communists (one-third of the total party membership) were purged. The second was a strict censorship, thus allowing the party to control access to information and ideas. One aspect of the censorship was the reimposition of restriction on travel abroad, particularly necessary (from the Communist point of view) because of the increasing numbers who chose permanent emigration from Czechoslovakia. The third and final element was the reinstallation of centralised control over the economy, in other words the reimposition of the old command structure with all its stultifying effects.

Presiding over the death of Czechoslovak freedom was Dubcek's successor, the experienced Slovak Communist Gustav Husak. He became first secretary on 17 April 1969 and, in a manner reminiscent of Novotny, also became president of the country in May 1975. (Svoboda was increasingly marginalised, and resigned the presidency on grounds of ill health.) Held to be of dubious and questionable memory in the Czech lands, he commanded some respect in Slovakia for ratifying the federal constitution of 1969. By this new arrangement the Czech lands and Slovakia became equal republics, each with its own republican cabinet. The old national assembly was replaced by a federal body representing both parts of the country.

Husak had been preparing for power since August 1968, when he was a member of the Czechoslovak delegation summoned to the Kremlin to 'negoti-ate' the Moscow protocol. Although not identified overtly with either the reform Communists and the Dubcek leadership or the pro-Soviet faction of the party, he contrived to make a good impression on the Soviet leaders. Alexei Kosygin remarked to Zdenek Mlynar, 'Comrade Husak is such a competent comrade and a wonderful Communist. We didn't know him personally before, but he quite impressed us here.'[2]

Husak became the most powerful man in Czechoslovakia at Moscow's behest, and swiftly he exposed his Stalinist credentials. Take the case of Milan Hubl, historian and rector of the party academy. An adherent of reform Communism, Hubl persuaded the remnants of that wing of the party to vote for Husak as Dubcek's replacement, having been deceived into thinking that some elements of Prague Spring would be best preserved under Husak's lead-ership. His ungrateful candidate had him imprisoned in 1972 for six and a half years on the usual normalising charge of 'subversion of the state'; Hubl was released in 1976, and thereafter found work as a janitor.

Husak and his Soviet masters went to work swiftly to implement normal-isation. Naturally the party leadership and government ministers from 1968 had to be either expelled or neutralised. Jiri Hajek, the Foreign Minister, was deprived of his post under Soviet pressure in August 1968 and expelled from the party in the first great purge of 1970. A similar fate befell Josef Pavel, Minister of the Interior. Zdenek Mlynar voluntarily resigned all his party posts in November 1968, was expelled from the central committee in September 1969 and from the party in March 1970. Josef Smrkovsky was deprived of his post as speaker of the national assembly by Soviet displeasure which was largely articulated through Husak. Later he was likewise expelled from both the central committee and the party. Unique among the architects of Prague Spring in daring to voice criticism of the normalisation process, he was perse-cuted by the regime even beyond his death in 1974. Mlynar recounts how the urn containing Smrkovsky's ashes was stolen from the family vault in Prague and 'planted' by security agents in the lavatory of a train bound for Vienna. The story was given out that Smrkovsky's remains were to be reburied in Vienna as a 'provocation' to the Czechoslovak regime.

As was described in the last chapter, the members of the Czechoslovak delegation who were reform Communists signed the Moscow protocol in the hope that something of Prague Spring might be salvaged. All of them were to be quite swiftly disillusioned. Oldrich Cernik managed to retain the post of prime minister until January 1970, when he was demoted to hold the office of minister for culture and reconstruction. He was succeeded as premier by Lubomir Strougal. Cernik was the only one of those reform Communists whom it had been planned to try before the 'revolutionary tribunal' in August 1968 to denounce the Prague Spring and his own role in the reform process. In spring 1970, however, he was expelled from the party and stripped of all party functions. Later, though, he was deputy director of the office for normalisation.

Josef Spacek lost all his party functions in 1969 and his party membership in 1970; eventually he was employed on a road construction project. Dubcek himself ended his working life in the forestry commission in Slovakia, having moved from a job as unskilled labour to a minor management position.

Similarly, Bohumil Simon was stripped of both his party functions and his party card, and found employment as an economist in the institute for the restoration of monuments in Prague. Later he was joined on that body by Cestmir Cisar, who had lain low during the August invasion, but even so was deprived of all party functions in 1969. Frantisek Kriegel was forced into retirement. The economist Ota Sik, deputy prime minister in 1968, was stripped of all functions and expelled from the party in 1969. Wisely, he chose to remain in emigration in Switzerland, where the events of August 1968 had caught him. Eduard Goldstueker, chairman of the Czechoslovak union of writers in 1968, chose exile in England in 1969.

Perhaps the most abject and cowardly case was that of Radovan Richta, the party functionary who coined the phrase 'socialism with a human face' for Alexander Dubcek. Deciding to hunt with the hounds rather than run with the hare, Richta became an adherent of normalisation. After 1970, as director of the philosophical institute and member of its ruling body, he undertook the job of purging the social sciences in Czechoslovakia. His reward was to be named an academician and a regular member of the academy of sciences in 1977. Stefan Sadovsky, who attempted to join the normalisers, was not so fortunate. For a time he was Prime Minister of the Slovak republic, then First Secretary of the central committee of the Czechoslovak party. In 1971, however, he was stripped of all party functions and later relegated to industrial management.

Naturally a number of opportunists as well as opponents of reform within the party hoped to make good during normalisation. Among the most successful were Josef Lenart, Cernik's predecessor as prime minister, and Milos Jakes, who had been party to the Soviet plot to proclaim a revolutionary government in August 1968 and proved to be an enthusiastic upholder of normalisation, particularly distinguishing himself in the great party purge of

1970. Lubomir Strougal, deputy prime minister in 1968, took to normalisation like a duck to water and was rewarded with the post of premier, in succession to Cernik, in 1970. Karel Hoffman, who had collaborated with the invaders by printing misinformation in August 1968, when he had some access to the party press, became an active normaliser, chairman of the central council of trade unions and a presidium member of the Communist Party. Less successful was Jan Piller, an unwilling adherent of normalisation after August 1968. Though he held several party functions he was stripped of these in 1971 and obliged to work as a government employee.

The two chief plotters of 1968, who had tried to establish the revolutionary government and tribunal to assist the invaders' claims of counter-revolution in Czechoslovakia and to lend some credence to the claim that they had been invited to render 'fraternal assistance', did tolerably well. Vasil Bilak and Alois Indra became the representatives of Soviet commands and neo-Stalinism in the party, Indra being appointed to the now meaningless post of speaker of the federal assembly. Even they, however, were forced to realise that Husak meant to reinstate one-man rule.

The purge of the universities and strict censorship led to Czechoslovakia becoming what its dissidents later termed a 'cultural wilderness'; the French writer Louis Aragon described it as a 'Biafra of the soul', while native dissidents later called it 'Absurdistan'. As was noted above, students and schoolchildren were especial targets of the regime. In a particularly malevolent policy they were held as hostages for their parents' good behaviour; any deviation from the norm meant that their chances of study would disappear. In any case, the Communist authorities did not want a well-educated subject population. In 1990 Jan Urban wrote that Czechoslovakia had less post-secondary school provision per head of population than had Nepal, while Vaclav Havel in that same year said that Czechoslovakia ranked only 72nd in the world in terms of government spending on education.

The cultural policy of the Husak regime also had a pernicious effect on science and the economy. Two out of every three members of the writers' union lost their posts. Between 1969 and 1971 no literary journal was published in the Czech lands, for the first time since 1821. Writers who wished to be published, or wished their published works to remain in public libraries, were constrained to make a statement disavowing the reforms of Prague Spring. (This was also an obligatory condition for membership of the writers' union.) Other unions – those of the students, journalists, and film and television workers, as well as the coordinating committee of art unions – were simply dissolved and their funds confiscated by the state, or rather, the Communists.

There were also press campaigns against eminent figures associated with Prague Spring, which were usually the prelude to forcing them out of office or employment. Thus Dubcek's Foreign Minister, Jiri Hajek, was labelled a 'Gestapo agent' by the Soviet news agency TASS, which also hinted that he was a Jew by saying that his real name was Karpeles. Hajek responded by stating that his name had always been Hajek, and that he had spent the whole of the war in a Nazi concentration camp as an anti-fascist. TASS did not publish this refutation, and shortly thereafter Hajek resigned his ministerial post.

Equally insulting was the treatment accorded to Jiri Pelikan, director of Czechoslovak television and chairman of the parliamentary foreign affairs committee. On 31 August 1968 the Soviet party paper *Pravda* claimed that Pelikan had given an interview in which he expressed pro-western and anti-Communist sentiments in a Lebanese newspaper – which was proved to have no existence. The story about the imaginary interview was broadcast repeatedly by the Soviet-controlled radio, while Pelikan was dismissed from his television post. That autumn a Bulgarian newspaper claimed that pornographic literature and a bust of Hitler had been found in Pelikan's office, and within a year a Moravian newspaper deduced that he must have been a Gestapo agent, as he had managed to survive one year's imprisonment and three years in the underground resistance during the war. All this was contemptible stuff, meant to discredit the man who had controlled Czechoslovak television during Prague Spring and the August invasion.

Many intellectuals as well as ordinary citizens chose the option of emigration; 170,000 had fled the country by 1971, a figure that would rise to 244,000 by the time of the velvet revolution in November 1989. Among the more eminent exiles were the writers Josef Skvorecky and Milan Kundera and the film director Milos Forman. From the world of sport Martina Navratilova, the tennis-player, defected to the West in 1975; she was to be followed by Ivan Lendl. By contrast the runner Emil Zatopek chose to stay in Czechoslovakia, though his association with the Dubcek reforms resulted in his being stripped of his army rank of colonel.

Exile is never an easy option, and in the case of the Czechoslovak emigration the misery was compounded by the knowledge that reprisals would be taken against relatives left at home. These took the form of petty persecution rather than imprisonment or torture, for example, being moved to a less desirable flat or facing demotion at work. Nonetheless it was effective as a means of encouragement to conformity.

While many of the exiles kept silence about home affairs, a number of writers did work to keep Czechoslovakia in the forefront of the public consciousness. Milan Kundera settled in France in 1975, and his melancholy yet humorous novels evoked the absurdity and cruelty of Communist rule. (See in particular *The Unbearable Lightness of Being* and *The Book of Laughter and Forgetting.*) The married writers Josef Skvorecky and Zdena Salivarova emigrated to Canada. Skvorecky already had a more than suspect past in the eyes of the 'normalising' regime. In 1956 his first novel *End of the Nylon Age* was suppressed by the censor before publication. In 1958 he caused a literary scandal with *The Cowards*. Written ten years previously, this novel set in a small town in Bohemia (Skvorecky's native Nachod, thinly disguised as 'Kostelec'), presented an unheroic and satirical picture of Czech resistance during the Nazi occupation. The book was banned and used as an excuse for a thorough purge of Czechoslovak writers. Deeply distrusted and closely watched, Skvorecky continued to write his disrespectful and often hilarious satires. *The Republic of Whores*, an account of Czechoslovak military conscripts in the early 1950s whose behaviour was somewhat less than valiant, was banned by the censor prior to publication in 1966. Publication was permitted in 1969 but the book was again proscribed in 1970. Skvorecky and Salivarova settled in Toronto, where in 1971 they founded Sixty Eight Publishing, a Czech language press which published writings both from the emigration and from banned writers still in Czechoslovakia. Skvorecky himself continued to write stories and novels, among the most notable being *The Engineer of Human Souls* (the phrase is adapted from Stalin's description of the writer and his function) and *Miracle Game*.

A number of outstanding intellectual figures chose to stay in Czechoslovakia rather than flee abroad. One such was the novelist Ivan Klima. As editor of the journal of the Czech writers' union during Prague Spring he was suspect in the eyes of the regime. In 1969 he was visiting professor of literature at the university of Michigan, but he returned to Prague after a year. He was obliged to earn his living by manual labour, and his books could only be published abroad. Another was the philosopher, playwright and poet Vaclav Havel, who was to prove a real thorn in the side of the normalised regime. On 21 August 1969 – the first anniversary of the invasion – he was one of ten signatories of a document called 'Ten Points' which condemned normalisation and was addressed to the government, federal assembly and central committee of the Communist Party. Havel and his co-signatories were charged with subverting the Czechoslovak Socialist Republic, though their trial, planned for the following autumn, never did take place.

From then on Havel was blacklisted, his works banned from libraries. In May 1972 the new 'normalised' writers' association attacked Havel and other proscribed authors, who were naturally excluded from this new organisation. (It must have been especially irritating to both the authorities and the 'official' writers that Havel had received American and Austrian literary prizes.) The following December he signed a petition by Czech writers to President Svoboda, asking for an amnesty for political prisoners. Naturally this request was not granted. In common with other writers who were forbidden to prac- tise their craft Havel was permitted to work only in a manual occupation. He spent most of 1974 working in a brewery in the provincial town of Trutnov, an experience which gave him material for his one-act play *Audience*.

Although this was largely a dismal, uneventful period in the history of Czechoslovakia, there were compensations for conformity. As early as 1972 the western press was reporting that obesity threatened to become a national problem in Czechoslovakia. This was because the shops were relatively well- stocked with foodstuffs as the price of compliance. By comparison with Poland in the 1970s, which was poorly provisioned but marked by protest, Czechoslovakia presented an abject if well-fed picture, something which was reflected in the following joke:

> A Polish dog and a Czechoslovak dog meet on the border
> between their respective countries and eye each other sus-
> piciously. 'You!' says the Czechoslovak dog. 'Why on earth
> do you want to go to Czechoslovakia?' 'Because I want to
> eat meat,' the Polish dog replies. 'And you, why do you
> want to go to Poland?' 'Because I want to bark.'

Similarly, guaranteed full employment and low wages under the command economy led to the export to Czechoslovakia of the Soviet joke, 'We pretend to work and you pretend to pay us'.

An example of the authorities' cynicism in bribing the population is the country cottage phenomenon. Czechoslovaks who lived in towns and cities were permitted to build themselves weekend homes, partly as compensation for the cramped living conditions in urban apartment-house complexes. (These ugly conurbations of 'panel houses' or tower blocks can still be seen on the outskirts of all towns in the Czech and Slovak Republics.) With equal cyni- cism employees would pilfer building materials from the workplace and steal time from working hours to build their cottages; the authorities would obli- gingly turn a blind eye to such petty larceny, while the workers coined the slo- gan, 'If you don't steal from the state you rob your own family'.

Indeed, the ordinary citizen coped with life under 'actually existing social- ism' (to use the government's slogan) by what was known at the time as 'inner emigration'. The home and family became a refuge from the world outside, most aptly symbolised by the Czechoslovak habit, shared with the denizens of other Communist countries, of taking their shoes off on the threshold or in the hall of the home. In practical terms this was to avoid transferring the dirt from the polluted street into the domestic space; but its emblematic meaning is also evident.

While the bulk of the population complied at least outwardly with the regulations of normalisation there was both individual and organised dissent. Many proscribed or dissident authors 'wrote for the drawer'. As in the Soviet Union itself such work was sometimes circulated in *samizdat*, that is, hand-typed copies, though to pass such works to another person became a criminal offence. In April 1975 Vaclav Havel went a large step beyond *samizdat* when he sent an open letter to Husak which protested at the measures of normalisation. Havel exposed the outward conformity of the population as being insincere and inspired by fear. 'Dear Dr Husak' only circulated privately in Czechoslovakia, but news of it was quickly picked up by foreign radio broadcasts and it was published in translation in several countries of Western Europe. Whether Husak actually read it must remain a matter of conjecture, since the letter was returned to its author by the president's office with a note explaining that as he had revealed it to hostile press agencies he had exposed himself as an enemy of his country. Much later, after the foundation of Charter 77, the open letter would be used to charge Havel with subversion of the Republic and thus provide one of the pretexts for his trial and imprisonment.

Even more effective than 'Dear Dr Husak' in showing the hollowness of conformity under normalisation is Havel's famous image of the greengrocer in 'Power of the Powerless'. (This essay was written in 1978 and dedicated to the memory of Jan Patocka, a fellow dissident and philosopher who died under police questioning in 1977.) The greengrocer decorates his shop window with the slogan 'Workers of the World, Unite!' It means nothing to him, indeed, he has largely forgotten that it is there. But what would happen, asked Havel, if he removes the slogan?

> Let us now imagine that one day something in our green-grocer snaps and he stops putting up the slogans merely to ingratiate himself. He stops voting in elections he knows are a farce. He begins to say what he really thinks at political meetings. And he even finds the strength within himself to express solidarity with those whom his conscience commands him to support. In this revolt the greengrocer steps out of living within the lie. He rejects the ritual and breaks the rules of the game. He discovers once more his

suppressed identity and dignity. He gives his freedom a
concrete significance. His revolt is an attempt to *live
within the truth.*[3]

Havel recognised, however, that such courageous behaviour would be rare,
as 'The bill is not long in coming'. The greengrocer would be demoted from his
position as manager, would have to take a pay cut, would lose his chance of a
foreign holiday within the Communist world, and would find that his children's
chances of university education were threatened. Indeed, it was by such petty
acts of persecution that the normalised Husak regime kept a hold on the
population. As Havel had stated in his open letter, the country was peaceful
and calm, but so was a morgue.

Given the repression of any sign of dissent at home, it seems extraordinary
that the Czechoslovak authorities should sign the Helsinki final act of the
Conference on Security and Cooperation in Europe (CSCE) in the summer of
1975. Extraordinary, in that the human rights provisions of the final act automatically entered Czechoslovak law and in theory bound the regime to
upholding them. The duplicity, cynicism or overconfidence of the authorities
was shown just over a year later with the notorious 'rock stars' trial'.

The psychedelic 'underground' group Plastic People of the Universe had
been performing semi-legally for the past five years when suddenly its members were arrested and charged with 'disturbing the peace', which, along with
'hooliganism', was official-speak for nonconformity. Despite the attempts of
official propaganda to portray the musicians simply as long-haired, anti-
social drug addicts, their imprisonment was seen as over-harsh, and shocked
and alienated many in Czechoslovakia as well as abroad. After all, these young
people were not discredited old Communists or even overtly political opponents of the regime, and their detention was seen, quite rightly, as the outcome
of the totalitarian reaction to any form of self-expression, any deviation from
the officially-approved 'norm'. Seven Czechoslovak writers, Havel and the
renowned poet Jaroslav Seifert among them, signed an open letter to the
eminent German novelist Heinrich Boll asking for international artistic solidarity with the imprisoned musicians. The letter eventually became a sizeable
petition, with more than 70 signatures. The indefatigable Havel also wrote an
article about the trial which gave their cause widespread publicity.

The severe treatment of the Plastic People undoubtedly acted as a catalyst
to the discussions which led to the formation of Charter 77 on 1 January 1977,
the beginning of political prisoners' year. The earliest 'Chartists' were men of
diverse background and convictions: the Communist politicians Zdenek
Mlynar and Jiri Hajek, both ranked among Dubcek's reform Communists

in 1968; the veteran democratic politician Prokop Drtina; intellectuals like the writers Pavel Kohout and Vaclav Havel. The Charter itself protested at the violation of the Helsinki final act by the Czechoslovak government. It stated that the citizens of the state were denied freedom of expression and of religious confession, freedom from fear, the right to study and to have access to information. It also enumerated other breaches of civil rights. The first round of canvassing attracted 243 signatures, a number which rose to about 1200 by 1987. The original signatories appointed as their spokesmen the philosopher Professor Jan Patocka, Vaclav Havel, and former Foreign Minister Jiri Hajek.

Charter 77 was neither a political party nor even a closely-knit organisation. Rather, it was a pressure group concerned with drawing attention to human rights abuses. Its membership was broadly based, and included Catholics (such as Vaclav Benda) and reform Communists, liberals and Social Democrats. The Chartists made contact with similar groups in Poland and Hungary and, thanks to its interest in the Helsinki final act and its concern with environmental issues, with groups and individuals in the West. Since it merely asked that the Czechoslovak government respect its own laws, it can be described as legalistic opposition.

Quite in contravention of its adherence to the Helsinki agreement, the Czechoslovak government moved swiftly against the Chartists. Together with the writer Ludvik Vaculik (author in 1968 of the manifesto *2000 Words*) and the actor and playwright Pavel Landovsky, Havel tried on 6 January to deliver copies of the Charter with a list of its signatories to the federal assembly, government and official press agency. Immediately they were detained and subject to repeated interrogation, house searches and surveillance, though the Charter itself was published in a leading West German newspaper. Havel was held in detention from 14 January until 20 May and eventually charged with subversion as one of the organisers of Charter 77 and as the author of 'Dear Dr Husak'. As a gesture of solidarity Josef Skvorecky's Toronto press Sixty Eight Publishers issued a collected edition of Havel's plays that August.

Other Chartists were harassed by house searches and interrogation. Among these was Zdenek Mlynar, who was dismissed from his post at the national museum and departed for exile in Vienna in the summer of 1977. So thorough were the security forces in investigating his nefarious past – he had joined the party in 1946, when he was almost 16 – that they even extracted from the police files a letter he had written in 1950. As a naive young Communist he had been one of thousands to send letters to the authorities denouncing those accused in the show trials, in his case, Sling and Svermova. On 1 March 1977 *Rude Pravo*, the Communist party paper, published extracts from this letter to demonstrate Mlynar's opportunism and disregard for human rights so as to discredit his signature of the Charter. Such was the cynicism of the Husak regime.

Meanwhile on 13 March 1977 Jan Patocka died of a massive brain haemorrhage while in police custody. The 69-year-old philosopher, a friend of Edmund Husserl, had been repeatedly questioned by the police since January. Neither his academic and intellectual eminence nor his age were respected.

Eventually, in October, came the trial of Havel and three other Chartists. Havel was found guilty of attempting to damage the interests of the Czechoslovak Socialist Republic and received a prison sentence of 14 months, conditionally suspended for three years. In December he was among the signatories of an open letter from Czech writers to their foreign colleagues asking them to demand from the Belgrade meeting of the Helsinki signatories an explicit declaration on the right to free exchange of information and on the right to publish proscribed works. On 28 January 1978 he was arrested with some friends and charged with 'disturbing the peace' again, being held in custody until 13 March. Criminal proceedings against these dissidents were halted in April 1979.

Unabashed by all the attention they were receiving from the security forces, members of Charter 77 met with representatives of a Polish dissident group. The Committee for Workers' Defence (KOR) had been established in 1976 as an organisation to facilitate cooperation between workers and intellectuals; among its founders were such luminaries of Polish dissent as Jacek Kuron and Adam Michnik. In August and September 1978 the two groups held two meetings, quite illegally, on the Polish–Czechoslovak border. On 1 October a third meeting was raided by the Polish and Czechoslovak police, and broken up.

Meanwhile a new dissident venture had been launched, on 27 April 1978. This was the Committee for the Defence of the Unjustly Prosecuted, known by its Czech acronym of VONS. This group of 18 (once more including Havel and other Chartists) was an outgrowth from Charter 77 and was concerned with specific cases of injustice and abuse of human rights. It disseminated information about individual cases, and also gave legal advice. VONS circulated roughly 155 reports in typescript to both the general public and to official institutions.

The security police now concentrated their attention on VONS. In May 1979 fifteen of the committee members were arrested and their houses searched. Ten of them were charged with criminal subversion of the Republic; of these, six were put on trial in October, while the other four were released without charge in December. The six who were convicted and sentenced to prison were Otka Bednarova, Vaclav Benda, Jiri Dienstbier, Vaclav Havel, Dana Nemcova and Petr Uhl.

On 23 October the 'six' were convicted, as members of both VONS and Charter 77, for disseminating 'indictable' material both in Czechoslovakia and abroad. Nemcova, a child psychologist, received a suspended sentence of two years. Bednarova, a former television journalist, received a sentence of three years which she served in Opava women's prison. Dienstbier and Benda received three and four years respectively; Havel four and a half; while Petr Uhl, a revolutionary Trotskyist who was no stranger to the prisons of the regime, received five years, which he was to serve in a maximum security prison.

The plight of the VONS defendants attracted considerable international attention. A dramatic reconstruction of the trial of the six was performed at theatres in Paris, Munich and New York, and was shown on Austrian, German and Swiss television. In 1981 plays by Havel were performed in Paris and Warsaw, while in June a resolution of the European parliament called for the release of Czechoslovak political prisoners. Havel in particular became a cause célèbre. In February 1982 the International Committee for the Defence of Charter 77 awarded him the Jan Palach prize for both his literary work and his defence of human rights. In June he received the honorary degree of Doctor of Letters from York University, Toronto, the University of Toulouse conferring a second honorary doctorate on him in August. In July the Avignon International Theatre Festival honoured and commemorated him with a 'Night for Vaclav Havel'.

All this was doubtless galling to the Czechoslovak authorities; but they had learned from their Soviet masters that one way to deal with dissidents was to let them go abroad; once such turbulent people were in the free world, foreign media interest in them dwindled. While under interrogation in August Havel had been told of an invitation to spend a year in New York as a theatrical adviser. Knowing that if he left it would be impossible to return to Czechoslovakia, he refused to consider doing so. Vaclav Benda, a prominent Catholic layman, was repeatedly offered his freedom if he agreed to leave the country; he consistently refused, and was not released until 1983. Similar offers were made to Jiri Dienstbier. Pavel Kohout, novelist, playwright, poet and founder and signatory of Charter 77, became an involuntary exile. After spending a year in Austria he was stripped of his citizenship, and was therefore unable to return to Czechoslovakia.

Despite harassment and outright persecution many dissidents in Czechoslovakia proved irrepressible. Take the case of Rudolf Battek, one of the founders of KAN in 1968 and a deputy in the Czech assembly. After writing a letter to the federal assembly demanding an official investigation into the invasion of August, he was dismissed from his post as a sociologist in the academy of sciences and imprisoned. This was to be the first of four sentences he would serve. He was one of the first signatories of Charter 77 and one of the founders of VONS. In 1978 he was also one of the founders of the Independent Socialists, a social democratic group with no connection with the official party, which had been forcibly merged with the Communists after 1948. In 1980 he began a five-year prison sentence, but appeared again as one of the founders of the Movement for Civil Liberties in 1988.

Another Chartist was Pavel Bratinka, a physicist who lost his job at the academy of sciences when he was caught distributing literature about the Charter. He worked as a caretaker, then as a stoker on the metro railway in Prague. He also worked underground in another sense, in that he gave lectures to other dissidents and was involved in Havel's underground press. He, too, helped found the Movement for Civil Liberties in 1988.

In January 1980 Havel, Dienstbier and Benda were transferred from prison in Prague to the labour camp at Hermanice, near the town and mines of Ostrava, where they worked as welders. This area was one of the most notoriously polluted in Communist Czechoslovakia, and not surprisingly Havel fell ill, and had to spend a week in the prison hospital in July 1981. After this he was transferred to the prison at Plzen-Bory, where he was assigned slightly lighter work in the laundry. In January 1983 he was suddenly admitted to the Pankrac prison hospital in Prague suffering from high fever and severe pneumonia. Once the fever had abated Havel managed to send a detailed letter to his wife Olga Havlova about his illness. She made the news known to friends and sympathisers at home and abroad, and soon there were many public appeals for his release. Possibly the authorities were embarrassed by this; more likely they were afraid Havel would die in prison. In any event in February his sentence was suspended on the grounds of ill health, and he was transferred to an ordinary hospital in Prague, whence he was allowed to go home. His sentence was only abrogated in September 1985, as part of a general amnesty of political prisoners.

As the authorities very well knew, the worst punishment for intellectual dissidents is not to be able to use their minds professionally. Just as in the aftermath of Prague Spring purged artists and academics had had to find unskilled manual jobs, so it was for the Chartists. Dienstbier had been a television journalist, and one of those who had continued to broadcast during the Warsaw pact invasion. For this 'illegal' activity he lost both his job and his Communist Party membership. After his release from prison in 1982 he had to work as a night watchman and stoker, a job he held up to and during the velvet revolution of November 1989. Even so, he managed to publish extensively in the underground *samizdat* press, and produced a book of essays on international relations which was also published abroad. Petr Pithart, a professor of law, also lost his post for supporting the Dubcek reforms. He had to work at manual jobs both before and after he became a signatory of Charter 77. He, too, wrote for the underground press; his works included *Sixty Eight*, a reassessment of Prague Spring.

Jan Urban's case shows that persecution was transmitted across the generations. His father had been a Communist partisan in World War II, held a senior post in the central committee of the party but lost it for criticism of the Novotny regime's lack of reform. Urban senior died of a heart attack following three police interrogations in 1988. Jan Urban lost his teaching post in a secondary school in 1977 when he refused to sign a statement condemning Charter 77, of which he became a signatory. It was this experience, of being asked to condemn something he had not read and then losing his teaching post, that turned Urban into an active dissident. He held a variety of jobs, including bookbinder and building labourer, and in 1985 qualified as a skilled bricklayer.

Perhaps one of the most remarkable works of *samizdat* literature to be created in the era of normalisation was Havel's *Letters to Olga*. While in prison following the VONS trial a weekly four-page letter to his wife was the only form of writing permitted to Havel. Accordingly he decided to use this as a form of literary and philosophical expression. In all, between 4 June 1979 and 4 September 1982 he wrote 144 letters to Olga. Naturally there was strict censorship at Hermanice and Plzen-Bory; some of the letters were mutilated by the prison censor, a number did not reach their destination at all.

Even those citizens who were not outright dissidents suffered from the oppressive, dreary yet fearful atmosphere of the years of normalisation. The plight of ordinary people punished for the crimes of relatives who had made an 'illegal exit to the West'; corruption in high places to protect Communists from the consequences of non-political crimes; the ubiquitous presence of the secret police and informers; all these facets of existence are shown in *The End of Lieutenant Boruvka*. This was a book of connected short stories by the exiled Czech writer Josef Skvorecky first published in Toronto in 1975. Boruvka is an honest and melancholy officer in the criminal police, who both despises and fears the 'other police'. He is constantly thwarted in his work of bringing miscreants to justice by official 'cover-ups', and is forced to disavow the 'deformations of the Dubcek era' in which he had briefly rejoiced. Boruvka finally breaks the law in obedience to his conscience as he helps a small girl to escape from Czechoslovakia to join her parents abroad. The consequences of his attempt to 'live in truth' (to revert to Havel's phrase) are terrible for all concerned. Boruvka himself, the girl's aunt and aged grandparents are all imprisoned; his wife has a stroke under the shock of his arrest and dies; his daughter, married to an American Czech, is forbidden to join her husband in the United States. Skvorecky claimed that the five cases with which Boruvka deals were all loosely based on real incidents. Although Boruvka ends on a note of personal redemption in his prison cell, this only emphasises the horrors of normalisation.

In retrospect 1985 was a momentous year for the Soviet bloc, since it saw the appointment of Mikhail Gorbachev as General Secretary of the Communist Party of the Soviet Union. For the Chartists little changed in terms of police harassment. Havel was interrogated by the police three times that year. In January he was held for 48 hours and questioned about the nomination of new Charter 77 spokesmen; he was questioned twice in August, this time over the drafting of a Chartist statement on the Warsaw pact invasion.

It is not remarkable that the neo-Stalinist regimes of the Soviet bloc, Czechoslovakia's among them, should not have felt great enthusiasm for the new broom sweeping the Kremlin. In March 1986 the XVII Congress of the Czechoslovak party paid lip service to *perestroika* and *glasnost* and even promised increased economic and social reform. In January 1987 the normalising prime minister Lubomir Strougal spoke of rehabilitating some of the Dubcek reforms (though not Dubcek and the reformers of 1968, his own colleagues until he rushed to the aid of the victors). The opposition was encouraged by Gorbachev's visit to Prague in March, but the Soviet leader went no further than denying Brezhnev's dictum that the Soviet party had a monopoly on truth. Indeed, Gorbachev had plenty of domestic problems of his own without encouraging dissent, and therefore instability, in the Communist bloc.

Perhaps it was the security engendered by this knowledge, or perhaps it was merely customary arrogance that made the Communist authorities act against a particularly irksome source of nonconformity. The Jazz Section of the official Musicians' Union had since the late 1970s been promoting jazz through staging concerts for Czechoslovak and foreign groups and by publishing books and magazines. Just over a decade after the arrest and trial of the Plastic People of the Universe the Jazz Section was suppressed and its leaders imprisoned.

Even so, 1987 proved to be an active year for the opponents of normalisation. A group of Moravian workers demanded the resignation of President Husak, who blithely and stubbornly ignored both this and increasing hints from Moscow that some lessening of constraints and economic reform might not come amiss. In September an unofficial, liberal-democratic organisation, Democratic Initiative, was formed to encourage public discussion of reform.

In October the Slovak green movement published the first of a number of reports called 'Bratislava Aloud'. Based on official data, these sounded severe warnings about the region's dire environmental condition. In November Dubcek broke his silence on public affairs by sending a telegram to Gorbachev wishing him luck with his reforms.

Another matter which must have irritated the regime was the increasing international profile of Czechoslovak dissidents. After six years of secret existence the Friends of Czechoslovak–Polish Solidarity was officially established. Jan Urban attended the seminar on international human rights held in Moscow by Press Club Glasnost. There he met Andrei Sakharov and other prominent victims of Soviet repression. Urban was also one of the founders of the Eastern European Information Agency, which publicised material about dissent and its opponents throughout the Soviet bloc.

All this brought about a token change. At the end of the year Husak resigned as first secretary, though he kept the position of president. He was replaced by Milos Jakes, a pro-Soviet survivor from the party leadership of 1968, who proved to be as hardline a normaliser as his predecessor. Let Moscow do as it pleased; Prague, like East Berlin, would remain frozen and inert in Brezhnev's age of sclerosis. (Or so their leaders fondly imagined.)

The year 1988 saw the growth of dissent from a number of quarters and on several issues in Czechoslovakia. Religious liberty became a rallying cry. Since the days of Gottwald the fiction of freedom of worship had been cynically maintained by the authorities; despite the fact that clergy were persecuted for subversion and espionage and the laity found themselves penalised if they attended church services too frequently and noticeably. In March 1988 there were Catholic demonstrations in both Prague and Bratislava, this last involving 2000 protesting believers, elderly women in the main.

More than 600,000 people signed the petition formulated by Cardinal Frantisek Tomasek, archbishop of Prague. Entitled 'Suggestions of Catholics for the Solution of the Problems of the Faithful', this document protested at the state's treatment of worshippers and declared itself in favour of increased religious freedom. Tomasek also issued a clarion call to Catholics in his Easter address, 'Spiritual renewal of the nation', made at the start of preparations for the millennial anniversary of the early medieval bishop, missionary and martyr St Vojtech. Massive pilgrimages took place in Slovakia; more than 280,000 went to the shrine of Levoca in July, while 60,000 were pilgrims to Sastin in September. In early December about one thousand Moravian Catholics demonstrated in Olomouc.

Political discontent was also manifest. The twentieth anniversary of the Warsaw pact invasion on 21 August was marked by massive demonstrations in

Prague and other cities. In Prague 10,000 demonstrators conducted a peaceful march through the city centre. In Wenceslas Square a petition was read out by members of the Independent Peace Association which condemned the invasion of 1968 and called for a public enquiry about it, together with abolition of censorship, free and democratic elections and rehabilitation of political victims of the regime. The security forces reacted with great brutality, using water cannon and tear gas on the civilian crowds.

Nonetheless, human rights continued to be defended by dissenters. The Movement for Civil Liberties was founded on 15 October. This was an umbrella organisation for all kinds of clubs and associations which rejected the 'leading role' of the Communist Party and published a manifesto, 'Democracy for All'. Largely in response to growing public restiveness, the authorities announced that 28 October, the anniversary of the foundation of the First Republic, would once more be celebrated as Czechoslovak national day. By making the occasion a public holiday they hoped to lessen the turnout at unofficial demonstrations. Even so, they were obliged to try to prevent independent demonstrations in Prague by arresting nearly 200 of the organisers the night before. Despite these precautions a demonstration of 5000 people took place in Wenceslas Square, which was broken up by the usual brutality on the part of the security forces. On 10 December, which was international human rights day, Charter 77 and other organisations organised a mass demonstration in Prague, calling for freedom of association, the press, religion and travel, and for an amnesty of political prisoners. This demonstration alone was officially sanctioned, not least because of the state visit of Francois Mitterand, the French president, to Czechoslovakia and his announced intention of raising the question of human rights.

Any idea that change was in the air was, however, brutally quashed by the authorities. In January 1989 the twentieth anniversary of Jan Palach's suicide was marked by a week ('Palach week') of huge and spontaneous demonstrations. The protesters voiced demands for democracy over six days. Once more the police responded with tear gas, water cannon, beatings and arrests. Among those taken into custody were well-known dissidents, including Havel, who had committed the crime of trying to lay flowers on the site of Palach's self-sacrifice. There were international protests. The Conference on Security and Cooperation in Europe (CSCE) was meeting in Vienna, Czechoslovakia having sent delegates to the debates on an agreement on human rights. The American representative denounced Czechoslovakia for infringement of the Helsinki agreement of which it was a signatory. Such a condemnation by the major imperialist power might seem easy to dismiss. Less comfortable was the criticism of the Czechoslovak regime's handling of the protests which appeared in

*Pravda*, the newspaper of the Soviet Communist Party. Yet the Czechoslovak hardliners were obdurate. At least outwardly, it seemed that normalisation would carry on, and the hold of the hardliners seemed unbreakable.

## Notes

1   Quoted in Alan Levy, *So Many Heroes* (2nd ed., Sagonapack, New York 1980), p. 313.
2   Zdenek Mlynar, *Night Frost in Prague: The End of Humane Socialism* (London, 1980), p. 221.
3   Jan Vladislav, ed. *Vaclav Havel Living in Truth* (London and Boston, 1989), p. 55.

# 1989

# The Velvet Revolution

On 20 August the Viennese newspaper *Die Presse* carried a small item on its front page about Czechoslovakia. Demonstrations were expected in Prague and other cities on the twenty-first anniversary of the Soviet-led invasion. Riot police and troops had been put on standby; but the regime was confident of its ability to handle any protests. No doubt its confidence was largely based on the 13,000 troops, 790 officers and 155 tanks at its disposal. In the event, the mass demonstration which took place in Prague was broken up by the armed forces and police with the usual brutality.

Even further down the front page was an article about East German tourist-refugees. Holidaymakers in significant numbers were abandoning their Trabant and Wartburg cars and seeking asylum in West German embassies in Warsaw pact capitals. The West German constitution recognised all Germans as citizens of the Federal Republic, with rights of residence and employment. The East Germans were not only claiming these rights, but were also voting with their feet against Communism.

At the time there seemed little to connect the two articles, but within months democratic revolution would have raced like wildfire through the Soviet bloc. Within Czechoslovakia itself there had been patent signs of discontent ever since the demonstrations on the anniversary of Jan Palach's death in January. The following month a political club called *Obroda* ('Revival') was formed by former Communist officials from 1968. These reform Communists supported Gorbachev's policies in the Soviet Union and demanded similar reforms for Czechoslovakia. In a separate development in April, Dubcek himself gave an interview to the Hungarian television journalist Andras Sugar. Over the course of three hours he reviewed and defended Prague Spring, condemned the Warsaw pact invasion, and exonerated his own conduct in Moscow and after his return to Prague.

Naturally enough this astonishing and revelatory account provoked protest and denunciation from the Czechoslovak authorities. Another blow was dealt to the Communists in May, however, when the hitherto tame Socialist Party demanded greater freedom for non-Communist parties.

All this did not prevent the Husak regime from loudly approving the Chinese suppression of peaceful student demonstrators in Beijing in June.

In that same month, however, a petition appeared called 'A Few Sentences'. This was signed by writers and artists (eventually it bore more than 40,000 signatures), and it demanded democratic reform. The petition complained that, although the Czechoslovak authorities paid lip service to *perestroika* and democratisation, they used coercion and violence against their own citizens. It saw social and democratic reform as the necessary prelude to dealing with economic problems, and made some specific demands. These included: an immediate amnesty for political prisoners; the lifting of restrictions on freedom of assembly and of discussion; the end of censorship of the mass media and cultural life; freedom to express religious belief; public consultation on environmental matters; and free discussion of the events of the 1950s, Prague Spring, the 1968 invasion and normalisation.

The confidence of the Czechoslovak authorities was seriously misplaced, given the chronic state of the economy. In the time of the First Republic Czechoslovakia had been ranked seventh among the industrialised states of the world; by the 1980s it had fallen shockingly to seventieth place. In 1988 the Czechoslovak Institute for Economic Forecasting had produced an ominous report about the economy and social problems; it called for drastic reform and some degree of democratisation. The report was taken up by the then Prime Minister, Lubomir Strougal, who had supported the Dubcek reforms in 1968 but had then joined the winning, normalising side. In 1988 he used the report to advocate reform; but this would have involved major social changes, with large-scale redundancies in industries such as metallurgy and engineering, and so the recommendations of the report were not implemented.

Early in 1989 the government declared more than 100 major enterprises bankrupt but announced that it would continue to support them. In late August, however, the Czechoslovak State Planning Agency announced that 30 per cent of the country's enterprises were unprofitable and recommended that they be closed. The only profitable manufactured product seems to have been Semtex, a plastic explosive made near Pardubice and exported in large quantities to terrorists and repressive governments the world over.

If the Czechoslovak economy was in trouble, environmental damage was one of the major problems facing the country. The chief source of fuel was brown coal (lignite), which was neither economical nor environmentally friendly. Brown coal gives off sulphur dioxide, the pollutant which is the main cause of acid rain. In 1990 Misha Glenny reported that Czechoslovak industry produced about 18 million tonnes of sulphur dioxide per square kilometre a year, three quarters of it from Northern Bohemia, which also produced about

60 per cent of the country's electricity supply. Glenny discovered a number of disturbing facts. Life expectancy in the 'black belt' of Northern Bohemia was three to four years lower than in other parts of Czechoslovakia. Infant mortality was at least 12 per cent higher there than elsewhere in the country. Furthermore, during the winter 'temperature inversion' meant that pollution was trapped by hot air so that a choking smog lay over the region.

At one of the demonstrations on Letna Plain in November 1989 the economist Milos Zeman announced even more shocking statistics. He declared that Czechoslovakia was a third world country in terms of economic growth and further education, and that the Republic had the highest level of pollution and the second highest mortality rate in the whole of Europe.

As well as Northern Bohemia, Northern Moravia, Western Bohemia, Prague itself and Bratislava and Eastern Slovakia were all officially designated as 'ecological disaster zones'. The acid rain generated by sulphur dioxide had completely destroyed 30 per cent of the forests, while of the rest 50 per cent had suffered partial destruction. Official organisations such as the Czechoslovak Union of Environmentalists sounded warnings about ecological damage. 'Clean water, clean air, clean government!' demanded one street slogan in November. Concern with the environment and the growth of independent green movements like the group Brontosaurus were undoubtedly major contributory factors to the Czechoslovak revolution of 1989.

Though there were specific national grievances, the revolution which developed in Czechoslovakia was not unaffected by events elsewhere in Eastern Europe; specifically in Poland, Hungary, East Germany and the Soviet Union itself. Poland took the lead in the process of democratisation. In August 1988, following a massive wave of industrial strikes, the Polish authorities declared themselves willing to negotiate with the banned trade union Solidarity, which had spearheaded the dissident movement. There began round-table talks (that is, discussions between equals) between the Communists and the opposition. These culminated in the legalisation of Solidarity and in some constitutional changes in the spring of 1989. An executive presidency would be created, along with a second parliamentary chamber, the senate; its seats would be filled through 'semi-free' elections for both chambers of the parliament or *Sejm*. For the first time since the Communist seizure of power independent candidates would be allowed to stand for parliament, albeit only for a proportion of the seats.

The elections took place in June, and the independents won all the seats they contested. At the same time the Communist General Wojciech Jaruzelski was elected president of Poland; a sign that the struggle for democracy was not over yet. However the desertion of the previously compliant minor parties in the 'popular front' with the Communists to the side of the opposition meant that it was impossible for the Communists to get enough votes to form a government. Consequently in August a new government was formed by Solidarity with Tadeusz Mazowiecki as the first non-Communist prime minister since 1947; so overcome was he that he fainted when he stood up in the *Sejm* to make his inaugural speech.

There should have been warning signs for the Czechoslovak Communists in the developments in Poland. In July 1989 the former dissidents Adam Michnik and Zbygniew Bujak visited Prague as parliamentary representatives and made contact with the leaders of Czechoslovak dissent. As Jan Urban later recalled with some glee, the secret police could do nothing but film the meetings. On 11 August the Polish senate unanimously denounced the Warsaw pact invasion of 1968 and apologised to the Czechoslovak people for the participation of Polish troops.

If events in Hungary were less dramatic than in Poland, economic reform and a movement towards political democratisation were bound to have an effect on public opinion in Czechoslovakia. After the bloody repression which followed the Hungarian uprising of 1956 Janos Kadar had slowly and almost imperceptibly moved towards liberalisation of the economy and some social reforms. Indeed, Hungarian participation in the 1968 invasion of Czechoslovakia had been an unpleasant surprise, as Dubcek had considered Kadar to be a kindred spirit and his political programme for Hungary to be not unlike the reforms of Prague Spring.

Despite the relative liberalism of the Hungarian regime (liberal, that is, in relation to the hard line governments of Czechoslovakia and East Germany), popular discontent fuelled by economic and ecological problems prompted Kadar's fall. In May 1988 he was deposed and replaced by a collective leadership, which proceeded to implement 'goulash Communism'. This was a peculiarly Hungarian mixture of old-fashioned 'democratic centralism' and a new form of 'socialist pluralism' which allowed the expression of opinion but did not affect the 'leading role of the party'.

In the event the Hungarian opposition organised itself into groups and clubs, and in January 1989 came legislation which inaugurated political pluralism, in that in principle it allowed the formation of independent political parties. The Hungarian Democratic Forum achieved victory in the by-elections of August 1989. In October the Communist Party congress enacted a significant measure of restructuring, and the party renamed itself the Hungarian Socialist Party. A schism developed later in the year, with the old guard renaming itself the Communist Party. All this was quite academic, however, as it was plain that the Communists had lost control of Hungary.

Back in January an official reassessment of the events of 1956 had concluded that these did not constitute a counter-revolution, but a popular uprising. Kadar died on 15 June; the next day, in a highly symbolic gesture Imre Nagy and other Communist leaders from 1956 were ceremonially reburied with full state honours.

The German Democratic Republic, like Czechoslovakia, was ruled by hard-line Communists, and the survival of each regime was to an extent dependent on the other. The GDR was ruled by Erich Honecker, spiritual heir to 'Frozen Walter' Ulbricht who had intervened in Czechoslovak affairs with such enthusiasm in 1968. Honecker's inability either to stem the flow of refugees to West Germany or to still the calls for reform within East Germany obviously had an effect on neighbouring Czechoslovakia. More than 11,000 East Germans took refuge in the West German embassy in Prague in September 1989. They came so suddenly and in such numbers that tents and blankets had to be conveyed by lorry from Bavaria for those camping out in the embassy compound. The citizens of Prague helped them in practical ways, according to reminiscences of those autumn days, and cheered the busloads of East Germans bound for the West and gave them the 'v for victory' sign; possibly the first time that gesture had been used since 1945.

Honecker reacted to events with the arrogance born of long years of repression and unopposed government. He threatened the protesters in the GDR with a 'Chinese' solution (thus recalling the recent massacre of students in Beijing), and he hoped to use a visit by Gorbachev in October to bolster his own position and authority. In the event Gorbachev neither reproved nor encouraged the dissidents, thus indicating by his silence that he would do nothing to save the East German Communist regime. (In fact, he gave an oblique warning to Honecker that governments which did not respond to the popular will put themselves in grave danger.) Later that month Honecker was deposed as party secretary. In November the Berlin wall was breached; the GDR opened its borders officially and the entire government and East German politburo resigned. The last blows to Communist power came in December, when the Communist leadership resigned and renounced the 'leading role' of the party. By that time the Czechoslovak revolution was virtually over.

A final factor which encouraged the 'velvet revolutionaries' was a development in the Soviet Union itself. It became known in Czechoslovak dissident circles that the central committee of the Soviet party had set up a working party to reassess the invasion of 1968. Its findings were reported finally on 4 December, at a Warsaw pact meeting in Moscow.

The events which unfolded rapidly in Czechoslovakia late in 1989 were immediately called the 'velvet revolution' because, apart from one violent incident provoked by the police, protest was peaceful and, in retrospect at least, Communism apparently died an easeful death. The revolutionaries were doubtless encouraged by the mass demonstrations for democracy in the GDR in September, and the denunciation of the 1968 invasion by the Hungarian parliament. On 14 October the People's Party (the Catholic party once led by Jan Sramek, but since 1948 a partner of the Communists in the bogus national front) showed signs of opposition. A group was formed called 'Stream of Rebirth' which denounced the party leadership for betraying its Catholic principles.

Meanwhile, and despite the ominous omen of Honecker's resignation on 18 October, the authorities continued to persecute signatories of the petition 'A Few Sentences'. In protest at this official journalists and the Czech Philharmonic Orchestra, led by Vaclav Neumann, initiated a boycott of state television on 25 October. On 13 November a new political party, Democratic Initiative, applied for registration as an independent party, the first since the Communist coup of 1948. At roughly the same time there were demonstrations against ecological damage and the regime's environmental policy in both Prague and Western Bohemia.

The velvet revolution proper is commonly held to have begun on 17 November, with the only violent incident in its course. Students gathered in Prague to commemorate – with official permission – the fiftieth anniversary of the funeral of Jan Opletal. This, it will be recalled, had ended in anti-Nazi demonstrations, violence against the students of the day, and the closure by the Protectorate authorities on Nazi orders of all Czech universities and institutes of higher education. The commemoration attracted an estimated crowd of about 100,000, and it became a pro-democracy demonstration.

Student discontent and dissent had been growing in a subdued manner throughout the year. The monopoly of student organisation enjoyed by the Socialist Union of Youth patently infringed the higher education law of the CSCE (Conference on Security and Cooperation in Europe). Accordingly tentative steps were taken to form an independent students' organisation. This new union, together with the reform wing of the Socialist Union of Youth and other student bodies which derived from it planned the commemoration of Opletal's death to be something more than an anti-fascist demonstration.

In place of the 2000–4000 expected demonstrators about 15,000 assembled for the start of the march, and were joined by thousands more in due course. Many carried candles and flowers, others bore banners with political slogans. Among these was what was to become the watchword of the students during the velvet revolution: 'If not us, who? If not now, when?' Another *leitmotif* of the revolution first appeared here, in that the students rattled their keys at their 'jailors', the police. The protesters sang songs, among them the Czech national anthem, 'Where is my Home?', the anti-militarist Western protest song, 'Where have all the Flowers Gone?', and the favourite song of T.G. Masaryk, 'My Son, my Son'.

As the procession marched up National Avenue towards Wenceslas Square it was attacked by riot police and by special troops known as red berets. One of the most striking photographic images of the velvet revolution was the sight of the students holding out their hands, palms open, to the police to show that they were unarmed. This did not prevent hundreds of them being severely beaten up. Many ended up in hospital, and there was a rumour (later proved to be untrue, and to have been spread by the Communist authorities in order to discredit the veracity of the protestors) that one student had been killed. A monument to the victims, consisting of open and empty hands, now stands on National Avenue at the scene of the atrocity.

This typically brutal police action served as the catalyst for the velvet revolution. The following day the students went on strike (apparently on the initiative of the drama students) and occupied university buildings; they pleaded for a sign of popular solidarity by participation in a general strike, planned for 27 November. Although police appeared outside some of the occupied premises they did not attempt to enter. The students were soon joined in their protest by the actors of Prague, who effectively went on strike and occupied the theatres for political discussions. More to the point, actors from the provinces arrived in Prague within hours, so that strike notices appeared in many cities beyond the capital. This concerted action was vital in transmitting news of the police violence against the students and the concomitant strike from Prague to the provinces. Furthermore, the alliance of students and actors would be crucial in enabling the message to be conveyed to the industrial workers, who formed a large part of theatre audiences. In this way the authorities' distortion of the events of 17 November, which tried to depict the students as spoilt and idle troublemakers, could be corrected in the next few days and weeks.

On 19 November (such was the pace of events) Civic Forum (*Obcanske Forum, OF*) was formed in Prague as an umbrella organisation for the opposition. Like Charter 77, it embraced all forms of opposition. The proclamation of foundation listed the participating bodies. These were Charter 77 and VONS (many Chartists were prominent in the Forum, Jiri Dienstbier and Vaclav Havel among them); the Club of Independent Intelligentsia; Artforum and Revival (*Obroda*); the Independent Students; the Czechoslovak Democratic Initiative; the Independent Peace Association; Open Dialogue; and the Czechoslovak Centre of the PEN Club. Civic Forum also included members of the Socialist and People's Parties, former Communists and current reform

Communists, Catholics like Vaclav Benda and Vaclav Maly, and Thatcherite economists and free marketeers like Vaclav Klaus. On 20 November a parallel organisation was founded in Slovakia by the actor Milan Knazko. This was called the Public Against Violence (*Verejnost Proti Nasiliu, VPN*). Like the Czech organisation it drew support from a wide constituency.

The founding document of Civic Forum linked the crimes of 1968 with the more recent outrage of 17 November. It demanded the immediate resignation of those high ranking Communists who were directly implicated in the 'invitation' to the Warsaw pact armies to intervene in Czechoslovak affairs, and who were responsible for the long dreary years of normalisation. Specifically it named, among others, Gustav Husak, Milos Jakes, Karel Hoffman, and Alois Indra. It also demanded the resignations of Miroslav Stepan, first secretary of Prague city council, and Frantisek Kincl, Federal Minister of the Interior, as being responsible for the police action against the students on 17 November; and an official enquiry into the events of that night. Finally, it called for the immediate release of all 'prisoners of conscience'.

Also on that and the following day there was a mass demonstration in Prague of between 150,000 and 200,000 people calling for democratic reforms. The vast majority of the crowd was made up of university and high school students. As they marched past newspaper offices on Wenceslas Square they taunted the journalists for writing lies and demanded an end to censorship. There were protests in other Czech and Slovak cities, including Brno, Olomouc, Ostrava and Bratislava. In response the Czech and Slovak republican governments threatened to 'restore order'.

The velvet revolutionaries now faced a fundamental difficulty. For years the dissident intellectuals who led Civic Forum had been depicted by official propaganda as indolent troublemakers and enemies of the working class. The Forum itself did not have any prominent working class members until the recruitment to the leadership of Petr Miller, an engineering worker, and a miner, Milan Hruska. The revolution could not become more general unless the intellectuals and students attracted the support of the workers. If they failed in this there was a real threat of a 'Chinese solution' in Czechoslovakia. The previous June the Chinese Communist leadership had successfully used an army of peasant and working class conscripts against their own students by propaganda which declared them to be idle drones who were trying to subvert the peasants' and workers' revolution. The Czechoslovak Communist authorities still kept control of television in the provinces, and they were able to prevent the delivery of non-Communist newspapers outside the capital. This effective grip on censorship prevented most urban workers and country people outside Prague from receiving news of the true state of affairs.

Accordingly, from 22 November student agitators were despatched to factories and farms throughout Czechoslovakia to plead for support for their cause. A 'student' delegation was typically made up of one student, one teacher and one actor, though later students went into factories in twos and threes. Naturally enough the management of industrial concerns placed obstacles in the way of the delegations' addressing the workforce, and many workers themselves, while not necessarily hostile to the student demands, were initially reluctant to pledge themselves to strike. Most crucially, however, the majority of factories and other enterprises in the capital decided to join in the general strike on 27 November. Indeed, on 23 November a delegation of 10,000 workers from the gigantic CKD engineering plant joined in a mass demonstration in Prague.

Working-class suspicion of the students was harder to combat in the provinces than in the capital. Student delegations might be arrested by the regional police, held without charge for a number of hours and have their leaflets and other materials confiscated. The authorities were assisted by the widespread assumption that the students were spoilt and privileged loafers who preferred striking to studying. There was also fear of the economic disruption a general strike might entail. Much of this suspicion was allayed when the students, beginning on 23 November, offered to work an eight-hour shift without payment at any enterprise which would take them.

The workers were also reassured by Civic Forum's definition of the general strike. The aim was not economic disruption, but political protest; it would last a mere two hours, to minimise loss of production; and there was nothing to prevent the conscientious from working overtime to make good the loss in production. (In the event, many workers did precisely that.)

Public opinion surveys conducted in November and December 1989 are most illuminating of the concerns of ordinary citizens. (The opinion polls are summarised by Wheaton and Kavan in their study of the velvet revolution.) One set of surveys canvassed views throughout Czechoslovakia on what would most benefit or damage the situation: 88 per cent of those questioned thought that personnel changes in the Communist leadership would benefit the situation; 85 per cent were for working properly and continuing with *perestroika*; 84 per cent for calm and discretion; 81 per cent for negotiation between the authorities and the opposition; and 55 per cent for demonstrating against past policies. On the debit side, 58 per cent thought that strikes would be damaging, 74 per cent thought that crushing the opposition would be harmful, and (interestingly) 59 per cent believed that demonstrating in support of past policies would have a negative effect.

Another survey of a sample of 401 people conducted between 20 and 22 November concerned areas of major social problems. These were ranked as the environment (a staggering 98 per cent), the economy (92 per cent), the health system (90 per cent), the political system (88 per cent), the quality of senior management (78 per cent), education (76 per cent), public morality (70 per cent), social security (63 per cent), and human rights (58 per cent). Only 47 per cent saw culture as a problematic area, while 49 per cent voted for access to foreign travel and a mere 29 per cent found religious freedom to be an area of major problems.

There were several interesting developments, political and otherwise, before the strike took place. The centre of Prague and other towns was transformed by huge crowds of demonstrators and candles lit in memory of the victims of Communism; a shrine to Jan Palach was created in Wenceslas Square, and old photographs of Dubcek and the Masaryks appeared in shop windows and on the plinths of public monuments. Just as during the invasion of 1968, graffiti and posters abounded. As Jan Urban, who had emerged as a leading spokesman for Civic Forum, told *The New York Times*, 'It's a war on walls'. 'The street is the voice of the people', proclaimed one slogan. A hand-painted poster in Prague proclaimed, 'The heart of Europe beats again'; 'The truncheon – the beating heart of the Communist party' proclaimed another, while a graffito in English on a kiosk in Wenceslas Square later declared 'It's Over Czechs Are Free'.

In Bratislava the velvet revolution was as orderly, pacific and dignified as in Prague. At one demonstration a crowd of 80,000 people was orchestrated from the speakers' podium to move back a few paces gently; a woman who lost her purse containing a large sum of money recouped the sum through a spontaneous collection from the crowd. An attempt was made to intimidate the student body of Komensky university when a deputation of four students was summoned to appear before the faculty of 200 staff. The intention was thwarted when the entire faculty applauded the student representatives.

At a rally in Bratislava on 22 November Dubcek made his first public speech in Czechoslovakia in 20 years. The 80,000-strong crowd acclaimed him with great joy as the living embodiment of 'socialism with a human face' and as an outstanding victim of the repression of normalisation. Soon he was on the bus to Prague, to consult with the leaders of Civic Forum. Dubcek embodied the conscious connection people were making between Prague Spring and the velvet revolution. One popular poster showed the number 89 to be merely 68 turned upside down. When a journalist asked Eduard Shevardnadze, Gorbachev's spokesman for foreign affairs, what the difference was between Prague Spring and *perestroika*, he replied 'Twenty years'. On the same day as the Bratislava rally Czechoslovak television workers protested at the biased nature of the reportage of the protests; as a result the censorship broke down, and coverage of the demonstrations was shown.

The Slovak Communist Party was unnerved by the protests. At the demonstration in Bratislava on 22 November news came that the Catholic dissident Jan Carnogursky, who had been held in custody charged with publishing an unofficial journal, had been released without charge. The Slovak party also showed itself willing to negotiate with students at various universities throughout Slovakia.

The release of Carnogursky shows how far and how quickly the world had changed. A defence lawyer since 1970, who dealt mainly with religious and political cases, he lost his right to practice law in 1981 after defending a dissident who had committed the crime of circulating *samizdat* publications. After 1987 he was unable to find employment, in 1988 he joined the Movement for Civil Liberties, and was involved in the cooperative efforts of Czechoslovak and Polish dissidents. Immediately on his release he joined the leadership of Public Against Violence, becoming a spokesman of major stature.

Dubcek made his first public speech in Prague since 1969 on 24 November. Civic Forum had by now taken over the balcony of the *Svobodne Slovo* ('Word of Freedom') newspaper building which looked out on Wenceslas Square. (Presumably the Socialist Party, whose paper *Svobodne Slovo* was, expected to make a little political capital out of this.) Dubcek and Havel both stepped out onto the balcony, receiving a rapturous reception from the crowd below. There was another face – or rather, voice – from 1968. Before the speeches Marta Kubisova, the most memorable singer from Prague Spring, appeared on the balcony and sang, 'The Times They Are A-Changin'.

That same night the Communist authorities decided to make some changes in official positions. Milos Jakes and the entire presidium of the politburo resigned, or rather, were dismissed by the central committee of the party. Jakes released the reins of power only reluctantly, and not before attempting to fob off party and public opinion by suggesting that only Husak, Alois Indra and Karel Hoffman should have to resign. The personnel changes were not propitious for reform, however. Karel Urbanek, a hardline 'normaliser', was appointed general secretary of the party, while Miroslav Stepan, the official who had ordered the police brutality of 17 November, kept his post.

On 25 November the demonstrations had a religious and nationalist flavour. Cardinal Frantisek Tomasek, the Archbishop of Prague, said mass to celebrate the official canonisation of Anezka (Agnes of Bohemia), a medieval Premyslid princess, Franciscan nun and correspondent of Clare of Assisi, who had long been regarded as one of the patron saints of Bohemia. The canonisation had taken place in Rome on 12 November. In an attempt to win the support of Czechoslovak Catholics the Communists sought to associate themselves with this great patriotic event. The canonisation proceedings and mass in Rome were broadcast on state television, and thousands of Czechoslovak Catholics were allowed to travel to the Eternal City. Miroslav Stepan went so far as to praise Tomasek for his role in the canonisation, evidently hoping to persuade the Cardinal-Archbishop to use his influence with Catholic students and dissidents to avert the general strike. As Stepan was widely and accurately held to be responsible for the police attack on the student demonstrators of 17 November, and as Tomasek was somewhat seasoned in opposition to the regime, these efforts came to naught.

On 25 November tens of thousands of people took part in the Prague celebrations, while millions more saw the mass broadcast on television. Many Catholics from the provinces were in the cathedral in Prague. Afterwards there was a rally of nearly three quarters of a million people on Letna Plain in Prague. Dubcek and Havel were among the speakers. They denounced the recent official changes as cosmetic, and asked their audience to put pressure on the government to accede to the opposition's demands. Urbanek announced that the government was prepared to negotiate with the opposition, while Stepan and other hardline Communists resigned their posts.

Next day government representatives led by Ladislav Adamec, the prime minister, held a meeting with a delegation from Civic Forum led by Havel. They met on ostensibly neutral territory at the municipal house (*obecni dum*), where the document declaring Czechoslovak independence had been signed in 1918. It was almost as if the clocks were running backwards. As recently as September Adamec had referred to Havel as an 'absolute zero'; the irony of their changed circumstances cannot have been lost on at least one of them. Further talks were promised, and both parties addressed the crowd of 500,000 gathered on Letna. Mistrustful of government promises, Civic Forum and Public Against Violence carried on with preparations for the general strike.

That same day, 26 November, Civic Forum also published its manifesto. Entitled 'What We Want', this demanded radical change in the spheres of law, the political system, foreign policy, the economy, social justice, the environment and culture. A new constitution guaranteeing the rights of citizens was called for, along with an independent judiciary. The stultifying Communist monopoly of power should be replaced by a fully democratic system, with a plurality of parties having equal rights and standing. Czechoslovakia would remain a federation, but one where both Czechs and Slovaks and the national minorities would have equal rights. In foreign policy Gorbachev's concept of a 'common European home' should take precedence over membership of the Warsaw pact and ComEcon. The command economy should be swept away and replaced by a market economy, though the state would still have a role to play. In terms of social justice there should exist a safety net of benefits for those who needed help, though such a welfare system was predicated on a healthy, growing economy. The environment and the country's natural resources should be protected and cherished, and the structure and aims of industry must be adapted to lower the consumption of raw materials and energy. Finally art, literature and education must be democratised, with full freedom of expression and access to information available to all citizens.

Two days earlier the opposition in Slovakia had published the demands of the Citizens' Initiatives, Public Against Violence and the coordinating committee of Slovak universities. Among their twelve demands were free elections to the Slovak national council or regional parliament and the abolition of the 'leading role' of the Communist Party. They also called for full civil liberties, including freedom of expression, association, assembly, movement and conscience; and the removal of ideology from the educational system and the independence of culture from state control. There were also calls for legal reforms, independent trades unions and an independent student organisation, legalisation of all forms of ownership and the complete separation of church and state. Absolute guarantees were demanded of the right to a healthy environment. Czechoslovakia should be a truly democratic and equal federation, and everyone should have an equal chance both in the elections and in future life.

The general strike took place on Monday, 27 November, between twelve noon and two o'clock. It has been estimated that four-fifths of the population stopped work. Some 38 per cent were on strike for the full two hours; 9 per cent for a shorter time; while 24 per cent showed support for the strike in several ways, such as street demonstrations. Given the widespread fears about the economic impact of the strike, many of its supporters were scrupulous enough to work overtime that evening so as not to lose the two hours' productivity. In towns throughout the land church bells rang, motor horns were sounded, sirens wailed and people rattled their keys to add to the noise. The authorities should have been unnerved, but the confidence engendered by a 40-year monopoly of power was hard to dent. The Communists thought that popular displeasure could be appeased by gestures such as the release of books and films previously suppressed by the censorship.

In reality the Communist Party itself was being undermined by disunity and outright schism. The reform group *Obroda* (Revival) was gaining increasing support, as against the old guard. In addition, a breakaway group of younger members called themselves the Democratic Forum of Communists, their name a transparent attempt to steal Civic Forum's thunder. They demanded a number of basic reforms in their proclamation of 27 November, the very day of the general strike. These included the abolition of the 'leading

role' of the party, the complete political rehabilitation of the victims of normalisation and the formulation of an action programme for the party. Rather
belatedly, they condemned the Warsaw pact invasion of 1968.

The Communists generally had lost a valuable weapon against the protesters, in the form of the people's militia. From the early days of the velvet revolution the militia had been something of an uncertain quantity, with
militiamen in Prague and Brno effectively ignoring Stepan's order to mobilise
and disperse the students by force. The end came for the militia when law students publicised the fact that, as it had no legal or constitutional standing,
individual members could be accountable for their actions before the courts.
Thereafter various units of the militia began to dissolve themselves.

Despite all this the party hierarchy thought that the leaders of the protest
even now could be bought off with concessions. On 28 November representatives of the government and of Civic Forum met again for discussions.
Adamec promised to amend the constitution so as to abolish the 'leading role'
of the party by 29 November. A coalition government would be formed by the
following Sunday, 3 December. Some concessions were made to the dissidents, but not enough to satisfy them. There were public calls for Husak's
resignation as president.

On 29 November Urbanek, the hardline General Secretary, told the central
committee of the party that the Communists could no longer hold their
monopoly of power. The constitution was debated in the federal assembly.
There was an official questioning of the events of 1968, and a commission was
formed to investigate the violence of 17 November. The Communist Defence
Minister gave a guarantee that there would be no coup by the armed forces,
and Adamec proposed negotiations with the Kremlin over the withdrawal of
Soviet tanks and troops from Czechoslovak territory. Most chillingly, however,
came the revelation that the Communist old guard had considered imple-
menting a 'military solution' against the protesters as late as the previous
Friday, 24 November. It was the Minister of Defence, Milan Vaclavik, who had
proposed the use of force in the plenum of the central committee. The proposal was debated and narrowly defeated. Fortunately, too, for the protesters,
the chief of staff, General Miroslav Vacek, did not exercise the military option.
This was all the more important as members of the armed forces took an oath
of allegiance, not to the Czechoslovak Republic or to the constitution, but to
the Communist Party.

All the manoeuvrings of the Communist authorities were to no avail, however; a true revolution had taken place in political and cultural terms.
Wheaton and Kavan in their study of the velvet revolution observe that in the
week following the general strike the three main bases of Communist power

had been destroyed. The article of the constitution guaranteeing the 'leading role' of the party had been abrogated by 29 November. The basic party organisations in the workplace were soon dissolved; and Marxism–Leninism was rejected as the official ideology of the Czechoslovak state and as the basis for educational and cultural activity.

The last day of November saw some significant developments. In Prague, representatives of Civic Forum negotiated directly with the Communist Party (in the person of Vasil Mohorita, secretary of the central committee) for the first time. Mohorita was something of an opportunist. As chairman of the Socialist Union of Youth his had been among the first voices to condemn the police violence of 17 November; curiously, he had expressed support for police violence against demonstrators the previous January during 'Palach week'. He had enjoyed substantial popularity during the early days of the student strike, when his official student body was able to give the independent students access to materials and facilities. Suspicion grew, however, that he was planning to use his popular base among the young to further his own ambitions within the party. Indeed, he abandoned the Socialist Union of Youth when it proved to be redundant to the changed situation, and on 26 November was voted one of the new central committee members who replaced Jakes and his associates.

On that same day 30 November, in Bratislava, a delegation from Public Against Violence met with members of the Slovak republican government to discuss leadership changes. It was also announced that the fence along the border between neutral Austria and Communist Czechoslovakia would be dismantled. This frontier and the one with West Germany were actually opened respectively on 17 and 23 December. In a highly symbolic gesture the barbed wire between the states was cut by Jiri Dienstbier, the new non-Communist Foreign Minister, and his Austrian and German counterparts.

Indeed, by the beginning of December it was questionable how long Czechoslovakia would remain Communist. A public opinion survey conducted between 29 November and 1 December concerned the 'leading role of the party'. In the country as a whole only 2 per cent thought that this was very necessary, with 59 per cent finding it unnecessary. In the city of Prague the proportions were respectively 1 per cent and 71 per cent.

In a desperate attempt to gain some credibility, the Czechoslovak Communist party met on 1 December to denounce the invasion of 1968. In a press communique Mohorita declared that 'the entry onto our territory of five armies of the Warsaw pact in 1968 was not justified, and the decision to do so was wrong.' At the same time Gorbachev admitted that the Prague Spring had grown out of a yearning for democracy, and three days later the Soviet Union and its allies in the 1968 invasion condemned their own actions at a Warsaw pact meeting in Moscow attended by Adamec and Urbanek.

Meanwhile on the weekend of 2–3 December the Malta summit took place, with Gorbachev holding talks with the United States President George Bush. Change was patently in the international air; yet the Czechoslovak politburo thought it could still cling to power by making a few minor concessions to the opposition. On Sunday 3 December the politburo announced the formation of a new provisional government for Czechoslovakia, with a mere five out of 20 ministerial posts being allotted to non-Communists. This was quite unacceptable to Civic Forum, who called for demonstrations for the next day and a general strike on the following Monday. President Husak refused to resign his office, though later that same day hinted that he might.

On Monday 4 December demonstrations took place in Prague and other towns, and Czechoslovakia quite literally roared its anger at the inadequacy of the proposed governmental changes. It was felt to be outrageous that 1.6 million Communists in the country should be represented by 15 ministers while the remaining 14.5 million of the population had to make do with five. (Times, indeed, had changed rapidly.) 'Five new ministers, 15 merry old men', quipped one poster, while another derisively quoted Lenin in 1917; 'No support for the provisional government!' Hundreds of thousands of citizens joined in a rally on Wenceslas Square. Here Civic Forum demanded the dismissal of all compromised parliamentary deputies, including Vasil Bilak and Alois Indra, who had 'invited' the 'fraternal assistance' of the Warsaw pact armies in 1968, and Vaclav David, Novotny's former foreign minister. ('Send them to work!' chanted the crowd.) The Forum also demanded the formation of a more representative government, and free elections by June 1990.

The very next day there was a cabinet reshuffle, which resulted in the Communist ministers being outnumbered 9:8. Negotiations took place between Adamec, the Prime Minister, and a number of opposition groups, including Civic Forum, Public Against Violence, 'Revival' (*Obroda*) and the parties formerly in the national front with the Communists. Adamec was given an ultimatum to form a new government by next Sunday, or face the threatened general strike on Monday; the eminent economist Valtr Komarek, a prominent member of Civic Forum and shortly to be a deputy prime minister, observed that the government needed a higher IQ. Meanwhile the commission investigating the police violence of 17 November recommended that both Stepan and Jakes be ejected from the federal assembly, and thus lose their parliamentary immunity from prosecution. The Czechoslovak Communist Party also announced that rehabilitation proceedings would take place for the half a million party members purged in the wake of the Warsaw pact invasion. These were somewhat desperate measures, as that same day Civic Forum submitted a new draft constitution.

The next few days saw the momentum of the velvet revolution increase. On 6 December the trade unions announced their political independence from the old Communist Revolutionary Trade Union Movement, and a congress of independent unionists was planned for January 1990. On the same day a reshuffle of the cabinet of the Czech republic put the non-Communists in a majority. On 7 December Adamec resigned, to be replaced by the deputy premier Marian Calfa, a Slovak Communist. Negotiations between the government and Civic Forum continued through the night, and on 8 December it was announced that half the ministerial posts in the new Czechoslovak government would be filled by non-Communists. President Husak, already contemplating retirement, announced an amnesty for political prisoners; possibly this was intended to sweeten his memory once he had departed from power.

Indeed, increasing pressure was put on Husak to resign the presidency, and Vaclav Havel expressed a reluctant willingness to succeed him. Husak announced his decision to resign on 9 December. The new president was to be elected by the federal assembly, and Civic Forum put forward Havel as its candidate.

Husak finally resigned as president on Sunday 10 December, immediately after swearing in the new Czechoslovak government. His feelings can be imagined; he had to accord government posts to despised dissidents, some of them fresh from prison. Be that as it may, this 'government of national understanding' contained a decided minority of Communists, (ten out of 21 ministers), though Calfa was reappointed prime minister; he and two other government members, Valtr Komarek and Vladimir Dlouhy, would soon leave the party.

Of the non-Communist ministers there were two members of the People's (Catholic) Party, two Czech Socialists, and seven without party affiliation. The new deputy premier was Jan Carnogursky, the Slovak Catholic dissident and campaigner for human rights, while Komarek was one of three ministers in charge of internal affairs. Jiri Dienstbier, longstanding dissident and Chartist, became Foreign Minister; the look on his face at the swearing-in ceremony was one of delighted and disbelieving wonder, though immediately afterwards he rushed back to his boiler-stoker's job. (After all, the economy was still in crisis, and the velvet revolutionaries were anxious to avoid the impairment of productivity.) There was a huge and triumphant rally in Wenceslas Square. The next day throughout the country there was a five-minute demonstration of popular satisfaction; church bells were rung, motor horns sounded, and there was the by now familiar key-jangling.

The political struggle now centred on the presidency of Czechoslovakia. On Tuesday 12 December the Communist party proposed an amendment to the constitution which would provide for the election of the president by nationwide ballot. Apparently and despite all the recent changes the Communists thought they could still command a majority in the country as a whole, as they assumed that outside Prague dissidents like Havel were little known and not at all trusted. That same day, however, the Czechoslovak Public Opinion Institute published the results of a poll. This showed that Civic Forum had the trust of 75 per cent of those questioned, while the Communist Party only retained the trust of 16 per cent. As far as the presidency went, Havel had 18 per cent of popular support, far more than any other candidate.

It seemed that by Wednesday 13 December the matter of the presidency had been settled. All parties agreed that the election should take place before the end of January, and that the new incumbent would be a Czech and not a Communist. The following day, however, negotiations between Civic Forum and the Communists were in chaos, as the right wing of the party denounced the previous day's decision as invalid and requiring the ratification of the party congress, scheduled to meet in a week's time.

There were a number of potential presidential candidates besides Havel. The Communists fielded Ladislav Adamec, so lately prime minister, while the moribund Socialist Union of Youth nominated Cestmir Cisar, a reform Communist in Dubcek's government and one of the students' heroes in 1968. Alexander Dubcek himself was the candidate of the central committee of the national front of the Slovak republic.

There had been popular cries of 'Dubcek to the castle!' (the seat of the president) on his first reappearance in Prague, and it seems highly probable that the father of Prague Spring himself entertained presidential ambitions. Certainly, the Communists hoped to exploit differences within the opposition to ensure the election of one of their own. Dubcek, however, played an important role in preserving the national unity of Czechs and Slovaks. Even during the velvet revolution there was suspicion in Slovakia of the intentions of Prague. The leaders of Civic Forum were unknown to Slovaks and suspected as opportunists and troublemakers. This is why it was crucial that Dubcek should go to Prague to appear with the Forum's leaders and to represent the Slovaks in their counsels.

By 16 December Dubcek and Havel had come to an arrangement, and it was announced that Havel would stand for president with Dubcek 'at his side'. Acutely aware of Slovak grievances, Havel declared that he would only stand for president on condition that no attempt was made to divide either himself from Dubcek or Czechs from Slovaks when it came to the election. At the same time Civic Forum demanded that the election take place before Christmas, and that the ballot should be televised.

All in all, the writing was on the wall for Communist parties throughout the former Soviet bloc. On 18 December the first incredible news trickled through of protests and riots in Rumania; this was the prelude to the fall of Ceausescu. That same day it was announced that Calfa and Dienstbier would go to Moscow to negotiate the withdrawal of Soviet troops from Czechoslovak soil. On 19 December Calfa announced fundamental changes in government policy; the security forces were to be disbanded, and Czechoslovakia would join the world economy once more. In other words, the failed command economy was to be abandoned, and free market policies adopted. Calfa also announced that Havel was the only possible future president, and that his candidature had the government's endorsement.

On 20 December 50,000 people demonstrated against Ceausescu in Timisoara, and the Lithuanian Communists severed their links with the Soviet party. In Prague, the Communist Party congress went ahead, and desperately tried to cope with the revolutionary situation by tinkering with the party structure. The office of general secretary was abolished and replaced by two 'new' posts; Adamec was elected as party chairman and Mohorita as first secretary. People murmured about old wine in new wineskins.

The final events of the velvet revolution unfolded with scant reference to the old normalising Czechoslovak Communists. On 28 December the hitherto compliant federal assembly was reconstituted, with a number of deputies being compelled to resign and members of the opposition being co-opted to take their places. That such a reform was necessary was shown by television broadcasts and still photographs of the constitutional debate on the 'leading role' of the party. Many of the deputies looked nervous or bewildered, while some of the more eminent members of the party hierarchy actually slept through it all; a fitting metaphor for the Communists' loss of power, initiative and even sense of reality. Alexander Dubcek was elected chairman of the federal assembly by that body (now a body with rather more teeth than the one he had chaired back in 1969), and was awarded the Andrei Sakharov prize for human rights by the European parliament.

The following day Vaclav Havel became the first democratic, non-Communist president of Czechoslovakia since the death of Edvard Benes in 1948. He was elected unanimously by the 323 deputies of the federal assembly. He made a short, dignified speech to a crowd assembled outside Prague castle in which he promised not to betray the people's confidence and to lead the country to free elections. His own electoral victory was marked by a *Te Deum* and mass celebrated by Cardinal Tomasek. After all the vicissitudes of Czechoslovak history it seemed that truth had at last prevailed.

# Epilogue: 1992
## The Velvet Divorce

In December 1989 Czechoslovakia was swept by an understandable wave of euphoria. Communism had collapsed and, as in the days of Masaryk, a philosopher was once more president of the Republic. Yet at midnight on 31 December 1992 the country divided into its constituent parts, the Czech lands and Slovakia. The reasons for this 'velvet divorce' were ethnic, economic and political.

As president, Vaclav Havel deliberately modelled himself on Tomas Garrigue Masaryk, as a figure of high moral authority who embodied the democratic ideals and traditions of Czechoslovakia. (He even went to the lengths of taking riding lessons, so as to be able to imitate the dignified figure of the President Liberator on horseback.) Havel enjoyed enormous personal popularity. Opinion polls conducted in February and in April–May 1990 into public confidence showed that a staggering 88 per cent of respondents expressed their trust in him.

In terms of foreign policy orientation Havel and his Foreign Minister Dienstbier promoted a 'return to Europe'. What this actually meant was a return to Edvard Benes' vision of Czechoslovakia as a bridge between East and West. It was noteworthy that the new president did not visit Moscow until February 1990, when he also went to Washington. His earliest journeys abroad had been to Poland, Hungary, and both East and West Germany. While in Moscow he negotiated the treaty for the withdrawal of all Soviet troops from Czechoslovakia; this was achieved by May 1991.

The 'government of national understanding' which had taken office on 10 December 1989 at the climax of the velvet revolution was to stay in place until parliamentary elections could be held, in June 1990. Not having been democratically elected, it was a provisional or 'caretaker' government. Its provisional character was shared by the federal assembly and by the republican governments of the Czech lands and Slovakia. Even so, these new executive and legislative authorities could be said to govern by popular mandate, since opinion polls held in late January 1990 showed a high level of satisfaction with developments (86 per cent) and of support for the proposed social and economic reforms (84 per cent).

The new government and legislature faced a plethora of economic, social and political problems inherited from the corrupt and inept Communist regime. Chief among these was the environment which, as has been noted, was regarded by many Czechoslovak citizens as a more pressing problem than even the economy. In the first six months of non-Communist government considerable attempts were made to tackle all these issues.

A mass of legislation was passed to rectify the wrongs of the Communist era and to regulate positions of state. Laws which legalised freedom of assembly, the press and of petition effectively brought an end to censorship, and the death penalty was abolished. The need for educational reform was addressed. New laws increased the autonomy of universities and the authority of student organisations. Postgraduate studies were reformed along Western lines, and restrictions on foreign travel were lifted.

Legislation was also passed to regulate political life. The electoral law greatly reduced the number of parties that had mushroomed after the velvet revolution by stipulating that parties could only participate in elections if they had 10,000 members. Parties would only gain seats in parliament if they polled 5 per cent of the vote in one of the two republics.

Economic reform was obviously high on the list of priorities of the 'government of national understanding'. The team of experts which had to consider these issues was led by Valtr Komarek, a deputy prime minister and former head of the Institute for Economic Forecasting; Vladimir Dlouhy, also a deputy prime minister and head of the State Plannning Commission; and Vaclav Klaus, the Minister of Finance. All these were agreed on the desirability of a transition to a market economy; where they disagreed was on the speed of the proposed reforms. Klaus, a neo-liberal and admirer of Margaret Thatcher, favoured a rapid transition, the 'cold sharp shock' treatment of the economy. Komarek, on the other hand, felt that too swift a change would result in 'economic agony'. The issue was muddled by the fact that many Czechoslovaks (and indeed, former denizens of Communist Europe generally) believed that a completely free market was compatible with guaranteed full employment. By the time of the June elections, however, it was clear that Klaus and the radicals had won the economic argument.

Privatisation of state property would take place in two stages. Small businesses such as restaurants would be sold to private owners first. Larger state enterprises would be disposed of by a system of vouchers, chiefly distributed to their employees, which could be used to buy shares. The budget of March

1990 successfully turned a huge deficit into a surplus. It reduced subsidies to state enterprises by 10 per cent, cut defence spending by 12.5 per cent, and price and wage subsidies by 14 per cent. In addition, Czechoslovakia withdrew from ComEcon (Council for Mutual Economic Assistance).

The legacy of mistrust bequeathed by the Communists to Czechoslovakia was the most harmful, and is discussed below; but there were some other dark bequests, too. Under Communism there had been comparatively little non-political crime; not because of any innate virtue in the authoritarian system, but simply because, as many Czechoslovaks felt, the entire country was a prison. Naturally enough, when the fear and restrictions imposed by the Husak regime were lifted, incidences of crime increased markedly. This was particularly so in Prague, which experienced a huge influx of foreign visitors from December 1989. These tourists and other travellers, being blessed with hard currency, were comparatively wealthy and so naturally a temptation to petty criminals, from pickpockets to money-changers and other fraudsters.

In the eyes of the Czechoslovak public, however, there were two sources of blame for the perceived 'crime wave'. One was President Havel, who by his amnesty for about 25,000 prisoners had emptied the gaols, not just of prisoners of conscience, but of common criminals. (That such a perception was false, or at least exaggerated, goes without saying.) The other chief fount of criminality was felt to be the Roma (Gypsy) community.

This brings us to another pernicious aspect of the Communist legacy. Far from seriously attempting to inculcate transnational proletarian brotherhood and thus obviate ethnic conflict, the Communist regime had merely suppressed all manifestations of tension. The Roma were and are a small but highly visible minority, less than 1 per cent of the population. The Communists had made little effort to integrate them into the national community and had allowed them to remain under-educated. They were obvious targets for an emergent racism, and scapegoats for the increase in crime. Otherwise intelligent and well-educated people would state in all seriousness that the Roma were responsible for between 90 and 99 per cent of all crime. In reality, they were responsible for 7.5 per cent of crime over all, and about 15 percent of street crime.

Another target for racism was the foreign guest workers and students, chiefly Vietnamese, who had been invited by the Communists to reside in Czechoslovakia in the interests of international proletarian comradeship and cheap labour. Individuals now openly became victims of racial attack and abuse, while a large-scale race riot, mainly involving working class skinheads, erupted in Prague in May 1990. This was directed against both guest workers and Roma, and was a source of shame and embarrassment to the authorities. Plainly, the work of creating a civil society would not be an easy task.

Military reform and reductions in defence expenditure were essential if Havel was to implement his foreign policy of a 'return to Europe'. The army was no longer to be called the 'people's army', and military service was reduced from two years to 18 months. Conscientious objectors now had the option of civilian service, and women were no longer to be conscripted in peacetime, though they might volunteer for military service. The army was no longer to be used in agriculture and industry, and political activity within the armed forces was prohibited. Finally, the role of the armed forces in internal security was to be limited.

Indeed, one of the most pernicious aspects of the Communist legacy to Czechoslovakia was paradoxically a lack of security and mistrust. The StB or state security police was abolished at the end of January 1990, but its end was not clean and in fact stirred up a lot of mud. Though the secret police had only numbered some 8000 members, still it had been assisted and supported by a mass of paid informants from all walks of life and all regions of the Republic. It seems probable that as many as 140,000 out of a population of 15 million informed for the security police. The StB had infiltrated all official organisations and even some dissident circles, and after its abolition something of a witch-hunt began. The first political scandal of post-Communist Czechoslovakia was known as 'Sachergate'.

Richard Sacher, a Catholic and member of the People's Party, was Minister of the Interior and charged with abolishing the StB and investigating the past actions of its members. There was a public outcry when it was discovered that officers dismissed from state security were to be paid for a further six months. (The argument that these men were guaranteed severance pay by law was received with some scepticism.) Suspicion grew that Sacher was dragging his feet in the matter of the secret police and in the purge of his own ministry.

The Sachergate scandal really broke in April, with the first stage of *lustrace*. This 'lustration' or cleansing originally involved screening the past careers of officials and candidates to ensure that they were not tainted by any dealings with the secret police. Information was leaked by some of Sacher's subordinates about a Civic Forum official who was critical of Sacher and his doings. It was alleged that this man, Oldrich Hromadko, had worked as a guard at the notorious uranium mines in the 1950s. The Forum observed that such accusations had been made against Hromadko in the 1960s but had not been proved.

Suspicion grew that the 'exposure' of Hromadko was nothing more than a political tactic intended to discredit the Forum before the parliamentary elections. The People's Party, though lately made respectable again, had for decades been one of the Communists' partners in the bogus national front; it was suspected that Sacher would be glad to create a little dust about members of the government and federal assembly in order to cover his own and his party's tracks. In the event a compromise was reached, by which Sacher would remain in office until the elections in June.

In April 1990 the Sokol affair showed that the Communist Party itself was still widely distrusted, and that fears continued that it would seek to destroy the newly reclaimed Czechoslovak democracy. Tomas Sokol, the Prague state prosecutor, sent a letter to the central committee of the party which was soon after reported in the press. In this letter Sokol warned the Communists that their affairs would be subject to strict investigation under the article of the penal code that prohibited all activities which aimed to propagate fascism. He argued that in its suppression of political and personal liberties and inability to tolerate any opposition once in power, the Communist Party was anti-democratic and indeed, closely resembled a fascist organisation.

Sokol's attack on the Communists received widespread press and public support, and there were calls for the abolition of the party, confiscation of its property and investigation of its personnel. On the other hand, the state prosecutor's office distanced itself from what it took to be Sokol's personal view, and Civic Forum was equivocal in its reaction. While the leadership supported Sokol's right to interpret the law as he saw fit, they chose to believe that he was warning the Communists about future acts of illegality rather than threatening the party with dissolution. At the grass roots level, however, many local branches of the Forum espoused Sokol's viewpoint. On 11 April 1990 there was a general strike to demand the confiscation of Communist Party property which received a significant level of public support.

Perhaps surprisingly, the former dissidents who had suffered under the Communist regime were more forgiving about the past than the man and woman in the street. Jan Urban spoke of the compromises which every citizen had had to make in the Communist era. President Havel himself said that all Czechoslovak citizens, dissidents and conformists alike, were guilty of colluding in their own oppression simply by having existed under Communism. His generosity in associating himself with the collective 'guilt' did not, however, find an echo in public opinion.

In the event, the Communist Party survived to participate in the first free elections in June 1990. The party adopted as its new emblem a pair of cherries; opposition election propaganda depicted these as outwardly sound and sweet, but rotten inside.

The elections resulted in indisputable victory for Civic Forum in the Czech lands and Public Against Violence in Slovakia. Over 96 per cent of the electorate turned out; 53.15 per cent of Czechs voted for Civic Forum, and 32.4% of Slovaks for Public Against Violence. Surprisingly, the Communists emerged as the second strongest party, gaining more than 13 per cent in both the republics. In Slovakia, the Christian Democratic Union came third in the elections, while the Slovak National Party gained 10 per cent of the vote.

The Czechs and Slovaks, unlike the peoples of the former Yugoslavia, had no history of violent conflict or atrocities committed against each other. True, residual bitterness existed among Czechs about Slovak behaviour during World War II, though this was in part offset by the heroism of the Slovak national uprising of 1944. Each nation, however, had perceptions about itself and the other which were causes of disagreement, and even grievance.

Part of this goes back to the very concept of 'Czechoslovakism' as propagated by T.G. Masaryk, Edvard Benes and other luminaries of the First Republic. In theory, and according to the constitution, there was one Czechoslovak nation, and the official language of the state was Czechoslovak. Although the Slovaks had been led to expect some form of autonomy within the Republic, their political inexperience and the comparative backwardness of their region had made this impractical.

In their negotiations with President Benes during and after the war Slovak politicians tried to advance the notion of two nations, Czech and Slovak, and to use this as a basis for arguing for autonomy or federation. Such a theory fitted neither with Benes' profound and pragmatic Czechoslovakism, nor, later, with the Communists' centralising policy.

Nonetheless, one of the few enduring reforms of the Prague Spring was the federalisation of the Republic, effective from January 1969. On paper at least, this new constitution delegated a fair amount of power to the Czech and Slovak republican governments, though amendments introduced in 1971, particularly in the economic sphere, tended to reduce their freedom of action. Besides the governments of the two republics, there was a federal assembly for the whole state. This was bicameral, composed of a chamber of the people with 200 members and a chamber of the nations with 150 deputies. The members of the former chamber were chosen on the basis of population, those of the latter divided equally between Czechs and Slovaks. This apparent fairness was largely cosmetic, however. The federal assembly was largely symbolic in nature, meeting infrequently to approve decisions already taken by the Communist party and government.

Very soon after the velvet revolution Slovak grievances surfaced in the so-called 'hyphen debate'. In his new year speech for 1990 President Havel proposed changing the name of the country to remove the word 'Socialist' from between 'Czechoslovak' and 'Republic'. Immediately this triggered a debate among Slovak politicians and public about the 'visibility' of Slovakia. This tended to be obscured by the hybrid name of the country, and indeed, many foreigners said 'Czech' when they meant 'Czechoslovak'. It was therefore proposed that the name of the country be hyphenated, to become 'Czecho-Slovakia'.

This caused an outcry from the Czechs. Not only could they not see what was so upsetting to the Slovaks; the proposed hyphenation of the country brought back bitter memories of that other 'Czecho-Slovakia', the truncated Second Republic which had led a pitiful existence between the Munich agreement and the dismemberment of the country in March 1939. After much heated discussion a somewhat ungainly compromise was reached. Both names would be legal, and the Republic was called 'Czechoslovakia' by Czechs and 'Czecho-Slovakia' by Slovaks.

After the elections of June 1990 both Civic Forum and Public Against Violence, originally formed as umbrella organisations for various kinds of dissent, began to break down into their constituent parts. In October 1990 Vaclav Klaus was elected chairman of Civic Forum, and differences between his conservative group and the more liberal wing associated with Havel, Dienstbier and other former dissidents deepened. In February 1991 there was a formal separation between the Civic Movement and Klaus' Civic Democratic Party, though the two were still loosely united by a coordinating body.

At roughly the same time, divisions within Public Against Violence resulted in a schism. Conflict between supporters of Fedor Gal, head of the organisation, and Vladimir Meciar, the Slovak Prime Minister, resulted in the latter breaking away to form the Movement for Democratic Slovakia in March 1991. The following month Meciar and some of his supporters were removed from the Slovak government after allegations of dubious actions while Minister of the Interior, including military talks with the red army. Meciar was replaced as premier by the Christian Democrat Jan Carnogursky.

Both parts of the country were increasingly plagued by disunity and perceived national grievance. For the Czechs, the chairman of the federal assembly, Jan Kalvoda, was outspoken about the economic benefits of a 'divorce' from the Slovaks. Separatism even loomed in Moravia–Silesia, whose political representatives seemed uncertain whether they wanted autonomy or outright independence.

For the Slovaks, there were two main concerns, *lustrace* and the pace of economic change. In Slovakia the reforms of 1968 were valued; in the Czech republic they were increasingly depicted as the result of a quarrel between Communists. Dubcek himself, the father of Prague Spring, was denounced by Czech deputies in the federal assembly for his Communist past. (Interestingly,

Marian Calfa, who had been a Communist during the Brezhnev era and beyond, was not.) In economic terms the Slovaks were concerned that the 'sharp shock' treatment advocated by Klaus and the radicals would result in social injustice, with the more vulnerable members of society left unprotected from the cold blast of free market forces.

As far as Czechs and Slovaks were concerned, old attitudes persisted; the Czechs thought that they were still 'paying for Slovakia', as they had done since the days of the First Republic; the Slovaks felt that their country was still exploited and 'invisible'. Even so, opinion polls from 1991–92 show that there was little public support for an outright 'divorce'. Sovereignty was debated and rejected in Slovakia on four occasions between 1990 and 1992. Part of the problem lay in the use of terminology; for many nationalists and politicians, 'sovereignty' meant the same as 'autonomy', while the word 'federalisation' had multiple meanings.

The divorce between Czechs and Slovaks was brought about and negotiated by the politicians, chiefly (though not exclusively) Klaus and Meciar, whose parties had emerged as the victors in the 1992 elections in their respective parts of the country. Klaus saw Slovakia as an impediment to his plans for rapid and radical economic reform; Meciar's contradictory rhetoric makes it hard to discern what his aims were, though personal ambition seems to have been his main motor. Whatever the case, it seems that in the increasingly confrontational negotiations Meciar threatened Klaus with secession, and Klaus called his bluff.

Masaryk's Czechoslovakia came to an end at the stroke of midnight on 31 December 1992. Both of the new Republics, Czech and Slovak, would continue to struggle with economic and environmental problems, as well as social issues such as the rise of racism. Both, too, would have to confront and deal with the Communist past. Yet Masaryk's legacy of humanitarian democracy is perhaps reflected in the very nature of the demise of his state. For Czechs and Slovaks there would be no fratricidal war, as in Yugoslavia, but a velvet and quite amicable divorce. In that sense, perhaps the motto of Jan Hus and of the First Republic had proved veracious.

# Suggestions for Further Reading

## GENERAL BIBLIOGRAPHY

### Primary Sources
Eduard Benes, *Democracy To-Day and Tomorrow* (London, 1939).
Alexander Dubcek with Andras Sugar, *Dubcek Speaks* (London and New York, 1990).
Alexander Dubcek, *Hope Dies Last* (London, 1993).
George J. Kovun, ed., *The Spirit of Thomas G. Masaryk 1850–1937: An Anthology* (London, 1990).
Vera Laska, ed., *The Czechs in America 1633–1977, A Chronology and Fact Book* (New York, 1978).
Godfrey Lias, *Benes of Czechoslovakia* (London, 1940).
Compton MacKenzie, *Dr Benes* (London, 1946).
Frantisek Moravec, *Master of Spies: The Memoirs of General Moravec* (London, Sydney and Toronto, 1975).

### Secondary Sources
John F.N. Bradley, *Politics in Czechoslovakia, 1945–1990,* (Boulder, Colorado 1991).
Mark Cornwall, 'The Rise and Fall of a "Special Relationship"?: Britain and Czechoslovakia, 1930–48', in Brian Brivati and Harriet Jones, eds, *What Difference Did the War Make?* (Leicester and London, 1991).
R.J. Crampton, *Eastern Europe in the Twentieth Century and After* (London, 1996).
A. French, *Czech Writers and Politics 1945–1969* (Boulder, Colorado 1982).
Owen V. Johnson, *Slovakia 1918–1938: Education and the Making of a State* (Boulder, Colorado 1985).
Stanley J. Kirschbaum, *A History of Slovakia, The Struggle for Survival* (New York, 1995).
Erazim Kohak, *Jan Patocka, Philosophy and Selected Writings* (Chicago and London, 1989).
Josef Korbel, *Twentieth-Century Czechoslovakia, The Meanings of its History* (New York, 1977).
Carol Skalnik Leff, *National Conflict in Czechoslovakia* (Princeton, 1988).
Victor S. Mamatey and Radomir Luza, eds, *A History of the Czechoslovak Republic 1918–1948* (Princeton, 1973).
Robert B. Pynsent, *Questions of Identity: Czech and Slovak Ideas of Nationality and Personality* (Budapest, London and New York, 1998).
Derek Sayer, *The Coasts of Bohemia, A Czech History* (Princeton, 1998).
Peter Spafford, *Interference, The Story of Czechoslovakia in the Words of its Writers,* (Cheltenham, 1992).

Norman Stone and Eduard Strouhal, eds, *Czechoslovakia: Crossroads and Crises, 1918–1988* (London, 1989).

Edward Taborsky, *Communism in Czechoslovakia 1948–1960* (Princeton, 1961).

Mikulas Teich, ed., *Bohemia in History* (Cambridge, 1998).

Alice Teichova, *The Czechoslovak Economy 1918–1980* (London and New York, 1988).

E. Garrison Walters, *The Other Europe, Eastern Europe to 1945* (New York, 1988).

R.W. Seton-Watson, *A History of the Czechs and Slovaks* (London, 1943).

Sharon L. Wolchik, 'Czechoslovakia', in Sabrina P. Ramet, ed., *Eastern Europe Politics, Culture, and Society Since 1939* (Bloomington and Indianapolis, 1998).

Joseph F. Zacek, 'Nationalism in Czechoslovakia', in F.P. Sugar and I.J. Lederer, eds, *Nationalism in Easter Europe* (Washington, 1969).

Zbynek Zeman, *The Masaryks, The Making of Czechoslovakia* (London and New York, 1990).

Zbynek Zeman with Antonin Klimek, *The Life of Edvard Benes 1884–1938, Czechoslovakia in Peace and War* (Oxford, 1997).

Paul E. Zinner, *Communist Strategy and tactics in Czechoslovakia, 1918–48* (London and Dunmow, 1963).

## INTRODUCTION. CZECHS AND SLOVAKS IN AUSTRIA–HUNGARY

Peter Brock, *The Slovak National Awakening; an Essay in the Intellectual History of East Central Europe* (Toronto and Buffalo, 1976).

Ladislav Holy, *The Little Czech and the Great Czech Nation* (Cambridge, 1996).

Robert A. Khan, *A History of the Habsburg Empire 1526–1918* (Berkeley, Los Angeles and London, 1974).

Emil Niederhauser, *The Rise of Nationality in Eastern Europe* (Gyoma, 1982).

## CHAPTER 1. 1918: THE WORLD WAR AND THE MAKING OF A STATE

### Primary Sources

Edvard Benes, *My War Memories* (London, 1928).

T.G. Masaryk, *The Making of a State, Memories and Observations 1914–1918* (London, 1927).

T.G. Masaryk, *The Meaning of Czech History*, ed. Rene Wellek (Chapel Hill, 1974).

R.W. Seton-Watson, *Masaryk in England* (Cambridge, 1943).

### Secondary Sources

Mark Cornwall, *The Undermining of Austria–Hungary, the Battle for Hearts and Minds* (London, 2000).

John W. Mason, *The Dissolution of the Austro-Hungarian Empire 1867–1918* (London, 1990).

Alan Sked, *The Decline and Fall of the Habsburg Empire 1815–1918* (London and New York, 1989).

H. Gordon Skilling, *T.G. Masaryk: Against the Current, 1882–1914* (London, 1994).

## CHAPTER 2. THE FIRST CZECHOSLOVAK REPUBLIC, 1918–1938

### Primary Sources

Karel Capek, *President Masaryk Tells His Story* (London, 1934).
Robert J. Kerner, ed. *Czechoslovakia, Twenty Years of Independence* (Berkeley and Los Angeles, 1940).
Ferdinand Peroutka, 'A Portrait of Czechoslovak Democracy', in Karel Capek *et al.*, *At the Crossroads of Europe, An Historical outline of the Democratic Idea in Czechoslovakia* (Prague, 1938).

### Secondary Sources

John Hibberd, *Kafka in Context* (London, 1975).
Zdenek Lukes, *Architecture of the 20th Century*, Prague, 2001.
Joseph Rothschild, *East Central Europe between the Two World Wars* (Seattle and London, 1977).
Ronald M. Smelser, *The Sudeten German Problem 1933–1938* (Folkestone, 1975).
J.P. Stern, ed., *The World of Franz Kafka* (London, 1980).
Jaroslav Vogel, *Leos Janacek* (3rd ed., Prague, 1997).

## CHAPTER 3. FOREIGN POLICY AND THE MUNICH AGREEMENT

### Primary Sources

Eduard Benes, *Five Years of Czechoslovak Foreign Policy* (Prague, 1924).
*Documents on German Foreign Policy, 1918–1945* (Washington, DC 1949–1966).
*Documents on International Affairs, 1934–1950* (London, 1935–1954).
S. Grant Duff, *Europe and the Czechs* (Harmondsworth, 1938).
R.H. Haigh, D.S. Morris, A.R. Peters, eds, *The Guardian Book of Munich* (Aldershot, 1988).
Sir Nevile Henderson, *Failure of a Mission* (London, 1940).
Michael Killanin, ed., *Four Days* (London, 1938?).
Kamil Krofta, *Czechoslovakia and International Tension* (Prague, 1937).
R.G.D. Laffan, *Survey of International Affairs 1938 Volume II, The Crisis Over Czechoslovakia January to September 1938* (London, New York and Toronto, 1951).
Eugene Lennhoff, *In Defence of Dr Benes and Czech Democracy* (London, 1938).
Hubert Ripka, *Munich: Before and After* (London, 1939).
Elizabeth Wiskemann, *Czechs and Germans, A Study of the Struggle in the Historic Provinces of Bohemia and Moravia*, 2nd ed., London and New York, 1967).
E.L. Woodward and Rohan Butler, eds, *Documents on British Foreign Policy, 1919–1939* (3rd series, London, 1949).

### Secondary Sources

J.W. Bruegel, *Czechoslovakia before Munich: The German Minority Problem and British Appeasement Policy* (Cambridge, 1973).

John Charmley, *Chamberlain and the Lost Peace* (London, 1989).

Keith Eubank, *Munich* (Norman, Oklahoma 1963).

Robert Kee, *Munich: The Eleventh Hour* (London, 1988).

Igor Lukes, *Czechoslovakia Between Stalin and Hitler: the Diplomacy of Edvard Benes in the 1930s* (New York and Oxford, 1996).

Anita J. Prazmowska, *Eastern Europe and the Origins of the Second World War* (London and New York, 2000).

Keith Robbins, *Munich 1938* (London, 1968).

F.P. Walters, *A History of the League of Nations* (London, 1960).

Kurt Weisskopf, *The Agony of Czechoslovakia 1938/68* (London, 1968).

John W. Wheeler-Bennett, *Munich: Prologue to Tragedy* (London, 1948).

## CHAPTER 4. WORLD WAR II: RESISTANCE, PROPAGANDA AND NATIONAL SURVIVAL

### Primary Sources

Edvard Benes, *Memoirs of Dr Edvard Benes: From Munich to New War and New Victory* (London 1954).

Bohumil Bilek, *Fifth Column at Work* (London, 1945).

Czechoslovak Republic, Ministry of Foreign Affairs, *Czechoslovak Documents and Sources*, nos 1–10 (London, 1942–44).

—— *Two Years of German Oppression* (London, 1941).

—— *Four Fighting Years* (London, 1943).

—— *On the Reign of terror in Bohemia and Moravia under Reinhard Heydrich* (London, 1942).

Shiela Grant Duff, *A German Protectorate* (London, 1942).

E.V. Erdely, *Germany's First European Protectorate* (London, 1941).

E.V. Erdely, *Prague Braves the Hangman* (London, 1942).

G.J. George [Jiri Hronek], *They Betrayed Czechoslovakia* (London, 1938).

Jiri Hronek, *Volcano Under Hitler, The Underground War in Czechoslovakia* (London, 1941).

Franz Koegler, *Oppressed Minority?* (London, c. 1943).

Alexander Kunosi, *The Basis of Czechoslovak Unity* (London, 1944).

Jan Masaryk, *Speaking to My Country* (London, 1943).

Hubert Ripka, *East and West* (London, 1944).

Karel Sedivy, *Why We Want to Transfer the Germans* (London, 1946).

Eduard Taborsky, *The Czechoslovak Cause* (London, 1944).

### Secondary Sources

Asa Briggs, *The History of Broadcasting in the United Kingdom, Volume III, The War of Words* (London, New York and Toronto, 1970).

Miroslav Ivanov, *Target: Heydrich* (New York, 1974).

Lewis M. White, ed., *On All Fronts: Czechoslovaks in World War II* (New York, 1995).

Callum MacDonald, *The Killing of SS Obergruppenfuhrer Reinhard Heydrich* (London and New York, 1989).

Edward Taborsky, *President Edvard Benes Between East and West, 1938–1948* (Stanford, 1981).

Piotr S. Wandycz, *Czechoslovak-Polish Confederation and the Great Powers, 1940–1943* (Bloomington, 1956).

# CHAPTER 5. 1948: COMMUNIST COUP AND STALINIST RULE

## Primary Sources

Shiela Grant Duff *et al.*, *Czechoslovakia: Six Studies in Reconstruction* (London, 1946).

Josef Josten, *Oh My Country* (London, 1949).

Eugen Loebl, *Sentenced and Tried* (London, 1969).

Artur London, *On Trial (L'Aveu)* (London, 1970).

Jiri Pelikan, ed., *The Czechoslovak Political Trials, 1950–1954* (London, 1971).

Dana Adams Schmidt, *Anatomy of a Satellite* (London, 1953).

Josefa Slanska, *Report on My Husband* (London, 1969).

Marian Slingova, *Truth Will Prevail* (London, 1968).

Jan Stransky, *East Wind Over Prague* (London, 1950).

## Secondary Sources

Karel Kaplan, *The Short March, The Communist Takeover in Czechoslovakia 1945–1948*, (London, 1987).

Josef Korbel, *The Communist Subversion of Czechoslovakia 1938–1948* (Oxford, 1959).

Radomir Luza, *The Transfer of the Sudeten Germans* (London, 1964).

Caroline Kennedy-Pipe, *Stalin's Cold War, Soviet Strategies in Europe, 1943 to 1956* (Manchester and New York, 1996).

# CHAPTER 6. 1968: PRAGUE SPRING AND THE SOVIET INVASION

## Primary Sources

*Dubcek's Blueprint for Freedom*, with a profile by Hugh Lunghi and commentary by Paul Ello (London, 1969).

Alan Levy, *So Many Heroes* (2nd ed., Sagaponack, NY, 1980).

Jaromir Navratil, ed., *The Prague Spring 1968, A National Security Archive Documents Reader* (Budapest, 1998).

Robert Little, ed., *The Czech Black Book* (New York, Washington and London, 1969).

Zdenek Mlynar, *Night Frost in Prague: The End of Humane Socialism* (London, 1980).

Ladislav Mnacko, *The Seventh Night* (London, 1969).

Jiri Pelikan, ed., *The Secret Vysocany Congress* (London, 1971).

Radoslav Selucky, *Czechoslovakia: The Plan That Failed* (London, 1970).

Ivan Svitak, *The Czechoslovak Experiment: 1968–1969* (New York and London, 1971).

Pavel Tigrid, *Why Dubcek Fell* (London, 1969).

Z.A.B. Zeman, *Prague Spring: A Report on Czechoslovakia, 1968* (Harmondsworth, 1968).

**Secondary Sources**

William Shawcross, *Dubcek* revised ed. (London, 1990).

H. Gordon Skilling, *Czechoslovakia's Interrupted Revolution* (Princeton, 1976).

Kieran Williams, *The Prague Spring and its Aftermath* (Cambridge, 1997).

Philip Windsor and Adam Roberts, *Czechoslovakia, 1968* (London, 1969).

## CHAPTER 7. NORMALISATION AND DISSENT: 1968–1988

**Primary Sources**

Vaclav Havel, *Disturbing the Peace* (London and Boston, 1990).

—— *Letters to Olga* (London New York and Toronto, 1990).

—— *Open Letters* (London and Boston, 1991).

Vaclav Havel et al., *The Power of the Powerless* (New York, 1985).

Jan Vladislav, ed., *Vaclav Havel Living in Truth* (London and Boston, 1989).

**Secondary Sources**

Frantisek Silnitsky, Lara Silnitsky and Karl Reyman, eds, *Communism and Eastern Europe, A Collection of Essays* (Brighton, 1979).

H. Gordon Skilling, *Charter 77 and Human Rights in Czechoslovakia* (London, 1981).

H. Gordon Skilling ed., *Czechoslovakia, 1968–1988* (London, 1991).

## CHAPTER 8. 1989: THE VELVET REVOLUTION

**Primary Sources**

Bernard Gwertzman and Michael T. Kaufman, eds, *The Collapse of Communism* (revised ed., New York, 1991).

**Secondary Sources**

Misha Glenny, *The Rebirth of History, Eastern Europe in the Age of Democracy* (2nd ed., London, 1993).

Richard Sakwa, 'The Age of Paradox: the Anti-revolutionary Revolutions of 1989–91', in Moira Donald and Tim Rees, eds, *Reinterpreting Revolution in Twentieth-Century Europe* (London and New York, 2001).

Jan Urban, 'Czechoslovakia: the Power and Politics of Humiliation', in Gwyn Prins, ed., *Spring in Winter, the 1989 Revolutions* (Manchester and New York, 1990).

Bernard Wheaton and Zdenek Kavan, *The Velvet Revolution, Czechoslovakia, 1988–1991* (Boulder, San Francisco and Oxford, 1992).

## EPILOGUE. 1992: THE VELVET DIVORCE

### Primary Sources
Tim D. Whipple, ed., *After the Velvet Revolution, Vaclav Havel and the New Leaders of Czechoslovakia Speak Out* (New York, 1991).

### Secondary Sources
Abby Innes, 'The Breakup of Czechoslovakia: the Impact of Party Development on the Separation of the State', *East European Politics and Societies* 11 (1997).

Jiri Musil, ed., *The End of Czechoslovakia* (Budapest, London and New York, 1995).

Robin Shepherd, *Czechoslovakia, the Velvet Revolution and Beyond* (London, 2000).

Eric Stein, *Czecho/Slovakia: Ethnic Conflict, Constitutional Fissure, Negotiated Breakup*, Ann Arbor (1997).

Sharon L. Wolchik, *Czechoslovakia in Transition, Politics, Economy and Society* (London and New York, 1991).

# Index

Action programme 1968  107, 109–10,
  111, 120
Activism  28, 48
Adamec, Ladislav  152, 154, 156, 157,
  158, 159
Agnes of Bohemia, *see* Anezka
Agrarian Party  23, 25, 30, 33, 81
Agriculture, *see* Economy
Albania  45
Ales, Mikulas  xvii
Alexander of Yugoslavia  45
Alexandrovsky, Sergei  55
American Czechs and Slovaks, *see*
  Emigration, Czechs and Slovaks in
Anezka (Agnes of Bohemia)  151–1
Ankara  121
'Anthropoid', Operation  72
Anti-Semitism  2, 27, 28, 50, 95, 118, 127
Appeasement  9, 19, 49–56, 71
Aragon, Louis  126
Architecture  xvii–xviii, 37–8
Artforum  147
Arthur  x
Arts  xvii–xviii, 36–8, 153
Atlantic charter  68
*Ausgleich* (Compromise)  xv, xix
Austria  19–20, 21, 35, 39, 40, 42, 43, 44,
  45, 50, 62, 64, 77, 83, 134, 155
Austria–Hungary  ix–xix passim, 1–16
  passim, 19, 24, 26, 29, 40, 47–8,
  49, 68
Austro-Slavism  xiv, xv, 2, 7, 8
Avignon  134

Badeni, Kasimir  xvii
Banska Bystrica  78
Barbarossa, Frederick  x
Barbarossa Operation  70
Barnard, Christian  115
Barrandov film studios  36
Barthou, Louis  45

Barton family  37
Bata, Tomas  37–8
Battek, Rudolf  134
Bavaria  78, 145
Beck, Josef  45, 58, 74
Bednarova, Otka  133–4
Beijing  142, 145
Belgium  45, 61
Belgrade  20, 133
Benda, Vaclav  132, 133–4, 135, 148
Benes, Edvard  xvi, xix, 1, 2, 3, 4, 6–7, 9,
  11, 14, 16, 21–2, 24, 25–6, 27, 31, 34,
  39, 41–2, 44–5, 51, 52, 54, 55, 56, 58,
  61, 64–78 passim, 80, 81, 82, 83, 84,
  86, 87, 88–9, 94, 108, 159, 160, 165
Benes, Hanna (Benesova)  5
Beran, Josef  92
Berchtesgaden  52
Beria, Lavrenty  77, 82, 95
Berlin  35, 36, 40, 49, 50, 53, 60, 66, 69,
  138, 145
Bernard, Vilem  88
Bernolak, Antonin  xi, xii
Beveridge Plan  31
Bierut, Boleslav  94
Bilak, Vasil  105, 108, 113–14, 116–17,
  119, 126, 156
Bilek, Bohumil  71
Bismarck, Otto von  7, 52
Blaho, Pavol  xvi
Blanik, knights of  x
Blum, Leon  46
Boll, Heinrich  131
Bolsheviks  11, 40
Bonnet, Georges  50, 52, 53–4
Bratinka, Pavel  135
Bratislava  xv, 31, 33, 34, 60, 77, 78, 87, 97,
  113, 138, 143, 148, 150, 155
Brest–Litovsk, treaty of  11
Brezhnev, Leonid  105, 106, 110, 113,
  115–16, 118, 120, 137, 138, 167

Briand, Aristide 36
Brno 1, 49, 62, 78, 91, 154
Brod, Max 36
Brontosaurus 143
Brusilov 39
Buchal, Jan 89
Budapest xvi, 12, 21, 28, 43, 99
Bujak, Zbygniew 144
Bukharin, Nikolai 95
Bulgaria 112, 114
Bush, George 156

Calfa, Marian 157, 159, 167
Canada 128
Capek, Josef 36, 37, 61
Capek, Karel 22, 36, 37, 38
Carnogursky, Jan 151, 157, 166
Cavour, Camillo 5
Ceausescu, Nicolae 159
Censorship, *see* Press and newspapers
Cernik, Oldrich 106, 108, 114, 116, 120,
   124–5, 126
Cervinka, Vincenc 5
Chamberlain, Neville 50, 51, 52–4, 59
Charles IV xii, xviii
Charles V xii
Charter 77, 131–6, 137, 139, 147
Chicago 12, 65
China 142, 145, 148
Christian Democratic Union 165, 166
Chrysanthemum revolution 42–3
Churches, *see* Religion
Churchill, Winston 54–5, 71
Chvalkovsky, Frantisek 60
Cieszyn, *see* Tesin
Ciena nad Tisou 113
Cihost, 'miracle' at 92
Cisar, Cestmir 106, 125, 158
Citizens' Initiatives, Slovakia 153
Civic Democratic Party 166
Civic Forum (*Obcanske Forum*) 147–8,
   150, 151, 152–3, 154, 155, 156, 157,
   158, 163, 164, 165, 166
Civic Movement 166
Clare of Assisi 151
Class warfare 90–1, 109
Clemenceau, Georges 11
Clementis, Vladimir 77, 84, 94, 95–6
Cleveland, Ohio 12
Club of Independent Intelligentsia 147
Collective security 41–2, 44–5, 55

ComEcon (Council for Mutual Economic
   Assistance) 110, 152
Comenius, *see* Komensky
Cominform 84, 94
Comintern 26, 27, 84
Communist Party, Czechoslovak 25, 26,
   27, 28, 34, 55, 70, 71, 74, 76, 77, 80,
   82, 83, 84, 86; from 1948, 86 passim
Concentration camps and forced labour
   36, 37, 61, 62, 73, 90–1, 92, 127
Conference on Security and Cooperation
   in Europe (CSCE) 131, 139, 146
Constance xviii
Constitution and constitutional change
   23, 24, 64, 101, 110, 123, 154, 157,
   158, 165
Corfu crisis 45
Corporatism 28, 64
Crane, Charles R. 37
Crime 162
Czech National Camp (fascist) 28
Czech Philharmonic Orchestra 241
Czech Socialist party, *see* National
   Socialist Party (Czechoslovak)
Czernin, Otakar 8

Daladier, Edouard 50, 52, 53–4
Daluege, Kurt 73
David, Vaclav 101, 156
De Gaulle, Charles 71
Delacroix, Eugene 115
Democratic Forum of Communists 153
Democratic Initiative 137, 146, 147
Denis, Ernest 6
Derer, Ivan xvi
Dienstbier, Jiri 133–4, 135–6, 147, 155,
   157, 159, 160, 166
Djilas, Milovan 85
Dlouhy, Vladimir 157, 161
Dobrovsky, Josef xiii
Dollfuss, Englebert 42, 64
Dresden 106
Drtina, Prokop 85, 87, 132
Dual Monarchy, *see* Austria–Hungary
Dubcek, Alexander 103, 105, 106, 107,
   108, 109, 110–11, 112, 113–14, 116,
   117, 118, 119, 120, 121, 122, 123,
   125, 127, 131, 136, 137, 138, 141,
   142, 144, 150, 151, 152, 158, 159, 166
Dubcek, Julius 107
Dukla 10

Dulles, Allen 94
Durciansky, Ferdinand 63
Durich, Jaroslav 5
Dvorak, Antonin xvii
Dyk, Viktor 27

East European Information Agency 138
Ecology, *see* Environment
Economy 29, 33, 48–9, 99–100, 103, 104,
　　105, 109, 110, 142–3, 150, 152, 153,
　　157, 159, 161–2, 166–7
Eden, Anthony 46
Education and literacy xv–xvi, 1, 2, 7,
　　33–4, 47–8, 62, 91, 92, 123, 126, 130,
　　146, 153, 155, 161
Eisenhower, Dwight D. 77, 78
Elections
　　1906 xvi
　　1910 xvi
　　1911 23
　　1912 36–7
　　1919 (Austrian) 23
　　1920 24
　　1935 28, 47
　　1946 82–3, 100
　　1990 160, 161, 164–5
　　1992 167
Elias, Alois 61, 69, 72, 73
Elisabeth xv
Emigration, Czechs and Slovaks in xv,
　　3–4, 5, 6, 9, 10, 12–13, 22, 34, 65, 66,
　　123, 127–8
England, *see* Great Britain
Environment 132, 138, 142–3, 146, 150,
　　152, 153, 161
Epiphany convention 14
European parliament 159

Fabian Society 83
Fascism
　　Czech 25, 27–8, 61
　　Foreign 27, 28, 45, 63, 84
　　Slovak 62–4
Federal assembly 121, 124, 126, 132, 134,
　　154, 156, 159, 164, 165, 166
Federalisation 105, 110, 123, 165
Ferdinand I xii
Ferdinand II xiii, 7
Fichte, Johann Gottlieb ix
Field, Noel and Hermann 94, 99
Fierlinger, Zdenek 75, 77, 80, 86

Forced labour, *see* Concentration camps
　　and forced labour
Forman, Milos 213
France 2–3, 5, 6, 10, 11, 15, 39, 40, 43,
　　44–5, 51–6, 59, 64, 65, 66, 67, 69, 70,
　　71, 83, 84, 89, 127
Franco, Francisco 46, 47
Frank, Karl Hermann 60
Frankfurt assembly 1848 xiv
Franz Josef xv
Friedjung, Heinrich 2
Fugner, Jindrich xvii

Gabcik, Jozef 72
Gahura, Frantisek 38
Gajda, Radola 27–8, 61
Gal, Fedor 166
Geneva 4, 16, 27, 41, 42, 44, 56
Germany ix, xiv, 2, 3, 7, 11, 15, 28,
　　29, 36, 39, 40, 41, 45, 46, 48,
　　49–56, 58–78 passim, 81, 83, 101,
　　112, 114, 115, 141, 143, 145, 146,
　　155, 160
Gestapo 72, 127
*Glasnost* 137
Gocar, Josef xviii, 38
Godesberg 53
Goldstueker, Eduard 125
Gomulkka, Wladislav 112
Gorbachev, Mikhail 137, 138, 141, 145,
　　150, 152, 155, 156
Gottwald, Klement 27, 55, 74, 77, 82,
　　83, 84, 86, 87–8, 94, 95, 96, 97, 101,
　　109, 138
'Goulash Communism' 144
Graeco-Turkish war 45
Graffiti 115, 117, 150
Grant Duff, Shiela 83
Great Britain 5, 39, 40, 41, 43, 44, 46,
　　50–6, 59, 64, 65, 66, 69, 70, 71, 72,
　　73, 77, 83, 97, 125
Great Moravia x, xi, 7
Greece 45, 59
Guest workers 267

Habsburg authorities and Empire, *see*
　　Austria–Hungary
Hacha, Emil 60, 61, 66, 69
Hajek, Jiri 124, 127, 131, 132
Halifax, Lord 50, 53
Hasek, Jaroslav 36–7

Havel, Vaclav 91, 101, 108, 126, 128–9, 130–2, 133–4, 135, 136, 137, 139, 147, 152, 157, 158, 159, 160, 162, 163, 164, 165, 166
Havlova, Olga (Havel) 135, 136
Havlicek-Borovsky, Karel xiii, xiv, xv
Helsinki final act 131, 132, 133, 139
Henlein, Konrad 47, 50, 53, 60
Herder, Johann Gottfried von ix, xi
Hermanice 135, 136
Heydrich, Reinhard 62, 69, 72, 73
Hilsner, Leopold 2
Hitler, Adolf ix, 28, 47, 49–56, 58, 59, 60, 62, 68, 127
Hitler's behind 70
Hlasists xvi, 32
Hlinka, Andrej xvi, 13, 26, 33, 63
Hlinka Party, *see* People's Parties
Hodza, Milan xvi, 21, 25, 33, 50, 65
Hoffman, Karel 116, 126, 148, 151
Hohenzollern dynasty 5
Holly, Jan xi
Honecker, Erich 145
Horakova, Milada 89–90
Horthy, Miklos 28, 43
Hradec Kralove 38
Hromadko, Oldrich 163
Hronek, Jiri 61, 69, 71
Hruska, Milan 148
Hrusovsky, Igor xvi
Hubl, Milan 124
Human rights issues 132–40, 148
Humour 36–7, 61, 129, 156
Hungarian Democratic Forum 144
Hungarian Soviet Republic 21, 40, 43
Hungary x, xi, xii, 7, 9, 13, 20, 21, 24, 28, 34, 39, 40, 42–3, 44, 45, 52, 58, 59, 60, 81, 83, 94, 99, 112, 114, 132, 143, 144–5, 146, 160
Hus, Jan xviii–xix, 4, 6, 24, 53, 111, 121, 167
Husak, Gustav 85, 87, 97, 98, 101, 106, 108, 120, 121, 123, 124, 126, 130, 137, 142, 148, 151, 154, 156, 157, 162
Husserl, Edmund 132
Hussites x, xii, 6, 11
Hyphen debate 165–6

Ice hockey riots 122
Independent Peace Association 139, 147
Independent Socialists 135

Independent Students 147, 155
Indra, Alois 105, 108, 113, 114, 116–17, 119, 126, 148, 151, 156
Industry, *see* Economy and Environment
Israel 95, 97, 101, 115
Italy 2, 5, 10, 15, 40, 44, 45, 54, 56
Ivanka, Milan xvi

Jachymov 90
Jakes, Milos 105, 113, 125, 138, 148, 151, 155, 156
Jaksch, Wenzel 51
Janacek, Leos xvii, 36, 37
Janak, Pavel 38
Janko, General 106
Janousek, Antonin 21
Jaruzelski, Wojciech 143
Jaszi, Oszkar 42–3
Jazz Section 137
Jehlicka, Fr xvi
Jellacic, Ban Josip xiv
Jesenska, Milena 36, 49
Jews 36, 40, 61, 62, 63, 72, 73, 81
Jirasek, Alois xvii, 13, 14
Jiri of Podebrady xii
Joseph II 7
Jungmann, Josef xiii
Juriga, Ferdinand xvi

Kadar, Janos 144–5
Kafka, Franz 36, 37, 119
Kalandra, Zavis 89
Kalvoda, Jan 166
KAN 108, 121, 134
Kaplan, Karel 83, 109
Kapp Putsch 44
Karl von Habsburg 8, 14, 42, 43, 44
Karlovy Vary (Karlsbad) 47, 50
Karolyi, Mihaly 42–3
Karlsbad programme 47, 50, 51, 110
Kerensky, Alexander 11
Khrushchev, Nikita 99, 104
Kiev 10
Kincl, Frantisek 148
Kladno 61
Klaus, Vaclav 148, 161, 166, 167
Kleinerova, Antonie 90
Klima, Ivan 62, 128
Klofac, Vaclav 5, 26
Klub 231, 108, 121
Knazko, Milan 148

Koegler, Franz 71
Koerber, Ernst von 3
Kohout, Pavel 132, 134
Kokoschka, Oskar xix
Kolder, Drahomir 106, 108, 113, 114, 119
Kollar, Jan xi, xii
Komarek, Valtr 156, 157, 161
Komensky, Jan Amos (Comenius) xviii–
    xix, 33, 122–3
Kopriva, Ladislav 95
KOR 133
Korbel, Joseph 82, 83, 88
Kosice 76, 77, 78, 97
Kossuth, Lajos xiv, 8
'Kossuth gallows' xv
Kosygin, Alexei 110, 118, 124
Kotera, Jan 38
Kramar, Karel 3, 5, 8, 16, 21, 24, 25
Kremlin 54, 55, 95, 101, 105, 113, 121,
    124, 137, 154
Kriegel, Frantisek 108, 114, 118–19, 125
Krofta, Kamil 41
Krtiny 92
Kubis, Jan 72
Kubisova, Marta 122–3, 151
Kun, Bela 21, 23, 43
Kundera, Milan 96, 127–8
Kuron, Jacek 133
Kutna Hora xviii

Lada, Josef 37
Landovsky, Pavel 132
Land reform, *see* Legislation
Lausman, Bohumil 86, 87
Laval, Pierre 45
League of Nations 27, 34, 40, 41, 42, 44,
    45, 55, 56
Legions and Legionaries 9–12, 15, 21, 27,
    37, 38, 72, 111
Legislation
  Censorship 108, 123, 161
  Child labour 30
  Clergy 92
  Death penalty, abolition of 161
  Educational reform 161
  Eight-hour day 30
  Electoral 161
  Emergency 122
  Employment and labour 66
  Freedom of assembly, press and
      petition 161

Human rights, *see* Helsinki final act
Insurance, sickness and accident
    30–1
Land reform 29–30, 47, 48
Language xvii, 47, 49
Minority school law 48
Nationalization 144, 171–2
Old age pensions 30–1
Privatisation 161–2
Public libraries 48
University education 161
Lenart, Josef 125
Lendl, Ivan 127
Lenin, Vladimir Ilyich 40, 156
Letna, Prague 99, 143, 152
Levoca 138
Levy, Alan 115
Lezaky 73, 122
Liberec (Reichenberg) 49
Libuse xviii
Lidice 73, 121
Liptovsky Svaty Mikulas 13
Literacy, *see* Education and literacy
Literature 153
Lithuania 159
Little Entente 41, 44, 45
Litvinov, Maxim 55
Ljubljana 13
Lloyd George, David 11
Locarno, treaty of 41, 45
Lockhart, Robert Bruce 55, 67, 88
Lodz 73
London 4, 6, 12, 31, 47, 53, 58, 65, 67, 71,
    73, 74, 75, 96
London, Artur 94, 95–6, 98
Lublin committee 76
Lusatia 22
*Lustrace* 163–4, 166–7
Lvov, Georgy 11

Mach, Sano (Alexander) 63
Madeira 43
'Maffia' 3, 5, 6, 8
Magyarisation x, xiv, xv, 7, 26
Maisky, Ivan 70
Malta 156
Maly, Vaclav 148
Manes, Josef xvii
Mann, Erica 37
Maria Theresia 7, 62
Marseilles 45

Marshall aid  84
Martinu, Bohumil  36, 37
Masaryk, Alice (Masarykova)  5
Masaryk, Charlotte Garrigue
    (Masarykova)  2
Masaryk, Jan  52, 53, 67, 70, 77, 80, 83,
    84, 85, 88, 94, 107–8, 150
Masaryk, Tomas Garrigue  xvi, xviii,
    1–2, 3, 4, 5, 6, 8, 9, 10–11, 12,
    14–16, 19, 22, 23–4, 26, 31, 32,
    34, 35, 36, 37, 41, 50, 53, 75, 88,
    106, 147, 150, 160, 165, 167
*Matica Slovenska*  xv, 33
Mazowiecki, Tadeusz  144
Mazzini, Giuseppe  5
Meciar, Vladimir  166, 167
Metternich, Clemens von  xiv
Mexico  4
Michigan  128
Michnik, Adam  133, 144
Militia, people's or workers'  82, 86, 92,
    109, 116, 154
Miller, Petr  148
Milyukov, Pavel  11
Mitterand, Francois  139
Mlada Benesov  10
Mlynar, Zdenek  91, 98–9, 103–4, 105,
    108, 109, 112, 119, 124, 131,
    132–3
Mohorita, Vasil  155, 159
Molotov, Vyacheslav  71, 78
Moravec, Emanuel  72
Moravec, Frantisek  51, 73
Moravska Ostrava  51
Moscow  9, 12, 26, 70, 73, 74, 75, 76, 77,
    80, 82, 84, 99, 101, 106, 107, 114,
    118, 119, 120, 124, 137, 138, 141,
    145, 156, 159, 160
Movement for Civil Liberties  135,
    139, 151
Movement for Democratic Slovakia
    166, 167
Mucha, Alfons  36, 37
Munich  25, 28, 37, 46, 49, 51, 53–6, 58,
    64–5, 66, 67, 68, 70, 73, 83, 89, 108,
    134, 166
Municipal house (*obecni dum*)  xvii,
    16, 152
Music  8, 20, 22, 205–6, 228–9
Mussolini, Benito  27, 40, 42, 44, 46,
    47, 53

Nachod  128
Nagy, Imre  145
National assembly  16, 23, 24, 30, 39,
    44–5, 68, 88, 89, 96, 124
National Avenue, Prague  147
National Democratic Party  8, 23, 25,
    82, 85
National Fascist League  25, 27–8, 61
National front  82, 84, 88, 92, 108, 146,
    156, 164
National Minorities  19, 23, 28–9, 31, 32,
    35, 40, 80, 152
    Germans  19–20, 23, 28, 29, 35, 40,
        47–56, 71, 80–1, 90, 91
    Hungarians  40, 52
    Poles  40, 52
    Roma  40, 162, 163
National museum  14
National Socialist Party (Czechoslovak)
    5, 23, 25–6, 82, 89–90
National theatre  xvii
Nationality census  48
Navratilova, Martina  127
Nazi-Soviet Non-Aggression Pact  70
Nemcova, Bozena  xvii
Nemcova, Dana  133–4
Nemec, Frantisek  76
Nepal  126
Neruda, Jan  xvii
Netherlands  62
Neumann, Vaclav  146
Neurath, Constantin von  60, 62, 72
New York  12, 13, 134
Newspapers, *see* Press and Newspapers
NKVD  77, 82
Nosek, Vaclav  85, 86, 94
Nove Mesto nad Metuji  37
Novomesky, Ladislav (Laco)  97, 101, 106
Novotny, Antonin  99, 100–1, 103, 104,
    105, 106, 107, 108, 109, 123, 136, 156
Nuremberg  51

*Obroda* (Revival)  141, 147, 153, 156
Old Czech Party  xvi, 1
Old Town Square, Prague  xix, 4, 16, 111
Olomouc  138, 148
Opava  134
Open Dialogue  147
Opinion polls  111, 112, 149–50, 155,
    158, 160, 161
Opletal, Jan  62, 146

Ostrava 135, 148
Osusky, Stefan 65
Otto von Habsburg 43, 68
Ottoman Empire 40

Palach, Jan 121–2, 134, 139, 141, 150, 155
Palacky, Frantisek xi, xii–xiv, xv, xvii, 2, 7
Pan-Germanism xiv, 28, 46, 47, 50, 59
Pankrac prison, Prague 89, 135
Pan-Slavism x, xii, xiv, xv, 10, 27
Papacy, *see* Vatican
Pardubice 73, 142
Paris 2, 5, 6, 12, 14, 16, 21, 22, 65, 66, 134
Paris peace conference and settlement
      12, 20, 21–2, 26, 31, 35, 47
Patocka, Jan 130, 132, 133
Patton, George Smith 78
Pauker, Ana 85
Pavel, Josef 108, 124
Pavlovsky, Oldrich 105
Pecl, Oldrich 89
Pelikan, Jiri 127
PEN Club, Czechoslovak Centre 147
People's Parties 13, 16, 23, 25, 26, 60,
      63–4, 92, 146, 147, 163–4
*Perestroika* 137, 142, 150
Peroutka, Ferdinand 24, 38
Petrograd 10
Piedmont-Sardinia xiv
Piller, Jan 126
Pilsudski, Josef 27, 73
Pinpricks, policy of 61, 62, 66, 69, 74,
      117–18
Pisek 10
Pithart, Petr 136
Pittsburgh 12–13, 33
Plastic People of the Universe 131, 137
Plojhar, Josef 92
Plzen (Pilsen) 10, 91, 135, 136
Poincare, Raymond 12, 15
Poland 9, 22, 24, 27, 29, 39, 40, 44, 45–6,
      52, 58, 59, 61, 70, 73, 81, 94, 99, 112,
      114, 132, 143–4, 160
Polisensky, J.V. 68
Portugal 64
Poszony, *see* Bratislava
Potsdam 81
Prague xi, xiv, xv, xvii–xix, 1, 4, 9, 10, 12,
      13, 14, 15–16, 21, 24, 31, 32, 33, 35,
      36, 37, 38, 42, 47, 51, 55, 59, 60, 61,
      62, 66, 68, 69, 72, 73, 77, 78, 80, 85,

86, 87, 91, 92, 94, 96, 97, 99, 101,
      104–5, 107, 109, 115, 116, 117, 119,
      121, 124, 125, 135, 137, 138, 139,
      141, 145, 146, 147, 148, 149, 150,
      151–2, 154, 155, 159, 162
Presov 21
Press and newspapers, censorship 8–9,
      12, 51–2, 71, 74, 101, 104, 107–8,
      109, 111, 112, 113, 115–16, 117, 119,
      121, 123, 126, 127, 128, 132, 133,
      139, 140, 141, 142, 148, 150, 151,
      153, 164
Pressburg, *see* Bratislava
Pribram 90
Progressive Party 1, 23
Propaganda
   Austrian 6
   Communist 81, 83, 100
   Czechoslovak 5, 6–7, 59, 65, 67–9,
      71–2
   German 68
   Soviet 78
Protection, treaty of (Slovakia and
      Germany) 63
Prussia 40, 62
Public Against Violence (*Verejnost Proti
      Nasiliu*) 148, 151, 152, 153, 155,
      156, 165, 166
Pulszky Ferenc xi

Racism 162–3
   *see also* Anti-Semitism
Radek, Karl 72
Radio and television 67, 71, 76, 112, 116,
      117, 127, 134, 135, 146, 150, 152,
      158, 159
Rajhrad 92
Rajk, Laszlo 94, 95
Rakosi, Matyas 94
Rapallo, treaty of 44
Rasin, Alois 3, 5, 16, 25, 27, 29
Realist Party 1
Red army 55, 75, 76, 77, 78, 82, 83, 87,
      95, 112, 114, 154, 159, 160
Red Cross 62
Reform Communism 98, 101, 103–4,
      105, 108, 109, 111, 113, 114, 117,
      118, 119, 120, 132, 141, 147–8
Religion and the Churches 14, 30, 33,
      62–3, 64, 89, 90, 92–3, 132, 138, 146,
      147–8, 150, 151–2, 153

Renner, Karl 42
'Revival', *see Obroda*
Richta, Radovan 107, 109, 125
Rieger, Frantisek xiii, xvi
Ripka, Hubert 67, 69, 71, 83, 88, 89
Roma, *see* National minorities
Romanov dynasty 8
Rome 13, 151
Roosevelt, Franklin Delano 65, 71
Rumania 9, 13, 43, 59, 159
Rumanova 33
Runciman, Lord and Lady 51
Russian Empire x, 2, 5, 7, 8, 9, 10, 12, 40
Russophilia xiv, 3, 8

Sachergate 163–4
Sadovsky, Stefan 125
Safarik, Pavol xi–xii
Saint Germain, treaty of 21
Sakharov, Andrei 138, 159
Salazar, Antonio de Oliveira 64
Salgovic, Viliam 116
Salivarova, Zdena 128
Salzburg 28, 64
Samal, Pavel 3
*Samizdat* 130, 135–6, 151
Sarajevo xiii
Sarka x
Sastin 138
Scheiner, Josef 3, 5
Schuschnigg, Kurt von 64
Scranton, Pennsylvania 13, 22, 34
Security or riot and secret police 104–5,
   110, 116, 121, 122, 132–3, 136, 139,
   144, 146–7, 159, 163
Sedivy, Karel 71
Seifert, Jaroslav 131
Sejna, Jan 106
Semtex 142
Separatism Czech 166–7
   Moravian 166
   Ruthenian 34
   Slovak xvi, 13, 33, 59–60, 62–4, 66, 85
Serbia xiii, 8
Seton-Watson, R.W. 6, 50, 60
Shevardnadze, Eduard 150
Show trials 89–90, 92–8, 99, 100, 107,
   108, 109, 132
Siberia 11
Sigismund (Zikmund) xviii
Sik, Ota 103, 105, 108, 109, 125

Sikorski, Wladislaw 24, 73, 74
Simon, Bohumil 109, 114, 125
Siroky, Viliam 77, 97
Sixtus of Bourbon-Parma 8
Skvorecky, Josef 127, 128, 132, 136–7
Slanska, Josefa (Slansky) 98, 108
Slansky, Rudolf 84, 94, 95–6
Sling, Otto 94, 95–6, 132
Slingova, Marian (Sling) 96, 98, 108
Slovak National Party
   before 1918 xvi, 13
   after 1989 165
Slovak national uprising 64, 74–5, 96, 97,
   107, 165
Slovak Soviet Republic 23, 40
Smeral Bohumir 27
Smetana, Bedrich x, xvii–xviii
Smrkovsky, Josef 86, 106, 108–9, 113,
   114, 116, 117, 124
Smutny, Jaroslav 88
Social Democratic Party 13, 23, 25–6, 27,
   77, 80, 86, 87, 89, 132
Socialist Party, Czechoslovak 141,
   147, 157
Socialist Union of Youth 146, 155
Sokol movement xvii, 3, 72, 88, 108
Sokol, Tomas 164
Solidarity 143–4
South Slavs ix, xii, 2, 4, 5, 8, 9, 10, 13, 40
Soviet–Czechoslovak treaty
   1935 46, 54
   1943 73, 84
Soviet Union ix, 39, 40–1, 44, 45, 47, 51,
   52, 54, 55, 65, 67, 69, 70, 71, 74, 77,
   80, 83, 84, 86, 87, 94, 95, 96, 97, 100,
   101, 106, 107, 110, 111, 112, 113,
   114, 117, 118, 130, 137, 141, 143,
   145, 155–6
Spacek, Josef 108, 114, 125
Spanish civil war 46–7, 95, 111
Spartacist uprising 40
Sramek, Jan 26, 146
Srobar, Vavro xvi, 13, 20–1, 23, 25,
   32–3, 88
Stalin, Joseph 27, 34, 54, 55, 65, 70, 73,
   74, 75, 76, 82, 84–5, 87, 88, 94–5, 96,
   98, 99, 104
State Rights Party, *see* National
   Democratic Party
StB, *see* Security police
Steed, H. Wickam 6

Stefanek, Antonin xvi
Stefanik, Milan Rastislav 1, 2–3, 5, 9, 10,
    11, 14, 31
Stepan, Miroslav 148, 151, 152, 154, 156
Stockholm 74, 122
Strahov, Prague 104
Strang, William 55
Stresemann, Gustav 27, 28, 45
Stribny, Jiri 26
Strougal, Lubomir 125, 126, 137, 142
Students 86, 104–5, 107, 108, 121, 123,
    126, 146–7, 148, 149, 150, 151, 152,
    154, 158, 162
Stur, Ludvit xii, xv
Sudeten German parties 28, 47
Sudeten Germans, *see* National
    Minorities
Suez canal 11
Sugar, Andras 141
Sulek, Josef 116
Svab, Karel 94, 95–6
Svehla, Antonin 25
Sverma, Jan 96
Svermova, Marie (Sverma) 96, 132
Svetla, Karolina xvii
Svitak, Ivan 108, 111
Svoboda, Ludvik 77, 80, 86, 95, 99, 106,
    116, 118, 123, 129
Switzerland 2, 4, 31, 43, 94, 125

Tabor x
Taborsky, Edward 64–5, 77, 88
Tahiti 3
TASS 116, 120, 127
Television, *see* Radio and television
Terezin (Theresienstadt) 62, 73, 89
Teschen, *see* Tesin
Tesin 21, 22, 39, 45
Thatcher, Margaret 161
Theresienstadt, *see* Terezin
Thirty Years War 12–13, 33
Timisoara 159
Tiso, Jozef 60, 63, 64, 69, 77, 85, 107
Tisza, Koloman xvi
Tito, Josip Broz 99
Tokyo 11
Tomasek, Frantisek 138, 151, 152, 159
Toronto 65, 128, 132, 134
Toulouse 134
Trade unions 27, 82, 85, 87, 126, 153, 157
Trans-Siberian railway 11

Transylvania 9, 13, 20
Trianon, treaty of 21, 42, 43
Trotsky, Leon 95
Trutnov 129
Tsarist regime, *see* Russian Empire
Tuka, Bela or Vojtech 63
Turciansky Svaty Martin 13, 16, 20, 26
Turkey 121
*2000 Words* 111, 132
Tyrs, Miroslav xvii

Uhl, Petr 133–4
Ukraine 11, 34, 76, 115
Ulbricht, Walter 106, 112, 145
United States of America 4, 5, 10, 11, 12,
    15, 34, 65, 70, 89, 93, 97, 106, 137,
    139, 156
Universities, *see* Education, Students
Uranium mines 90–1, 163
Urban, Jan 136, 138, 144, 150, 164
Urbanek, Karel 151, 152, 154, 156
USSR, *see* Soviet Union
Uzhorod 34

'V for victory' 61, 145
Vacek, Miroslav 154
Vaclav (Wenceslas), prince and saint
    xii, 53
Vaclav IV xii, xviii
Vaclavik, Milan 154
Vaculik, Ludvik 111, 132
Vatican and papacy 64, 92, 93
Versailles, treaty of ix, 40
Vienna xi, xii, xvi, 1, 12, 24, 35, 58, 124,
    132, 139
Viest, Rudolf 75
Vladivostok 11, 12
*Vlajka, see* Czech National Camp
*Volkssport* trial 28
Vojtech 138
VONS 133–5, 136, 147
Voska, Emanuel 3–4
Vysocany congress 117, 119, 121

Walters, F.P. 56 and n.
Warsaw 94, 112, 113
Warsaw pact (treaty) organisation 106,
    110, 112, 113, 114, 122, 123, 135,
    137, 138, 141, 144, 145, 148, 152,
    154, 155, 156
Washington DC 14, 16, 66, 73, 75, 160

Wenceslas, *see* Vaclav
Wenceslas Square, Prague  16, 87,
    121, 122, 139, 147, 148, 150,
    151, 156, 157
White Mountain, battle of  xiii, xviii, 7,
    16, 24, 122
Wilhelm II  52
Wilson, Woodrow  12, 15, 40
Windischgraetz, Alfred von  xv
Wiskemann, Elizabeth  47–9
Women, position of and rights  2, 30, 31,
    89, 91, 109, 163
Writers' union  101, 104, 107, 125,
    126, 128

Young Czech Party  xvi, 1, 25
Yugoslavia  22, 40, 42, 43, 44, 94, 97,
    165, 167

Zagreb  2
Zajic, Jan  121–2
Zapotocky, Antonin  84, 94, 99
Zatopek, Emil  127
Zavodsky, Osvald  94
Zay, Karolyi  x
Zborov, battle of  11, 27
Zdenka, 'daughter of the nation'  xv
Zeman, Milos  143
Zeminova, Frantiska  90
Zenkl, Petr  85
Zhivkov, Todor  112
Zikmund, *see* Sigismund
Zinoviev, Grigori  95
Zita von Habsburg  43
Zizka hill, Prague  99
Zlin  37–8
Zorin, Valerian  87